*Detroit Studies in Music Bibliography, No. 78*

*Editors*
*J. Bunker and Marilyn S. Clark*
University of Kansas

# A BIBLIOGRAPHY OF

## SOURCE READINGS IN

## MUSIC EDUCATION

*by*

## VINCENT J. KANTORSKI

*HARMONIE PARK PRESS* • *WARREN, MICHIGAN* • *1997*

Copyright 1997 by Harmonie Park Press

Printed and bound in the United States of America
Published by
Harmonie Park Press
23630 Pinewood
Warren, Michigan 48091

Editor, J. Bunker Clark
Book Design, Elaine Gorzelski
Typographer, Colleen McRorie


**Library of Congress Cataloging-in-Publication Data**

Kantorski, Vincent.
     A bibliography of source readings in music education / by Vincent
J. Kantorski.
          p.     cm. — (Detroit studies in music bibliography ; no. 78)
     Includes index.
     ISBN 0-89990-079-8
     1. Music—Instruction and study—Bibliography.     I. Series.
ML128.I64K36   1997
780'.71—dc21                                              97-33024

*To*

*Valrie, Brian, and Matthew*

*Joe and Paul*

*Marzia Paulina and John*

*and*

*in loving memory*
*of my father*
*Joseph John Kantorski*
*(1912-1960)*

# CONTENTS

## A Bibliography of Source Readings
## in Music Education

# FOREWORD

In the present age of increased information and information retrieval, it is important not only to have access to vast amounts of information, but to have access to information written for a specific audience that has been initially screened. Increased possibilities for information are burgeoning, yet the need for that special information that someone has carefully selected to "fit" a limited number of circumstances is especially beneficial. Vincent Kantorski has provided such a source.

Not unlike other distilled analyses provided by experts, this source material comes from one who has expended a great deal of effort and time discriminating among the vast resources available for music education students, and he has selected the best within several categories important for music scholarship. Kantorski's rationale for inclusion combined with his taxonomic structure are clear and straightforward, evidencing the necessary discrimination for appropriate student use.

Alternatively, I am often amazed, not only by the apparent lack of discrimination, but by the exuberance combined with an almost childish naivete that some evidence in our technological world. With great joy they are quick to demonstrate the newest computer search, or technological gadget, or special new "source" that is capable of permitting access to limitless information, or holding vast amounts of information, or specific data, or whatever. I am reminded of an old colleague who became enamored with the "new" technology of the 60s. Having laboriously copied by hand, and then by typing, an entire semester class schedule for a large music department, he would then type the schedule once more, but this time on IBM cards so that the cards could be fed through the new processing machines across campus. This process resulted in a computer printout, complete with holes on both edges of oversized computer paper. Instead of receiving the initial typed schedule, one received the computer printout schedule—it seemed very impressive.

I do not mean this to be a diatribe on technological advances or in any way disparage the wonderful opportunities available to students in the current technological age. Those of us who still remember writing everything on the ubiquitous "yellow pad" are especially grateful for the use of this technology. I do want to draw attention to the merits of this specific bibliographic source. Much like other issues concerning technological advancements, along with new, exciting and voluminous possibilities, we need greater discrimination as well.

Bombarded with greater levels of sophistication, one often fails to recognize that most often the student just needs "to get started." The student who is just starting to avail him/herself with an information base does not need yet another complete list; rather this person needs a selected list, a refined list, an expert's list. Something that narrows the field, something that focuses on specific issues, categories, and resources, yet is extensive enough to "cover the field." Such is the case with the present work, and I am pleased to write this foreword and recommend it to my colleagues.

CLIFFORD K. MADSEN

Florida State University

# ACKNOWLEDGMENTS

I am fortunate to have had the assistance and advice of valued friends and colleagues throughout this project. Each person's contribution was important in that it added to the mosaic of knowledge and experience needed for this book to evolve from an idea to reality. I extend special thanks to Brian Goslee for his important library and typing assistance in the early stages of compiling this bibliography; to Bonna Boettcher for her expertise concerning reference works, music bibliographies, and bibliographic formats; to my Department of Music Education colleagues Anna Belle Bognar, Victor Ellsworth, and Patrick Tallarico for the professionalism of their guidance and encouragement; to my former and current students who have enriched my academic life and inspired me to compile this bibliography; and especially to Clifford K. Madsen for his wise suggestions concerning many aspects of this book, for his continuous support of all my professional endeavors and for teaching me and many others fortunate enough to be associated with him the importance and satisfaction of pursuing long-term goals.

In the memory of Gwen Ohlinger, I gratefully acknowledge her generosity in offering me advice and important printed resources concerning the book publishing process. As assistant manager of the Bowling Green State University Bookstore, she patiently answered my questions and freely shared her wealth of knowledge and experience.

Finally, I thank my loving wife Valrie and sons Brian and Matthew; it is accurate to state that this book would not have come to fruition without their patience, understanding, and support.

*Vincent J. Kantorski*

Bowling Green State University
Bowling Green, Ohio
April 1997

# INTRODUCTION

This bibliography is a substantial augmentation of lists of required and suggested readings that I have prepared for students in several graduate music education courses over the past thirteen years.  As instructors often do on the first day of class, I typically begin each semester by distributing a bibliography of references for students to use as a point of departure in their research.  I have always thought it unfortunate, however, that graduate students have not had a single, more extensive bibliography in different but overlapping areas within music education (e.g., psychology of music, philosophical foundations, research practices, curriculum and instruction) to use during their coursework and while writing a thesis or other scholarly paper.  I compiled *A Bibliography of Source Readings in Music Education* primarily to address this situation.

Although this bibliography evolved from a need for graduate students to have an additional research tool, I also intended for other individuals who are interested in music education to use it for their own research.  With this in mind, I have tried to present a wide variety of materials in this bibliography, including many that seemed to merit the reader's attention because of their inclusion in other worthwhile sources.

Because the field of music education is far too vast to include every source that one may consider important, I set certain limitations when compiling this bibliography.  Specifically, it contains titles of books, journals, and standardized tests in music; reviews of journals; and chapters of edited books.  There are no titles of dissertations, theses, or journal articles.

I obtained the entries listed in this bibliography in three ways.  First, I accumulated numerous titles from years of teaching the following graduate music education courses: Psychology of Music, Research in Music Education, Source Readings in Music Education, and Building Instructional Programs in Music.  Second, I acquired additional titles from publishers' and professional music organizations' catalogs, and from music education and research books and texts.  I then verified bibliographic information concerning these titles by using library computer databases.  Third, I obtained the remaining titles through computer searches of university libraries' on-line catalogs (primarily OhioLINK and ILLINET), the Library of Congress on-line catalog, and various Gophers on the Internet.  As a result of these computer searches, I obtained numerous books through interlibrary loan systems—in particular, edited books and older titles.

## *Categories of the Bibliography*

Each title of the bibliography appears in one or more categories. For example, titles concerning research in the teaching of general music are in both the Research and in the Curriculum and Instruction categories. Additionally, nonmusic titles that offer a broader perspective of a subject area appear in the appropriate category (e.g., a general research methodology text within Research).

The bibliography's eight categories include the following content areas. The abbreviations of each category appear after entries in the bibliography and indicate the single or multiple categories that include them:

### (A) Arts
Arts education, artistic intelligences, arts education policy, and related topics.

### (BR) Bibliographic Resources
Bibliographies, directories, indexes, lists, guides, handbooks, and related topics.

### (CI) Curriculum and Instruction
Curriculum theory and design, methods, approaches, and related topics that are typically in music education curriculum texts and courses.

### (FPA) Foundations, Philosophy, and Aesthetics
Foundations, philosophy and aesthetics of music education, and related topics (including the history of music education) that typically appear in foundations and/or philosophy of music education texts and courses.

### (J) Journals
Selected reviews of music journals from *International Music Journals*\* and titles of other relevant music and nonmusic journals.

### (P) Psychology
Acoustics, music perception, musical abilities and evaluation (including representative standardized tests), and related topics that are typically in psychology of music texts and courses.

### (R) Research
Books or chapters of books that present substantive reviews of research, informational and/or instructional materials relating to research methodologies, and research oriented topics that typically appear in music education research texts and courses.

### (RSC) Reports, Symposia, and Conferences
Published reports or proceedings of professional gatherings such as meetings, symposia, and conferences, and related collections such as festschrifts.

---

\* Linda M. Fidler and Richard S. James, eds., *International Music Journals* (New York: Greenwood, 1990).

# A Bibliography of

## Source Readings in

### Music Education

# (A)

## ARTS

*America 2000 Arts Partnership.* Washington: U.S. Department of Education and the National Endowment for the Arts, 1992.

**A, CI**

American Council for the Arts. *Toward a New Era in Arts Education.* Reston, Va.: Music Educators National Conference, 1988.

**A, CI**

————. *Why We Need the Arts: Eight Quotable Speeches by Leaders in Education, Business, and the Arts.* Reston, Va.: Music Educators National Conference, 1989.

**A, CI, RSC**

*Americans and the Arts V: Highlights from a National Survey of Public Opinion.* New York: American Council for the Arts, 1988.

**A, RSC**

Arnheim, Rudolf. "What Is Art For?" In *Aesthetics and Problems of Education*, ed. Ralph A. Smith, 231-42. Urbana: University of Illinois Press, 1971.

**A, FPA**

Arnstine, Donald. "The Aesthetic as a Context for General Education." In *Aesthetics and Problems of Education*, ed. Ralph A. Smith, 402-13. Urbana: University of Illinois Press, 1971.

**A, CI, FPA**

*Arts Education Research Agenda for the Future.* Washington: U.S. Department of Education, 1994.

**A, CI, R, RSC**

*Arts Go to School: An Arts-in-Education Handbook.* New York: American Council for the Arts, 1983.
**A, BR, CI**

*Arts in Education: Research Report.* Washington: National School Boards Association, 1978.
**A, CI, R, RSC**

*Arts in Rural America.* Washington: National Endowment for the Arts, 1991.
**A, CI**

*Arts in Schools—Perspectives from Four Nations: A Report from the National Endowment for the Arts.* Washington: National Endowment for the Arts, 1993.
**A, CI, RSC**

Arts, Education, and Americans Panel. *Coming to Our Senses: The Significance of the Arts for American Education.* New York: McGraw-Hill, 1977.
**A, CI, FPA, RSC**

Aschner, Mary Jane. "Teaching the Anatomy of Criticism." In *Aesthetics and Problems of Education*, ed. Ralph A. Smith, 425-34. Urbana: University of Illinois Press, 1971.
**A, CI, FPA**

Aspin, David. "Assessment and Education in the Arts." In *The Aesthetic Imperative: Relevance and Responsibility in Arts Education*, ed. Malcolm Ross, 25-52. New York: Pergamon, 1981.
**A, CI, FPA, P**

Balfe, Judith H., and Joni Cherbo Heine. "On the Necessity of Adult Arts Education beyond the Classroom." In *Arts Education beyond the Classroom*, ed. Judith H. Balfe and Joni Cherbo Heine, 3-6. New York: American Council for the Arts, 1988.
**A, CI**

————, eds. *Arts Education beyond the Classroom.* New York: American Council for the Arts, 1988.
**A, CI, RSC**

Ball, Charles H. "Thoughts on Music as Aesthetic Education." In *Toward an Aesthetic Education: A Report*, 57-62. Washington: Music Educators National Conference, 1971.
**A, CI, FPA**

Barresi, Anthony L. "Public Policy and Music Education: Policy Analysis as a Pathway to Professional Understanding." In *Policy Issues in Music Education: A Report of the Proceedings of the Robert Petzold Symposium*, ed. Gerald Olson, Anthony L. Barresi, and David Nelson, 1-15. Madison: School of Music, University of Wisconsin, 1991.
**A, FPA**

Beardsley, Monroe C. *The Aesthetic Point of View: Selected Essays of Monroe C. Beardsley.* Ed. Michael J. Wreen and Donald M. Callen. Ithaca, N.Y.: Cornell University Press, 1982.
**A, FPA**

_____. *Aesthetics from Classical Greece to the Present: A Short History.* New York: Macmillan, 1975.
**A, FPA**

_____. *Aesthetics: Problems in the Philosophy of Criticism.* 2nd ed. Indianapolis, Ind.: Hackett, 1981.
**A, FPA**

_____. "The Classification of Critical Reasons." In *Aesthetics and Problems of Education*, ed. Ralph A. Smith, 435-44. Urbana: University of Illinois Press, 1971.
**A, FPA**

Beardsley, Monroe C., and Herbert M. Schueller, eds. *Aesthetic Inquiry: Essays on Art Criticism and the Philosophy of Art.* Belmont, Calif.: Dickenson, 1967.
**A, FPA**

Bell, Clive. *Art.* Ed. J. B. Bullen. 1914. Reprint, New York: Oxford University Press, 1987.
**A, FPA**

Berger, Arthur. "Music as Imitation." In *Perspectives on Musical Aesthetics*, ed. John Rahn, 302-12. New York: Norton, 1994.
**A, FPA, P**

Berlyne, D. E. *Aesthetics and Psychobiology.* New York: Appleton-Century-Crofts, 1971.
**A, FPA, P**

_____, ed. *Studies in the New Experimental Aesthetics: Steps toward an Objective Psychology of Aesthetic Appreciation.* Washington: Hemisphere, 1974.
**A, FPA, P**

Black, Max. "Education as Art and Discipline." In *Aesthetics and Problems of Education*, ed. Ralph A. Smith, 529-36. Urbana: University of Illinois Press, 1971.
**A, CI, FPA**

Blacking, John. "A False Trail for the Arts?" In *The Aesthetic in Education*, ed. Malcolm Ross, 1-27. New York: Pergamon, 1985.
**A, FPA**

Blacking, John, and Joann W. Kealiinohomoku, eds. *The Performing Arts: Music and Dance.* New York: Mouton, 1979.
**A, CI, RSC**

Blaustein, Susan. "The Survival of Aesthetics: Books by Boulez, Delio, Rochberg." In *Perspectives on Musical Aesthetics*, ed. John Rahn, 333-64. New York: Norton, 1994.
**A, FPA**

Bloom, Kathryn. "Development of Arts and Humanities Programs." In *Toward an Aesthetic Education: A Report*, 89-99. Washington: Music Educators National Conference, 1971.
**A, CI, FPA**

_____. "Research and Development Needs for Comprehensive Programs in the Arts in Education at the Precollegiate Level." In *Arts and Aesthetics: An Agenda for the Future*, ed. Stanley S. Madeja, 317-30. St. Louis, Mo.: CEMREL, 1977.
**A, CI, R**

Boston, Bruce O., ed. *Perspectives on Implementation: Arts Education Standards for America's Students.* Reston, Va.: Music Educators National Conference, 1994.
**A, CI, FPA**

*British Journal of Aesthetics.* London: Oxford University Press, 1960-.
**A, FPA, J, R**

Broudy, Harry S. "Arts Education - Praise May Not Be Enough." In *The Crane Symposium: Toward an Understanding of the Teaching and Learning of Music Performance*, ed. Charles B. Fowler, 37-43. Potsdam: Potsdam College of the State University of New York, 1988.
**A, FPA**

_____. *Enlightened Cherishing: An Essay on Aesthetic Education.* 1972. Reprint, Urbana: University of Illinois Press, 1994.
**A, CI, FPA**

_____. "Enlightened Preference and Justification." In *Aesthetics and Problems of Education*, ed. Ralph A. Smith, 305-19. Urbana: University of Illinois Press, 1971.
**A, CI, FPA**

_____. "On Cognition and Emotion in the Arts." In *The Arts, Cognition and Basic Skills*, ed. Stanley S. Madeja, 18-22. St. Louis, Mo.: CEMREL, 1978.
**A, P**

_____. "Some Duties of a Theory of Educational Aesthetics." In *Aesthetics and Problems of Education*, ed. Ralph A. Smith, 103-16. Urbana: University of Illinois Press, 1971.
**A, CI, FPA**

_____. "Some Reactions to a Concept of Aesthetic Education." In *Arts and Aesthetics: An Agenda for the Future*, ed. Stanley S. Madeja, 251-61.  St. Louis, Mo.: CEMREL, 1977.
**A, CI, FPA**

_____. *The Whys and Hows of Aesthetic Education.*  St. Louis, Mo.: CEMREL, 1977.
**A, CI, FPA**

Bruhn, Karl.  "Advocacy: Getting to 'How to'."  In *Perspectives on Implementation: Arts Education Standards for America's Students*, ed. Bruce O. Boston, 9-18.  Reston, Va.: Music Educators National Conference, 1994.
**A, CI, FPA**

Bussis, Anne M., Edward A. Chittenden, and Marianne Amarel.  "Collaborative Research."  In *The Teaching Process, Arts and Aesthetics*, ed. Gerard L. Knieter and Jane Stallings, 70-91.  St. Louis, Mo.: CEMREL, 1979.
**A, R**

Canada, Benjamin O.  "Building Support for the Arts Standards among School Administrators."  In *Perspectives on Implementation: Arts Education Standards for America's Students*, ed. Bruce O. Boston, 63-69.  Reston, Va.: Music Educators National Conference, 1994.
**A, CI, FPA**

Chagy, Gideon, ed.  *The State of the Arts and Corporate Support.*  New York: P. S. Eriksson, 1971.
**A**

Clifford, Geraldine Joncich.  "An Historical Review of Teaching and Research: Perspectives for Arts and Aesthetic Education."  In *The Teaching Process, Arts and Aesthetics*, ed. Gerard L. Knieter and Jane Stallings, 11-39.  St. Louis, Mo.: CEMREL, 1979.
**A, FPA, R**

Coleman, Earle J., ed.  *Varieties of Aesthetic Experience.*  Lanham, Md.: University Press of America, 1983.
**A, FPA**

Conklin, Kenneth R.  "The Aesthetic Dimension of Education in the Abstract Disciplines."  In *Aesthetics and Problems of Education*, ed. Ralph A. Smith, 537-54.  Urbana: University of Illinois Press, 1971.
**A, CI, FPA**

Consortium of National Arts Education Associations.  *National Standards for Arts Education: Dance, Music, Theatre, Visual Arts.  What Every Young American Should Know and Be Able to Do in the Arts.*  Reston, Va.: Music Educators National Conference, 1994.
**A, CI, FPA**

Csikszentmihalyi, Mihaly, and Ulrich Schiefele. "Arts Education, Human Development, and the Quality of Experience." In *The Arts, Education, and Aesthetic Knowing: 91st Yearbook of the National Society for the Study of Education (Part II)*, ed. Bennett Reimer and Ralph A. Smith, 169-91. Chicago: University of Chicago Press, 1992.

**A, CI, P**

Curl, G. "R. K. Elliott's 'As-If' and the Experience of Art." In *The Arts: A Way of Knowing*, ed. Malcolm Ross, 85-100. New York: Pergamon, 1983.

**A, FPA**

Davis, Donald J. "Evaluation and Curriculum Development in the Arts." In *Toward an Aesthetic Education: A Report*, 117-27. Washington: Music Educators National Conference, 1971.

**A, CI, P**

Davis, Jessica, and Howard Gardner. "The Cognitive Revolution: Consequences for the Understanding and Education of the Child as Artist." In *The Arts, Education, and Aesthetic Knowing: 91st Yearbook of the National Society for the Study of Education (Part II)*, ed. Bennett Reimer and Ralph A. Smith, 92-123. Chicago: University of Chicago Press, 1992.

**A, CI, FPA, P**

Dearden, R. F. "The Aesthetic Form of Understanding." In *Aesthetics and Problems of Education*, ed. Ralph A. Smith, 285-304. Urbana: University of Illinois Press, 1971.

**A, CI, FPA**

*Design for Arts in Education*. Washington: Heldref, 1989-.

**A, CI, FPA, J**

Dewey, John. *Art as Experience*. 1934. Reprint, New York: Perigee Books, 1980.

**A, CI, FPA**

Dewey, John, Albert C. Barnes, and Laurence Buermeyer. *Art and Education: A Collection of Essays*. 1929. 3rd ed., rev. Merion, Pa.: Barnes Foundation, 1978.

**A, CI, FPA**

Dykema, Peter W. "Significant Relationships of Music to Other Subjects." In *Music Education: 35th Yearbook of the National Society for the Study of Education (Part II)*, ed. Guy Montrose Whipple, 23-33. Bloomington, Ill.: Public School Publishing, 1936.

**A, CI, FPA**

Eaton, Marcia Muelder. "Teaching through Puzzles in the Arts." In *The Arts, Education, and Aesthetic Knowing: 91st Yearbook of the National Society for the Study of Education (Part II)*, ed. Bennett Reimer and Ralph A. Smith, 151-68. Chicago: University of Chicago Press, 1992.
**A, CI, FPA**

Ecker, David W. "The Development of Qualitative Intelligence." In *Aesthetics and Problems of Education*, ed. Ralph A. Smith, 172-77. Urbana: University of Illinois Press, 1971.
**A, CI, FPA, P**

Eddy, Junius. "Beyond 'Enrichment': Developing a Comprehensive Community-School Arts Curriculum." In *Arts and the Schools*, ed. Jerome J. Hausman and Joyce Wright, 157-204. New York: McGraw-Hill, 1980.
**A, CI**

Edelfelt, Roy A. "Staff Development and Teaching in the Arts." In *The Teaching Process, Arts and Aesthetics*, ed. Gerard L. Knieter and Jane Stallings, 129-47. St. Louis, Mo.: CEMREL, 1979.
**A, CI, FPA**

Efland, Arthur. "Conceptions of Teaching in the Arts." In *The Teaching Process, Arts and Aesthetics*, ed. Gerard L. Knieter and Jane Stallings, 152-86. St. Louis, Mo.: CEMREL, 1979.
**A, CI, FPA, P**

Egan, Robert F. *Music and the Arts in the Community: The Community Music School in America*. Metuchen, N.J.: Scarecrow, 1989.
**A, CI, FPA**

Eggleston, John. "The Arts and the Whole Curriculum." In *The Arts and Personal Growth*, ed. Malcolm Ross, 58-68. New York: Pergamon, 1980.
**A, CI**

Eisner, Elliot W. "Implications of Artistic Intelligences for Education." In *Artistic Intelligences: Implications for Education*, ed. William J. Moody, 31-42. New York: Teachers College, 1990.
**A, CI, P**

_____. "Thoughts on an Agenda for Research and Development in Arts Education." In *Arts and Aesthetics: An Agenda for the Future*, ed. Stanley S. Madeja, 411-22. St. Louis, Mo.: CEMREL, 1977.
**A, CI, R**

_____, ed. *The Arts, Human Development, and Education*. Berkeley, Calif.: McCutchan, 1976.
**A, CI**

Engel, Martin. "An Informal Framework for Cognitive Research in Arts Education." In *The Arts, Cognition and Basic Skills*, ed. Stanley S. Madeja, 23-30. St. Louis, Mo.: CEMREL, 1978.
**A, P, R**

_____. "Toward a Federal Policy for the Arts in Education." In *Arts and Aesthetics: An Agenda for the Future*, ed. Stanley S. Madeja, 202-19. St. Louis, Mo.: CEMREL, 1977.
**A, CI**

Engel, Martin, and Jerome J. Hausman, eds. *Curriculum and Instruction in Arts and Aesthetic Education*. St. Louis, Mo.: CEMREL, 1981.
**A, FPA, R, RSC**

Evans, David. "Aesthetic Development: A Psychological Viewpoint." In *The Development of Aesthetic Experience*, ed. Malcolm Ross, 48-66. New York: Pergamon, 1982.
**A, FPA**

Fehrs-Rampolla, Barbara. "Opportunities in the Classroom: A Teacher's Perspective." In *Perspectives on Implementation: Arts Education Standards for America's Students*, ed. Bruce O. Boston, 31-37. Reston, Va.: Music Educators National Conference, 1994.
**A, CI, FPA**

Fosburg, Linda. "Arts Councils and Arts Education." In *Arts and Aesthetics: An Agenda for the Future*, ed. Stanley S. Madeja, 170-77. St. Louis, Mo.: CEMREL, 1977.
**A, CI**

Foshay, Arthur W. "Inquiry into Aesthetics Education for Curriculum-Making." In *Arts and Aesthetics: An Agenda for the Future*, ed. Stanley S. Madeja, 243-50. St. Louis, Mo.: CEMREL, 1977.
**A, CI, FPA, R**

Fowler, Charles B. "Arts Education for Tomorrow: Straight Talk about the Future of Music Education." In *Toward Tomorrow: New Visions for General Music*, ed. Sandra L. Stauffer, 21-29. Reston, Va.: Music Educators National Conference, 1995.
**A, CI, FPA**

_____. *Can We Rescue the Arts for America's Children: Coming to Our Senses Ten Years Later*. New York: American Council for the Arts, 1988.
**A, FPA**

————. "One Nation, Undercultured and Underqualified." In *Artistic Intelligences: Implications for Education*, ed. William J. Moody, 159-69. New York: Teachers College, 1990.
**A, FPA**

————, ed. *An Arts in Education Source Book.* New York: The Fund, 1980.
**A, BR, CI**

————, ed. *Arts in Education, Education in Arts: Entering the Dialogue of the 80's.* Washington: Charles B. Fowler, 1984.
**A, CI, FPA**

————, ed. *Summit Conference on the Arts and Education: A Report.* Washington: Alliance for Arts Education, 1980.
**A, CI, RSC**

Gans, Eric. "Art and Entertainment." In *Perspectives on Musical Aesthetics*, ed. John Rahn, 40-53. New York: Norton, 1994.
**A, FPA**

Gardner, Howard. *Art, Mind, and Brain: A Cognitive Approach to Creativity.* New York: Basic Books, 1982.
**A, CI, P**

————. *Artful Scribbles: The Significance of Children's Drawings.* New York: Basic Books, 1980.
**A, P**

————. *The Arts and Human Development: A Psychological Study of the Artistic Process.* 1973. Reprint, New York: Basic Books, 1994.
**A, CI, P**

————. *Creating Minds: An Anatomy of Creativity Seen through the Lives of Freud, Einstein, Picasso, Stravinsky, Eliot, Graham, and Gandhi.* New York: Basic Books, 1993.
**A, CI, P**

————. "Multiple Intelligences: Implications for Art and Creativity." In *Artistic Intelligences: Implications for Education*, ed. William J. Moody, 11-27. New York: Teachers College, 1990.
**A, CI, P**

————. "Sifting the Special from the Shared: Notes toward an Agenda for Research in Arts Education." In *Arts and Aesthetics: An Agenda for the Future*, ed. Stanley S. Madeja, 267-78. St. Louis, Mo.: CEMREL, 1977.
**A, CI, R**

Gardner, Howard, and David N. Perkins, eds. *Art, Mind, and Education: Research from Project Zero*. Urbana: University of Illinois Press, 1989.
**A, CI, P, R**

Gary, Charles L., and Wade M. Robinson. "Implications of Aesthetic Education for Professional Action." In *Toward an Aesthetic Education: A Report*, 129-34. Washington: Music Educators National Conference, 1971.
**A, CI, FPA**

Geahigan, George. "The Arts in Education: A Historical Perspective." In *The Arts, Education, and Aesthetic Knowing: 91st Yearbook of the National Society for the Study of Education (Part II)*, ed. Bennett Reimer and Ralph A. Smith, 1-19. Chicago: University of Chicago Press, 1992.
**A, CI, FPA**

*Generation of Fellows: Grants to Individuals from the National Endowment for the Arts*. Washington: National Endowment for the Arts, 1993.
**A, CI, RSC**

Gfeller, Kate. "Arts Education Policies for Students with Disabilities." In *Policy Issues in Music Education: A Report of the Proceedings of the Robert Petzold Symposium*, ed. Gerald Olson, Anthony L. Barresi, and David Nelson, 76-87. Madison: School of Music, University of Wisconsin, 1991.
**A, CI, FPA**

Gingrich, Arnold. *Business and the Arts: An Answer to Tomorrow*. New York: P. S. Eriksson, 1969.
**A**

Golby, Michael. "The Responsive School." In *The Arts and Personal Growth*, ed. Malcolm Ross, 16-26. New York: Pergamon, 1980.
**A, CI, FPA**

Goodlad, John I. "Beyond the Rhetoric of Promise." In *Arts and the Schools*, ed. Jerome J. Hausman and Joyce Wright, 205-36. New York: McGraw-Hill, 1980.
**A, CI, P**

————. "Toward a Place in the Curriculum for the Arts." In *The Arts, Education, and Aesthetic Knowing: 91st Yearbook of the National Society for the Study of Education (Part II)*, ed. Bennett Reimer and Ralph A. Smith, 192-212. Chicago: University of Chicago Press, 1992.
**A, CI, FPA**

Goodlad, John I., and Jack Morrison.  "The Arts and Education."  In *Arts and the Schools*, ed. Jerome J. Hausman and Joyce Wright, 1-21.  New York: McGraw-Hill, 1980.
**A, CI**

Gotshalk, D. W.  "Aesthetic Education as a Domain."  In *Aesthetics and Problems of Education*, ed. Ralph A. Smith, 117-25.  Urbana: University of Illinois Press, 1971.
**A, CI, FPA**

Greene, Maxine.  "Art, Technique, and the Indifferent Gods."  In *Aesthetics and Problems of Education*, ed. Ralph A. Smith, 555-63.  Urbana: University of Illinois Press, 1971.
**A, CI, FPA**

————.  "Arts Education in the Humanities: Toward a Breaking of the Boundaries." In *Artistic Intelligences: Implications for Education*, ed. William J. Moody, 147-58.  New York: Teachers College, 1990.
**A, CI**

————.  "Teaching for Aesthetic Experience."  In *Toward an Aesthetic Education: A Report*, 21-43.  Washington: Music Educators National Conference, 1971.
**A, CI, FPA**

Gurin, Richard S.  "The Arts Education Standards: A Payoff for Business."  In *Perspectives on Implementation: Arts Education Standards for America's Students*, ed. Bruce O. Boston, 82-88.  Reston, Va.: Music Educators National Conference, 1994.
**A, CI, FPA**

Hanshumaker, James.  "The Art of Recognizing Artistic Teaching in the Arts."  In *The Teaching Process, Arts and Aesthetics*, ed. Gerard L. Knieter and Jane Stallings, 223-39.  St. Louis, Mo.: CEMREL, 1979.
**A, CI, FPA**

Hanslick, Eduard.  *On the Musically Beautiful: A Contribution towards the Revision of the Aesthetics of Music.*  Transl. and ed. Geoffrey Payzant from 8th ed., 1891.  Reprint, Indianapolis, Ind.: Hackett, 1986.
**A, FPA, P**

Hargreaves, D. H.  "Dr. Brunel and Mr. Denning: Reflections on Aesthetic Knowing."  In *The Arts: A Way of Knowing*, ed. Malcolm Ross, 127-60.  New York: Pergamon, 1983.
**A, FPA**

Hargreaves, David J.  "Developmental Psychology and the Arts."  In *Children and the Arts*, ed. David J. Hargreaves, 3-21.  Philadelphia: Open University Press, 1989.
**A, P**

Hargreaves, David J., and Maurice J. Galton. "Aesthetic Learning: Psychological Theory and Educational Practice." In *The Arts, Education, and Aesthetic Knowing: 91st Yearbook of the National Society for the Study of Education (Part II)*, ed. Bennett Reimer and Ralph A. Smith, 124-50. Chicago: University of Chicago Press, 1992.
**A, CI, P**

Hargreaves, David J., ed. *Children and the Arts*. Philadelphia: Open University Press, 1989.
**A, P**

Hausman, Jerome J. "A Contemporary Aesthetics Curriculum." In *Toward an Aesthetic Education: A Report*, 45-55. Washington: Music Educators National Conference, 1971.
**A, CI, FPA**

————. "The Domain of the Arts." In *Arts and the Schools*, ed. Jerome J. Hausman and Joyce Wright, 23-45. New York: McGraw-Hill, 1980.
**A, FPA**

Hausman, Jerome J., and Joyce Wright, eds. *Arts and the Schools*. New York: McGraw-Hill, 1980.
**A, CI, FPA**

Heyfron, Victor. "Artistic Creativity." In *The Aesthetic in Education*, ed. Malcolm Ross, 29-53. New York: Pergamon, 1985.
**A, FPA**

————. "The Concept of Art." In *The Arts and Personal Growth*, ed. Malcolm Ross, 79-95. New York: Pergamon, 1980.
**A, FPA**

————. "The Objective Status of Aesthetic Knowing." In *The Arts: A Way of Knowing*, ed. Malcolm Ross, 43-72. New York: Pergamon, 1983.
**A, FPA, P**

Hobbs, Jack A., and Robert L. Duncan. *Arts, Ideas and Civilization*. 2nd ed. Englewood Cliffs, N.J.: Prentice-Hall, 1992.
**A, FPA**

Hodgkinson, Harold L. "Arts in the Future: A Pragmatic Analysis." In *Arts and Aesthetics: An Agenda for the Future*, ed. Stanley S. Madeja, 28-45. St. Louis, Mo.: CEMREL, 1977.
**A, CI, FPA**

Hodsoll, Frank S. M. "Arts Education and the Arts Endowment." In *The Future of Musical Education in America: Proceedings of the July 1983 Conference*, ed. Donald J. Shetler, 1-10. Rochester, N.Y.: Eastman School of Music Press, 1984.
**A**

Hoffa, Harlan Edward. "Implementing the National Standards: Developing Professional Resources." In *Perspectives on Implementation: Arts Education Standards for America's Students*, ed. Bruce O. Boston, 19-30. Reston, Va.: Music Educators National Conference, 1994.
**A, CI, FPA**

Hoffer, Charles R. "Artistic Intelligences and Music Education." In *Artistic Intelligences: Implications for Education*, ed. William J. Moody, 135-40. New York: Teachers College, 1990.
**A, CI, P**

Hoffman, Mary E. "The Potential for MENC as a Leader in Arts Education Policy." In *Policy Issues in Music Education: A Report of the Proceedings of the Robert Petzold Symposium*, ed. Gerald Olson, Anthony L. Barresi, and David Nelson, 172-84. Madison: School of Music, University of Wisconsin, 1991.
**A, FPA**

Hope, Samuel. "Making Disciplinary Connections." In *Perspectives on Implementation: Arts Education Standards for America's Students*, ed. Bruce O. Boston, 38-46. Reston, Va.: Music Educators National Conference, 1994.
**A, CI, FPA**

Horowitz, Harold. "The Research Division of the National Endowment for the Arts: Background and Highlights of the First Year." In *Arts and Aesthetics: An Agenda for the Future*, ed. Stanley S. Madeja, 178-201. St. Louis, Mo.: CEMREL, 1977.
**A, R**

Inglefield, Ruth K. "International Review of the Aesthetics and Sociology of Music." In *International Music Journals*, ed. Linda M. Fidler and Richard S. James, 172-74. New York: Greenwood, 1990.
**A, FPA, J, P, R**

_____. "Journal of Aesthetics and Art Criticism." In *International Music Journals*, ed. Linda M. Fidler and Richard S. James, 187-88. New York: Greenwood, 1990.
**A, FPA, J, R**

Jenkins, Iredell. "Aesthetic Education and Moral Refinement." In *Aesthetics and Problems of Education*, ed. Ralph A. Smith, 178-99. Urbana: University of Illinois Press, 1971.
**A, CI, FPA**

Johnson, Nancy Jo. "Involving School Boards in Implementing the Arts Standards." In *Perspectives on Implementation: Arts Education Standards for America's Students*, ed. Bruce O. Boston, 70-74. Reston, Va.: Music Educators National Conference, 1994.
**A, CI, FPA**

Johnson, Philip. "Black Music, the Arts and Education." In *The Claims of Feeling: Readings in Aesthetic Education*, ed. Malcolm Ross, 37-63. Philadelphia: Falmer, 1989.
**A, CI, FPA**

*Journal of Aesthetic Education*. Urbana: University of Illinois Press, 1966-.
**A, CI, FPA, J, R**

*K-12 Arts Education in the U.S.: Present Context, Future Needs*. Reston, Va.: Music Educators National Conference, 1986.
**A, CI**

Kaagan, Stephen S. *Aesthetic Persuasion: Pressing the Cause of Arts Education in American Schools*. Los Angeles: Getty Center for Education in the Arts, 1990.
**A, CI**

Kaelin, Eugene F. "Aesthetic Education: A Role for Aesthetics Proper." In *Aesthetics and Problems of Education*, ed. Ralph A. Smith, 144-61. Urbana: University of Illinois Press, 1971.
**A, CI, FPA**

Kaelin, Eugene F., and David W. Ecker. "The Institutional Prospects of Aesthetic Education." In *Arts and Aesthetics: An Agenda for the Future*, ed. Stanley S. Madeja, 229-42. St. Louis, Mo.: CEMREL, 1977.
**A, CI, FPA**

Kapinus, Barbara, et al. "National Standards: Implications and Strategies for the States." In *Perspectives on Implementation: Arts Education Standards for America's Students*, ed. Bruce O. Boston, 89-95. Reston, Va.: Music Educators National Conference, 1994.
**A, CI, FPA**

Karafelis, Plato, and Robert I. Hugh. "Integrated Arts and Music Composition at Wolcott Elementary School." In *Toward Tomorrow: New Visions for General Music*, ed. Sandra L. Stauffer, 111-20. Reston, Va.: Music Educators National Conference, 1995.
**A, CI**

Katz, Jonathan, ed. *Arts and Education Handbook: A Guide to Productive Collaborations*. Washington: National Assembly of State Arts Agencies, 1988.
**A, BR, CI**

Keppel, Francis. "The Arts and Education Today Compared to the Sixties." In *Arts and Aesthetics: An Agenda for the Future*, ed. Stanley S. Madeja, 25-27. St. Louis, Mo.: CEMREL, 1977.

**A, CI, FPA**

Keyserling, Harriet. "The Politics of Mainstreaming Arts in Education." In *Artistic Intelligences: Implications for Education*, ed. William J. Moody, 63-68. New York: Teachers College, 1990.

**A, CI, FPA**

Kimpton, Jeffrey. *Public Education and the Arts: Linked by Necessity.* Reston, Va.: Music Educators National Conference, 1985.

**A, CI, FPA**

Knieter, Gerard L. "The Nature of Aesthetic Education." In *Toward an Aesthetic Education: A Report*, 3-19. Washington: Music Educators National Conference, 1971.

**A, CI, FPA, P**

Knieter, Gerard L., and Jane Stallings, eds. *The Teaching Process, Arts and Aesthetics.* St. Louis, Mo.: CEMREL, 1979.

**A, CI, FPA, RSC**

Koehler, Virginia. "Research on Teaching: Implications for Research on the Teaching of the Arts." In *The Teaching Process, Arts and Aesthetics*, ed. Gerard L. Knieter and Jane Stallings, 40-63. St. Louis, Mo.: CEMREL, 1979.

**A, R**

Langer, Susanne Katherina. "The Cultural Importance of the Arts." In *Aesthetics and Problems of Education*, ed. Ralph A. Smith, 86-94. Urbana: University of Illinois Press, 1971.

**A, FPA**

_____. *Feeling and Form: A Theory of Art Developed from "Philosophy in a New Key."* New York: Scribner, 1953.

**A, FPA**

_____. *Philosophy in a New Key: A Study in the Symbolism of Reason, Rite, and Art.* 3rd ed. Cambridge: Harvard University Press, 1976.

**A, FPA**

_____. *Problems of Art: Ten Philosophical Lectures.* New York: Charles Scribner's Sons, 1957.

**A, FPA**

_____, ed. *Reflections on Art: A Source Book of Writings by Artists, Critics, and Philosophers*. 1958. Reprint, New York: Arno, 1979.
**A, BR, FPA**

Lasch, Christopher. "The Degradation of Work and the Apotheosis of Art." In *The Future of Musical Education in America: Proceedings of the July 1983 Conference*, ed. Donald J. Shetler, 11-20. Rochester, N.Y.: Eastman School of Music Press, 1984.
**A, FPA**

Lashley, Horace. "Arts Education, the Curriculum and the Multi-Cultural Society." In *The Arts and Personal Growth*, ed. Malcolm Ross, 27-36. New York: Pergamon, 1980.
**A, CI**

Lehman, Paul R. "Issues of Assessment." In *Perspectives on Implementation: Arts Education Standards for America's Students*, ed. Bruce O. Boston, 47-54. Reston, Va.: Music Educators National Conference, 1994.
**A, CI, P**

Leonhard, Charles. *The Status of Arts Education in American Public Schools: Report of a Survey Conducted by the National Arts Education Research Center at the University of Illinois*. Urbana: Council for Research in Music Education, School of Music, University of Illinois, 1991.
**A, BR, CI, RSC**

Lipman, Samuel. "On Adult Arts Education." In *Arts Education beyond the Classroom*, ed. Judith H. Balfe and Joni Cherbo Heine, 7-10. New York: American Council for the Arts, 1988.
**A, CI**

List, Lynne K. *Music, Art, and Drama Experiences for the Elementary Curriculum*. New York: Teachers College, Columbia University, 1982.
**A, CI**

Lynch, Robert L. "Implementing the Standards: Making Use of the Arts Community." In *Perspectives on Implementation: Arts Education Standards for America's Students*, ed. Bruce O. Boston, 75-81. Reston, Va.: Music Educators National Conference, 1994.
**A, CI, FPA**

Madeja, Stanley S. "Structuring a Research Agenda for the Arts and Aesthetics." In *Arts and Aesthetics: An Agenda for the Future*, ed. Stanley S. Madeja, 374-91. St. Louis, Mo.: CEMREL, 1977.
**A, FPA, R**

————, ed. *Arts and Aesthetics: An Agenda for the Future.* St. Louis, Mo.: CEMREL, 1977.
**A, CI, FPA, RSC**

————, ed. *The Arts, Cognition and Basic Skills.* St. Louis, MO.: CEMREL, 1978.
**A, CI, P, RSC**

Madeja, Stanley S., and Harry T. Kelly. "A Curriculum Development Model for Aesthetic Education." In *Aesthetics and Problems of Education*, ed. Ralph A. Smith, 345-56. Urbana: University of Illinois Press, 1971.
**A, CI, FPA**

————. "The Process of Curriculum Development for Aesthetic Education." In *Toward an Aesthetic Education: A Report*, 101-15. Washington: Music Educators National Conference, 1971.
**A, CI, FPA**

Maus, Fred Everett. "Recent Ideas and Activities of James K. Randall and Benjamin Boretz: A New Social Role for Music." In *Perspectives on Musical Aesthetics*, ed. John Rahn, 107-15. New York: Norton, 1994.
**A, FPA, P**

McLaughlin, John, ed. *A Guide to National and State Arts Education Services.* New York: ACA Books, 1987.
**A, BR**

Metz, Donald. *Teaching General Music in Grades 6-9.* Columbus, Ohio: Merrill, 1980.
**A, CI**

Meyer, Leonard B. *Music, the Arts, and Ideas.* 1967. Reprint, Chicago: University of Chicago Press, 1994.
**A, FPA, P**

Miller, Louise. "Working with State Legislatures." In *Perspectives on Implementation: Arts Education Standards for America's Students*, ed. Bruce O. Boston, 96-100. Reston, Va.: Music Educators National Conference, 1994.
**A, CI, FPA**

Mills, E. Andrew, and D. Ross Thompson. *A National Survey of Arts Education, 1984-85: A National Report on the State of the Arts in the States.* Reston, Va.: National Art Education Association, 1986.
**A, RSC**

Mitchell, Ruth, ed. *Measuring Up to the Challenge: What Standards and Assessment Can Do for Arts Education.* New York: ACA Books, 1994.
**A, CI, P, RSC**

Moody, William J. "Summary and Coda." In *Artistic Intelligences: Implications for Education*, ed. William J. Moody, 170-79. New York: Teachers College, 1990.
A, FPA

———, ed. *Artistic Intelligences: Implications for Education*. New York: Teachers College, 1990.
A, CI, FPA, P, RSC

Murfee, Elizabeth. *The Value of the Arts: Written for the President's Committee on the Arts and the Humanities*. Washington: The Committee, 1993.
A, RSC

Myers, Rose Maree. "The Theory Is Realized: A Creative Arts Elementary School." In *Artistic Intelligences: Implications for Education*, ed. William J. Moody, 72-76. New York: Teachers College, 1990.
A, CI

Narmour, Eugene, and Ruth A. Solie, eds. *Explorations in Music, the Arts, and Ideas: Essays in Honor of Leonard B. Meyer*. Stuyvesant, N.Y.: Pendragon, 1988.
A, BR, FPA, RSC

Newman, Warren Bennett. "The Effect of Standardized Testing in the Arts." In *Artistic Intelligences: Implications for Education*, ed. William J. Moody, 52-56. New York: Teachers College, 1990.
A, P

Olson, David R. "The Arts as Basic Skills." In *The Arts, Cognition and Basic Skills*, ed. Stanley S. Madeja, 59-81. St. Louis, Mo.: CEMREL, 1978.
A, CI

Osborne, Harold. "Appreciation as Percipience." In *Aesthetics and Problems of Education*, ed. Ralph A. Smith, 445-72. Urbana: University of Illinois Press, 1971.
A, FPA

Overby, Lynnette Young, Ann Richardson, Lillian S. Hasko, and Luke Kahlich, eds. *Early Childhood Creative Arts: Proceedings of the International Early Childhood Creative Arts Conference*. Reston, Va.: Music Educators National Conference and National Dance Association, 1991.
A, CI, P, RSC

Pankratz, David. "Adults and Arts Education: A Literature Review." In *Arts Education beyond the Classroom*, ed. Judith H. Balfe and Joni Cherbo Heine, 11-22. New York: American Council for the Arts, 1988.
A, R

Pankratz, David, and Kevin V. Mulcahy, eds. *The Challenge to Reform Arts Education: What Role Can Research Play?* New York: ACA Books, 1989.
**A, CI, FPA, R**

Pankratz, David, and Valerie B. Morris, eds. *The Future of the Arts: Public Policy and Arts Research.* New York: Praeger, 1990.
**A, FPA**

Parsons, Michael J. "Cognition as Interpretation in Art Education." In *The Arts, Education, and Aesthetic Knowing: 91st Yearbook of the National Society for the Study of Education (Part II)*, ed. Bennett Reimer and Ralph A. Smith, 70-91. Chicago: University of Chicago Press, 1992.
**A, CI, P**

*Performing Together: The Arts and Education.* Washington: Alliance for Arts Education, 1985.
**A, CI**

*Perspectives on Education Reform: Arts Education as Catalyst.* Santa Monica, Calif.: Getty Center for Education in the Arts, 1993.
**A, CI**

Phenix, Philip H. "The Aesthetic Realm of Meaning." In *Aesthetics and Problems of Education*, ed. Ralph A. Smith, 265-84. Urbana: University of Illinois Press, 1971.
**A, FPA**

Porter, Robert, ed. *Arts Advocacy: A Citizen Action Manual.* New York: American Council for the Arts, 1980.
**A, BR**

Pring, Richard. "Creative Development at 14 + ." In *The Aesthetic in Education*, ed. Malcolm Ross, 115-31. New York: Pergamon, 1985.
**A, P**

Rahn, John. "What Is Valuable in Art, and Can Music Still Achieve It?" In *Perspectives on Musical Aesthetics*, ed. John Rahn, 54-65. New York: Norton, 1994.
**A, FPA**

Ree, Henry. "Education and the Arts: Are Schools the Enemy?" In *The Aesthetic Imperative: Relevance and Responsibility in Arts Education*, ed. Malcolm Ross, 90-99. New York: Pergamon, 1981.
**A, CI, FPA**

Regelski, Thomas A. *Arts Education and Brain Research.* Reston, Va.: Music Educators National Conference, 1978.

**A, CI, P**

Reid, Louis Arnaud. "Aesthetic Knowledge in the Arts." In *The Arts: A Way of Knowing*, ed. Malcolm Ross, 19-41. New York: Pergamon, 1983.

**A, FPA, P**

_____. "Assessment and Aesthetic Education." In *The Aesthetic Imperative: Relevance and Responsibility in Arts Education*, ed. Malcolm Ross, 8-24. New York: Pergamon, 1981.

**A, CI, FPA, P**

_____. "The Concept of Aesthetic Development." In *The Development of Aesthetic Experience*, ed. Malcolm Ross, 2-26. New York: Pergamon, 1982.

**A, FPA**

_____. "Knowledge and Aesthetic Education." In *Aesthetics and Problems of Education*, ed. Ralph A. Smith, 162-71. Urbana: University of Illinois Press, 1971.

**A, CI, FPA**

_____. "Meaning in the Arts." In *The Arts and Personal Growth*, ed. Malcolm Ross, 1-15. New York: Pergamon, 1980.

**A, FPA**

_____. *Meaning in the Arts.* New York: Humanities Press, 1969.

**A, CI, FPA, P**

Reimer, Bennett. "Aesthetic Behaviors in Music." In *Toward an Aesthetic Education: A Report*, 65-87. Washington: Music Educators National Conference, 1971.

**A, CI, FPA, P**

_____. "Designing Effective Arts Programs." In *Arts and the Schools*, ed. Jerome J. Hausman and Joyce Wright, 117-56. New York: McGraw-Hill, 1980.

**A, CI, FPA, P**

_____. "What Knowledge Is of Most Worth in the Arts?" In *The Arts, Education, and Aesthetic Knowing: 91st Yearbook of the National Society for the Study of Education (Part II)*, ed. Bennett Reimer and Ralph A. Smith, 20-50. Chicago: University of Chicago Press, 1992.

**A, CI, FPA, P**

Reimer, Bennett, and Ralph A. Smith, eds. *The Arts, Education, and Aesthetic Knowing: 91st Yearbook of the National Society for the Study of Education (Part II)*. Chicago: National Society for the Study of Education, 1992.

**A, BR, CI, FPA, P**

Robinson, Doris. *Music and Dance Periodicals: An International Directory and Guidebook.* Voorheesville, N.Y.: Peri, 1989.

**A, BR, J**

Rockefeller, David, Jr. "The State of Arts Education in American Public Schools." In *Arts and Aesthetics: An Agenda for the Future*, ed. Stanley S. Madeja, 46-50. St. Louis, Mo.: CEMREL, 1977.

**A, CI**

Ross, Malcolm. "The Arts and Personal Growth." In *The Arts and Personal Growth*, ed. Malcolm Ross, 96-119. New York: Pergamon, 1980.

**A, CI, FPA**

————. "Knowing Face to Face: Towards Mature Aesthetic Encountering." In *The Development of Aesthetic Experience*, ed. Malcolm Ross, 78-91. New York: Pergamon, 1982.

**A, FPA**

————. "The Last Twenty-Five Years: The Arts in Education, 1963-1988." In *The Claims of Feeling: Readings in Aesthetic Education*, ed. Malcolm Ross, 3-23. Philadelphia: Falmer, 1989.

**A, FPA**

————. "You Are the Music." In *The Aesthetic Imperative: Relevance and Responsibility in Arts Education*, ed. Malcolm Ross, 147-72. New York: Pergamon, 1981.

**A, FPA**

————, ed. *The Aesthetic Imperative: Relevance and Responsibility in Arts Education.* New York: Pergamon, 1981.

**A, CI, FPA, RSC**

————, ed. *The Aesthetic in Education.* New York: Pergamon, 1985.

**A, CI, FPA**

————, ed. *The Arts and Personal Growth.* New York: Pergamon, 1980.

**A, FPA, RSC**

————, ed. *The Arts: A Way of Knowing.* New York: Pergamon, 1983.

**A, FPA, RSC**

————, ed. *Assessment in Arts Education: A Necessary Discipline or a Loss of Happiness?* New York: Pergamon, 1986.

**A, CI, P**

————, ed. *The Claims of Feeling: Readings in Aesthetic Education.*  Philadelphia: Falmer, 1989.

**A, CI, FPA, RSC**

————, ed. *The Development of Aesthetic Experience.*  New York: Pergamon, 1982.

**A, CI, FPA, RSC**

Schoen, Max. *Art and Beauty.*  New York: Macmillan, 1932.

**A, FPA**

————. *The Enjoyment of the Arts.*  1944.  Reprint, Freeport, N.Y.: Books for Libraries, 1971.

**A, FPA**

*Schools and the Fine Arts: What Should Be Taught in Art, Music, and Literature?*  Washington: Council for Basic Education, 1965.

**A, CI, RSC**

Schwartz, Delmore.  "Poetry as Imitation."  In *Perspectives on Musical Aesthetics*, ed. John Rahn, 297-301.  New York: Norton, 1994.

**A, FPA**

Scott-Kassner, Carol.  "Music, the Arts, and Other Subjects: Maintaining Musical Integrity in the Integrated Curriculum."  In *Toward Tomorrow: New Visions for General Music*, ed. Sandra L. Stauffer, 103-09.  Reston, Va.: Music Educators National Conference, 1995.

**A, CI**

Sesonske, Alexander.  *What Is Art? Aesthetic Theory from Plato to Tolstoy.*  New York: Oxford University Press, 1965.

**A, FPA**

Shaw, Sir Roy.  "Education and the Arts."  In *The Arts and Personal Growth*, ed. Malcolm Ross, 69-78.  New York: Pergamon, 1980.

**A, CI**

Shuler, Scott C.  "Assessment in General Music: Trends and Innovations in Local, State, and National Assessment."  In *Toward Tomorrow: New Visions for General Music*, ed. Sandra L. Stauffer, 51-66.  Reston, Va.: Music Educators National Conference, 1995.

**A, CI, P**

————. *Making Arts Education Curricular.*  Reston, Va.: Music Educators National Conference, 1990.

**A, CI**

Shulman, Lee S. "Research on Teaching in the Arts: Review, Analysis, Critique." In *The Teaching Process, Arts and Aesthetics*, ed. Gerard L. Knieter and Jane Stallings, 244-64. St. Louis, Mo.: CEMREL, 1979.

**A, CI, R**

Silvers, Anita. "Show and Tell: The Arts, Cognition, and Basic Modes of Referring." In *The Arts, Cognition and Basic Skills*, ed. Stanley S. Madeja, 31-50. St. Louis, Mo.: CEMREL, 1978.

**A, P**

Simpson, Alan. "Utilitarianism, the Arts and Education." In *The Aesthetic in Education*, ed. Malcolm Ross, 187-212. New York: Pergamon, 1985.

**A, CI, FPA**

Sinor, Jean. "Policy Development in Arts Education for Early Childhood Programs." In *Policy Issues in Music Education: A Report of the Proceedings of the Robert Petzold Symposium*, ed. Gerald Olson, Anthony L. Barresi, and David Nelson, 92-106. Madison: School of Music, University of Wisconsin, 1991.

**A, CI, FPA**

Smith, C. M. "The Aesthetics of John Dewey and Aesthetic Education." In *Aesthetics and Problems of Education*, ed. Ralph A. Smith, 64-85. Urbana: University of Illinois Press, 1971.

**A, CI, FPA**

Smith, Louis M., and Sally Schumacher. *Extended Pilot Trials of the Aesthetic Education Program: A Qualitative Analysis and Evaluation.* St. Louis, Mo.: CEMREL, 1972.

**A, CI, FPA**

Smith, Nancy R. "Classroom Practice: Creating Meaning in the Arts." In *Arts and the Schools*, ed. Jerome J. Hausman and Joyce Wright, 79-115. New York: McGraw-Hill, 1980.

**A, CI, P**

Smith, Ralph A. "Aesthetic Criticism: The Method of Aesthetic Education." In *Aesthetics and Problems of Education*, ed. Ralph A. Smith, 473-84. Urbana: University of Illinois Press, 1971.

**A, CI, FPA**

————. "Is Teaching an Art?" In *Aesthetics and Problems of Education*, ed. Ralph A. Smith, 564-69. Urbana: University of Illinois Press, 1971.

**A, CI, FPA**

_____. "The Philosophical Literature of Aesthetic Education." In *Toward an Aesthetic Education: A Report*, 137-69. Washington: Music Educators National Conference, 1971.
**A, CI, FPA**

_____. "Toward Percipience: A Humanities Curriculum for Arts Education." In *The Arts, Education, and Aesthetic Knowing: 91st Yearbook of the National Society for the Study of Education (Part II)*, ed. Bennett Reimer and Ralph A. Smith, 51-69. Chicago: University of Chicago Press, 1992.
**A, CI, FPA**

_____. "Trends and Issues in Policy-Making for Arts Education." In *Handbook of Research on Music Teaching and Learning*, ed. Richard J. Colwell, 749-59. New York: Schirmer Books, 1992.
**A, CI, FPA, R**

_____, ed. *Aesthetics and Problems of Education*. Urbana: University of Illinois Press, 1971.
**A, CI, FPA**

Smith, Ralph A., and Alan Simpson, eds. *Aesthetics and Arts Education*. Urbana: University of Illinois Press, 1991.
**A, CI, FPA**

Smith, Ralph A., and C. M. Smith. "Justifying Aesthetic Education." In *Aesthetics and Problems of Education*, ed. Ralph A. Smith, 126-43. Urbana: University of Illinois Press, 1971.
**A, CI, FPA**

Sparshott, F. E. "The Unity of Aesthetic Education." In *Aesthetics and Problems of Education*, ed. Ralph A. Smith, 243-57. Urbana: University of Illinois Press, 1971.
**A, CI, FPA**

Spector, Irwin. *Rhythm and Life: The Work of Emile Jaques-Dalcroze*. Stuyvesant, N.Y.: Pendragon, 1990.
**A, CI**

Stake, Robert E., ed. *Evaluating the Arts in Education: A Responsive Approach*. Columbus, Ohio: Merrill, 1975.
**A, CI**

Standifer, James A. "Policy Development in Multicultural Arts Education." In *Policy Issues in Music Education: A Report of the Proceedings of the Robert Petzold Symposium*, ed. Gerald Olson, Anthony L. Barresi, and David Nelson, 61-71. Madison: School of Music, University of Wisconsin, 1991.
**A, CI, FPA**

Steinel, Daniel V., comp. and ed. *Arts in Schools: State by State.* 2nd ed. Reston, Va.: Music Educators National Conference, 1988.

**A, BR**

Stevens, Louise K. *Planning to Make the Arts Basic: A Report to the National Endowment for the Arts on the Impact and Results of the Arts in Schools Basic Education Grants Program.* Marion, Mass.: Artsmarket Consulting, 1991.

**A, CI, RSC**

Swanwick, Keith, ed. *The Arts and Education: Papers from the National Association for Education in the Arts, 1983-1990.* Oakham, England: National Association for Education in the Arts, 1990.

**A, CI, RSC**

Taylor, Dorothy. "Aesthetic Development in Music." In *The Development of Aesthetic Experience*, ed. Malcolm Ross, 94-109. New York: Pergamon, 1982.

**A, CI, FPA**

Taylor, Fannie, and Anthony L. Barresi. *The Arts at a New Frontier: The National Endowment for the Arts.* New York: Plenum, 1984.

**A, FPA**

Taylor, Harold. "The Arts in a Democracy." In *Artistic Intelligences: Implications for Education*, ed. William J. Moody, 3-10. New York: Teachers College, 1990.

**A, FPA**

*These People Have Passed the Test of Time, Can You? A Report on Arts Education.* Washington: National Endowment for the Arts, 1988.

**A, CI, RSC**

Tikunoff, William J., and Beatrice A. Ward. "How the Teaching Process Affects Change in the School." In *The Teaching Process, Arts and Aesthetics*, ed. Gerard L. Knieter and Jane Stallings, 100-24. St. Louis, Mo.: CEMREL, 1979.

**A, CI**

Tolbert, Mary R., ed. *Evaluating the Arts in Schools: New Concepts.* Columbus: Ohio State University, 1974.

**A, P**

Tolstoy, Leo. *What Is Art?* Ed. W. Gareth Jones, transl. Aylmer Maude. 1898. Reprint, London: Bristol Classical, 1994.

**A, FPA**

*Toward an Aesthetic Education: A Report.* Washington: Music Educators National Conference, 1971.

**A, CI, FPA, RSC**

*Toward Civilization: A Report on Arts Education.* Washington: National Endowment for the Arts, 1988.

**A, CI, RSC**

Tweddell, Paul. "The Professional Development of Arts Teachers." In *The Claims of Feeling: Readings in Aesthetic Education*, ed. Malcolm Ross, 167-99. Philadelphia: Falmer, 1989.

**A, CI, FPA**

Vallance, Elizabeth. "Artistic Intelligences and General Education." In *Artistic Intelligences: Implications for Education*, ed. William J. Moody, 79-84. New York: Teachers College, 1990.

**A, CI, P**

*Vision for Arts Education in the 21st Century.* Reston, Va.: Music Educators National Conference, 1994.

**A, CI, FPA**

Waikart, Kitty. "A Nuts-and-Bolts Plan for Parents." In *Perspectives on Implementation: Arts Education Standards for America's Students*, ed. Bruce O. Boston, 55-62. Reston, Va.: Music Educators National Conference, 1994.

**A, CI, FPA**

Ward, David. "The Arts and Special Needs." In *The Claims of Feeling: Readings in Aesthetic Education*, ed. Malcolm Ross, 99-118. Philadelphia: Falmer, 1989.

**A, CI, P**

Warnock, M. "Imagination." In *The Arts: A Way of Knowing*, ed. Malcolm Ross, 73-83. New York: Pergamon, 1983.

**A, FPA**

Weber, Nathan, and Loren Renz. *Arts Funding: A Report on Foundation and Corporate Grantmaking Trends.* New York: Foundation Center, 1993.

**A, RSC**

Weitz, Morris. "Research on the Arts and in Aesthetics: Some Pitfalls, Some Possibilities." In *Arts and Aesthetics: An Agenda for the Future*, ed. Stanley S. Madeja, 223-28. St. Louis, Mo.: CEMREL, 1977.

**A, FPA, R**

Wheeler, D. K. "Aesthetic Education and Curriculum." In *Aesthetics and Problems of Education*, ed. Ralph A. Smith, 320-44. Urbana: University of Illinois Press, 1971.
**A, CI, FPA**

Wilson, Margaret Bush. "The Arts and the Minorities." In *Arts and Aesthetics: An Agenda for the Future*, ed. Stanley S. Madeja, 51-56. St. Louis, Mo.: CEMREL, 1977.
**A, CI**

Witkin, Robert W. "The Concept of 'Development' in Aesthetic Education." In *The Development of Aesthetic Experience*, ed. Malcolm Ross, 67-77. New York: Pergamon, 1982.
**A, CI, FPA**

————. "Expressivist Theories of Art and Ideologies of Arts Education." In *The Claims of Feeling: Readings in Aesthetic Education*, ed. Malcolm Ross, 24-36. Philadelphia: Falmer, 1989.
**A, FPA**

Wolf, Dennie, and Howard Gardner. "Beyond Playing or Polishing: A Developmental View of Artistry." In *Arts and the Schools*, ed. Jerome J. Hausman and Joyce Wright, 47-77. New York: McGraw-Hill, 1980.
**A, P**

Wolff, Janet. "Questioning the Curriculum: Arts, Education and Ideology." In *The Aesthetic in Education*, ed. Malcolm Ross, 213-30. New York: Pergamon, 1985.
**A, CI, FPA**

# (BR)

## Bɪʙʟɪᴏɢʀᴀᴘʜɪᴄ Rᴇsᴏᴜʀᴄᴇs

Abeles, Harold F. "A Guide to Interpreting Research in Music Education." In *Handbook of Research on Music Teaching and Learning*, ed. Richard J. Colwell, 227-43. New York: Schirmer Books, 1992.
**BR, R**

Althouse, Jay. *Copyright: The Complete Guide for Music Educators.* Reston, Va.: Music Educators National Conference, 1984.
**BR**

American String Teachers Association, National School Orchestra Association, and Music Educators National Conference. *The Complete String Guide: Standards, Programs, Purchase, and Maintenance.* Reston, Va.: Music Educators National Conference, 1988. **BR, CI**

Anderson, Jill Kuespert. *TIPS: Music in Our Schools Month (MIOSM).* Reston, Va.: Music Educators National Conference, 1988. **BR, CI**

Anderson, Lorin W., and Lauren A. Sosniak, eds. *Bloom's Taxonomy—A Forty-Year Retrospective: 93rd Yearbook of the National Society for the Study of Education (Part II).* Chicago: National Society for the Study of Education, 1994. **BR, CI, FPA, P**

Arneson, Arne Jon. *Music Educators Journal: Cumulative Index 1914-1987: Including Music Supervisors' Bulletin and Music Supervisors' Journal.* Stevens Point, Wisc.: Index House, 1987. **BR, J**

*Arts Go to School: An Arts-in-Education Handbook.* New York: American Council for the Arts, 1983. **A, BR, CI**

*Assessment of Community Education Programs in Music.* Reston, Va.: National Association of Schools of Music, 1988. **BR, CI, P, RSC**

*Assessment of Graduate Programs in Music.* Reston, Va.: National Association of Schools of Music, 1985. **BR, CI, P**

*Assessment of Undergraduate Programs in Music.* Reston, Va.: National Association of Schools of Music, 1991. **BR, CI, P**

Baird, Peggy Flanagan. *Music Books for the Elementary School Library.* Washington: Music Educators National Conference, 1972. **BR, CI**

Barron, John P., comp. *A Selected Bibliography of the Kodály Concept of Music Education.* Willowdale, Ontario: Avondale, 1979. **BR, CI**

Bartle, Graham A., comp. *International Directory of Music Education: Details of Higher Music and Music Education Institutions and Music Education Qualifications.* Nedlands, Western Australia: Callaway International Resource Centre for Music Education, 1991.
**BR**

Bergin, Bob. "The Role of Instruments: Preschool through Third Grade." In *Voices of Industry*, 33-40. Reston, Va.: Music Educators National Conference, 1990.
**BR, CI**

Bjorneberg, Paul, comp. *Exploring Careers in Music.* Rev. and exp. ed. Reston, Va.: Music Educators National Conference and American Music Conference, 1990.
**BR**

Block, Adrienne Fried, ed. *Women's Studies/Women's Status, 1987.* Boulder, Colo.: College Music Society, 1988.
**BR, RSC**

Bloom, Benjamin Samuel, J. Thomas Hastings, and George F. Madaus. *Handbook on Formative and Summative Evaluation of Student Learning.* New York: McGraw-Hill, 1971.
**BR, P**

Boney, Joan, and Lois Rhea. *A Guide to Student Teaching in Music.* Englewood Cliffs, N.J.: Prentice-Hall, 1970.
**BR, CI**

Brookhart, Edward. *Music in American Higher Education: An Annotated Bibliography.* Bibliographies in American Music, 10. Warren, Mich.: Harmonie Park Press, 1988.
**BR, CI**

Brown, Joseph D. *Strategic Marketing for Music Educators: A Complete Marketing Handbook for Music Educators.* Muncie, Ind.: Gemeinhardt, 1985.
**BR**

Butler, David. *The Musician's Guide to Perception and Cognition.* New York: Schirmer Books, 1992.
**BR, P**

Campbell, Don G., comp. *Music Physician for Times to Come: An Anthology.* Wheaton, Ill.: Theosophical Publishing House, 1991.
**BR, P**

Campbell, Patricia Shehan. *Lessons from the World: A Cross-Cultural Guide to Music Teaching and Learning.* New York: Schirmer Books, 1991.
**BR, CI**

Capurso, Alexander, ed. *Music and Your Emotions: A Practical Guide to Music Selections Associated with Desired Emotional Responses.* 1952. Reprint, New York: Liveright, 1970.

**BR, P, R**

Chall, Jeanne S., and Allan F. Mirsky, eds. *Education and the Brain: 77th Yearbook of the National Society for the Study of Education (Part II).* Chicago: University of Chicago Press, 1978.

**BR, CI, P**

Clark, J. Bunker. *Music at KU: A History of the University of Kansas Music Department.* Lawrence: Department of Music and Dance, University of Kansas, 1986.

**BR, CI**

Collins, Thomas Clark, ed. *Music Education Materials: A Selected Annotated Bibliography.* Washington: Music Educators National Conference, 1968.

**BR, CI**

Colwell, Richard J. *A Critique of Research Studies in Music Education.* Urbana: University of Illinois, 1972.

**BR, R**

————, ed. *Handbook of Research on Music Teaching and Learning.* New York: Schirmer Books, 1992.

**BR, CI, P, R**

*Comprehensive Dissertation Index, 1861-1972.* 37 vols. Ann Arbor, Mich.: Xerox University Microfilms, 1973.

**BR, R**

Cox, Richard C., and Nancy Jordan Unks. *A Selected and Annotated Bibliography of Studies Concerning the Taxonomy of Educational Objectives: Cognitive Domain.* Pittsburgh, Pa.: University of Pittsburgh, 1967.

**BR, CI**

Crawford, Richard. "Music at Michigan: A Historical Perspective." In *100 Years of Music at Michigan, 1880-1980,* 9-38. Ann Arbor: University of Michigan, 1979.

**BR, CI**

*Data Summary: Music.* Reston, Va.: Higher Education Arts Data Services and National Association of Schools of Music, 1990.

**BR**

Dillon, Jacquelyn. "How to Educate Parents for a Better String Program." In *Voices of Industry*, 25-31. Reston, Va.: Music Educators National Conference, 1990.
**BR, CI**

*Dissertation Abstracts International.* Ann Arbor, Mich.: University Microfilms International, 1938-.
**BR, R**

Doerksen, David P. *Guide to Evaluating Teachers of Music Performance Groups.* Reston, Va.: Music Educators National Conference, 1990.
**BR, CI, P**

Druesedow, John E., Jr. *Library Research Guide to Music: Illustrated Search Strategy and Sources.* Ann Arbor, Mich.: Pierian, 1982.
**BR, R**

Duckles, Vincent H., and Ida Reed. *Music Reference and Research Materials: An Annotated Bibliography.* 5th ed. New York: Schirmer Books, 1997.
**BR, R**

*Encyclopedia of Adolescence.* Ed. Richard Lerner, Anne C. Petersen, and Jeanne Brooks-Gunn. New York: Garland, 1991.
**BR, CI, R**

*Encyclopedia of Educational Research.* Ed. Marvin C. Alkin, Michele Linden, Jana Noel, and Karen Ray. 6th ed. New York: Macmillan, 1992.
**BR, CI, R**

Erbes, Robert L. *Certification Practices and Trends in Music Teacher Education.* 4th ed. Reston, Va.: Music Educators National Conference, 1992.
**BR, CI**

Feldstein, Sandy. "How to Get Your Music Published." In *Voices of Industry*, 59-63. Reston, Va.: Music Educators National Conference, 1990.
**BR**

Fidler, Linda M., and Richard S. James. "Jazz Index." In *International Music Journals*, ed. Linda M. Fidler and Richard S. James, 474-75. New York: Greenwood, 1990.
**BR, CI, J**

————. "Music Article Guide." In *International Music Journals*, ed. Linda M. Fidler and Richard S. James, 476. New York: Greenwood, 1990.
**BR, J**

————. "Music Index." In *International Music Journals*, ed. Linda M. Fidler and Richard S. James, 477-78. New York: Greenwood, 1990.
**BR, J**

————. "Popular Music Periodicals Index." In *International Music Journals*, ed. Linda M. Fidler and Richard S. James, 479. New York: Greenwood, 1990.
**BR, J**

————. "RILM Abstracts." In *International Music Journals*, ed. Linda M. Fidler and Richard S. James, 480. New York: Greenwood, 1990.
**BR, J**

————, eds. *International Music Journals.* New York: Greenwood, 1990.
**BR, J**

Flagg, Marion Elizabeth. *Musical Learning: A Guide to Child Growth.* Boston: C. C. Birchard, 1949.
**BR, CI, P**

Fowler, Charles B., ed. *An Arts in Education Source Book.* New York: The Fund, 1980.
**A, BR, CI**

Gary, Charles. "Working within the Copyright Law." In *Voices of Industry*, 65-72. Reston, Va.: Music Educators National Conference, 1990.
**BR**

Geerdes, Harold P. *Music Facilities: Building, Equipping, and Renovating.* Rev. ed. Reston, Va.: Music Educators National Conference, 1987.
**BR**

Godwin, Joscelyn, ed. *Music, Mysticism, and Magic: A Sourcebook.* New York: Arkana, 1987.
**BR, FPA, P**

Graham, Richard M., and Alice S. Beer. *Teaching Music to the Exceptional Child: A Handbook for Mainstreaming.* Englewood Cliffs, N.J.: Prentice Hall, 1980.
**BR, CI, P**

*Guidelines for Performances of School Music Groups: Expectations and Limitations.* Reston, Va.: Music Educators National Conference, 1986.
**BR, CI**

Harris, Ernest E. *Music Education: A Guide to Information Sources.* Detroit, Mich.: Gale Research, 1978.
**BR**

Heintze, James R. *American Music Studies: A Classified Bibliography of Master's Theses,* Bibliographies in American Music, 8. Detroit: Information Coordinators, 1984.
**BR, R**

Heller, George N. *Historical Research in Music Education: A Bibliography.* 2nd ed. Lawrence: University of Kansas Department of Art and Music Education and Music Therapy, 1992.
**BR, FPA, R**

_____. *Music and Music Education History: A Chronology.* 2nd ed. Lawrence: University of Kansas Department of Art and Music Education and Music Therapy, 1993.
**BR, FPA**

Henry, Nelson B., ed. *Basic Concepts in Music Education: 57th Yearbook of the National Society for the Study of Education.* Chicago: University of Chicago Press, 1958.
**BR, CI, FPA**

Herman, Joan L., Pamela R. Aschbacher, and Lynn Winters. *A Practical Guide to Alternative Assessment.* Alexandria, Va.: Association for Supervision and Curriculum Development, 1992.
**BR, CI, P**

Herz, Beverley, and Craig D. Northrup. "Planning a Successful Concert Tour." In *Voices of Industry,* 13-18. Reston, Va.: Music Educators National Conference, 1990.
**BR, CI**

Hilgard, Ernest Ropiequet, ed. *Theories of Learning and Instruction: 63rd Yearbook of the National Society for the Study of Education.* Chicago: University of Chicago Press, 1964.
**BR, CI, P**

Hodges, Donald A., ed. *Handbook of Music Psychology.* Lawrence, Kans.: National Association for Music Therapy, 1980.
**BR, P, R**

Houston, W. Robert, Martin Haberman, and John P. Sikula, eds. *Handbook of Research on Teacher Education.* 2nd ed. New York: Macmillan, 1996.
**BR, CI, R**

*International Directory of Approved Music Education Dissertations in Progress.* Urbana, Ill.: Council for Research in Music Education, 1989-.
**BR, J, R**

*International Directory of Music Education Institutions.* Paris: UNESCO, 1968.
**BR**

Jackson, Philip W., ed. *Handbook of Research on Curriculum: A Project of the American Educational Research Association.* New York: Macmillan, 1992.
**BR, CI, R**

Katz, Jonathan, ed. *Arts and Education Handbook: A Guide to Productive Collaborations.* Washington: National Assembly of State Arts Agencies, 1988.
**A, BR, CI**

Kowall, Bonnie C., ed. *Perspectives in Music Education: Source Book III.* Washington: Music Educators National Conference, 1966.
**BR, CI, FPA**

Kramer, Jack J., and Jane Close Conoley, eds. *The Eleventh Mental Measurements Yearbook.* Lincoln: University of Nebraska Press, 1992.
**BR, P**

Landon, Joseph W. *Clinical Practice in Music Education: A Guide to Field Experiences in the Preparation of Teachers.* Fullerton, Calif.: Music Education Publications, 1988.
**BR, CI**

Langer, Susanne Katherina, ed. *Reflections on Art: A Source Book of Writings by Artists, Critics, and Philosophers.* 1958. Reprint, New York: Arno, 1979.
**A, BR, FPA**

Larson, William S., ed. *Bibliography of Research Studies in Music Education, 1932-1948.* Chicago: Music Educators National Conference, 1949.
**BR, R**

———, ed. *Bibliography of Research Studies in Music Education, 1949-1956.* Chicago: Music Educators National Conference, 1958.
**BR, R**

Lawrence, Vera Brodsky. *CMP Library: Contemporary Music Project for Creativity in Music Education.* 2nd ed. Washington: Music Educators National Conference, 1969.
**BR, CI, RSC**

Leonhard, Charles. *The Status of Arts Education in American Public Schools: Report of a Survey Conducted by the National Arts Education Research Center at the University of Illinois.* Urbana: Council for Research in Music Education, School of Music, University of Illinois, 1991.
**A, BR, CI, RSC**

Lieberman, Ann, ed. *The Changing Contexts of Teaching: 91st Yearbook of the National Society for the Study of Education (Part I).* Chicago: National Society for the Study of Education, 1992.
**BR, CI**

Lieberman, Julie Lyonn. *You Are Your Instrument: The Definitive Musician's Guide to Practice and Performance.* 3rd ed. New York: Huiksi Music, 1995.
**BR, CI, P**

Lincoln, Harry B., comp. *Index to Graduate Degrees in Music, U.S. and Canada.* Binghamton, N.Y.: College Music Society, 1971.
**BR**

Livingston, Robert Allen, ed. *The Music Information and Education Guide.* Cardiff by the Sea, Calif.: La Costa Music Business Consultants, 1983.
**BR**

Madsen, Clifford K. *Music Therapy: A Behavioral Guide for the Mentally Retarded.* Lawrence, Kans.: National Association for Music Therapy, 1981.
**BR, CI, P**

Mark, Michael L. *Source Readings in Music Education History.* 1982. Reprint, Charlottesville, Va.: Lincoln-Rembrandt, 1994.
**BR, FPA**

May, William V., and Craig Tolin. *Pronunciation Guide for Choral Literature.* Reston, Va.: Music Educators National Conference, 1987.
**BR, CI**

Mayer, Frederick R., ed. *The String Orchestra Super List.* Reston, Va.: Music Educators National Conference, 1993.
**BR, CI**

McLaughlin, John, ed. *A Guide to National and State Arts Education Services.* New York: ACA Books, 1987.
**A, BR**

McPherson, Bruce. *Measure by Measure: A History of the New England Conservatory from 1867.* Boston: New England Conservatory, 1995.
**BR, CI**

Mills, Elizabeth. *In the Suzuki Style: A Manual for Raising Musical Consciousness in Children.* Berkeley, Calif.: Diablo, 1974.
**BR, CI**

Mixter, Keith E. *General Bibliography for Music Research.* 3rd ed. Detroit Studies in Music Bibliography, 75. Warren, Mich.: Harmonie Park Press, 1996.
**BR, R**

Morgan, Hazel Nohavec, ed. *Music Education Source Book: A Compendium of Data, Opinion and Recommendations.* Chicago: Music Educators National Conference, 1951.
**BR, CI, FPA**

————, ed. *Music in American Education: Music Education Source Book II.* Chicago: Music Educators National Conference, 1955.
**BR, CI, FPA**

Murphy, Linda L., Jane Close Conoley, and James C. Impara, eds. *Tests in Print IV: An Index to Tests, Test Reviews, and the Literature on Specific Tests.* Lincoln: University of Nebraska Press, 1994.
**BR, P**

*Music Booster Manual.* Reston, Va.: Music Educators National Conference, 1989.
**BR**

*Music Education Materials: A Selected Bibliography.* Chicago: Music Educators National Conference, 1959.
**BR, CI**

*Music Psychology Index.* Vol. 2. Ed. Charles T. Eagle, Jr. Denton, Tex.: Institute for Therapeutics Research, 1978.
**BR, J, P, R**

*Music Psychology Index.* Vol. 3. Ed. Charles T. Eagle, Jr., and John J. Miniter. Phoenix, Ariz.: Oryx, 1984.
**BR, J, P, R**

*Music Scholarship Guide.* 3rd ed. Reston, Va.: Music Educators National Conference, 1994.
**BR**

*Music Schools and Music Education.* New York: Foundation Center, 1986.
**BR, CI**

*Music Therapy Index.* Vol. 1. Ed. Charles T. Eagle, Jr. Lawrence, Kans.: National Association for Music Therapy, 1976.
**BR, J, P, R**

Narmour, Eugene, and Ruth A. Solie, eds. *Explorations in Music, the Arts, and Ideas: Essays in Honor of Leonard B. Meyer.* Stuyvesant, N.Y.: Pendragon, 1988.
**A, BR, FPA, RSC**

National Coalition for Music Education. *Building Support for School Music: A Practical Guide.* Reston, Va.: Music Educators National Conference, 1991.

**BR, FPA**

Neiman, Marcus L., comp. *Life in the Music Classroom.* Reston, Va.: Music Educators National Conference, 1992.

**BR, CI**

Phelps, Roger P., Lawrence Ferrara, and Thomas W. Goolsby. *A Guide to Research in Music Education.* 4th ed. Metuchen, N.J.: Scarecrow, 1993.

**BR, R**

Porter, Robert, ed. *Arts Advocacy: A Citizen Action Manual.* New York: American Council for the Arts, 1980.

**A, BR**

Potosky, Alice. *Promoting School Music: A Practical Guide.* Reston, Va.: Music Educators National Conference, 1984.

**BR, CI, FPA**

Probasco, Jim. *A Parent's Guide to Band and Orchestra.* White Hall, Va.: Betterway, 1991.

**BR, CI**

————. *A Parent's Guide to Teaching Music.* White Hall, Va.: Betterway, 1992.

**BR, CI**

Rao, Doreen. *Choral Music for Children: An Annotated List.* Reston, Va.: Music Educators National Conference, 1990.

**BR, CI**

Reimer, Bennett, and Ralph A. Smith, eds. *The Arts, Education, and Aesthetic Knowing: 91st Yearbook of the National Society for the Study of Education (Part II).* Chicago: National Society for the Study of Education, 1992.

**A, BR, CI, FPA, P**

*Restructuring and Reform: Selected Bibliography.* Reston, Va.: Music Educators National Conference, 1993.

**BR, CI, R, RSC**

Robinson, Doris. *Music and Dance Periodicals: An International Directory and Guidebook.* Voorheesville, N.Y.: Peri, 1989.

**A, BR, J**

Rossman, R. Louis. *The Business of Administration and Supervision in Music: A Selective Annotated Bibliography.* Sioux City, Iowa: Dabec Educational Products, 1989.
**BR, CI, FPA**

Schiller Institute. *A Manual on the Rudiments of Tuning and Registration.* Washington: Schiller Institute, 1992.
**BR, P**

Schulberg, Cecilia H. *The Music Therapy Sourcebook: A Collection of Activities Categorized and Analyzed.* New York: Human Sciences, 1981.
**BR, CI, P**

Schurk, William L. "Recorded Sound." In *International Music Journals*, ed. Linda M. Fidler and Richard S. James, 360-62. New York: Greenwood, 1990.
**BR, J, R**

Shrude, Marilyn. "Source: Music of the Avant Garde." In *International Music Journals*, ed. Linda M. Fidler and Richard S. James, 401-03. New York: Greenwood, 1990.
**BR, J**

Silverberg, Ann L. *A Sympathy with Sounds: A Brief History of the University of Illinois School of Music to Celebrate Its Centennial.* Urbana: School of Music, University of Illinois, 1995.
**BR, CI**

Simons, Gene M. *Early Childhood Musical Development: A Bibliography of Research Abstracts, 1960-1975, with Implications and Recommendations for Teaching and Research.* Reston, Va.: Music Educators National Conference, 1978.
**BR, CI, P, R**

Small, Arnold M., ed. *Bibliography of Research Studies in Music Education, 1932-1944.* Iowa City: State University of Iowa Press, 1944.
**BR, R**

*Sourcebook for Futures Planning.* Reston, Va.: National Association of Schools of Music, 1990.
**BR, FPA**

Standifer, James A., and Barbara Reeder. *Source Book of African and Afro-American Materials for Music Educators.* Washington: Contemporary Music Project, 1972.
**BR, CI**

Stebbing, Lionel, comp. *Music Therapy: A New Anthology.* Sussex, England: New Knowledge Books, 1975.
**BR, P**

Steinel, Daniel V., comp. *Data on Music Education.* Reston, Va.: Music Educators National Conference, 1990.
**BR, R**

————, comp. *Music and Music Education: Data and Information.* Reston, Va.: Music Educators National Conference, 1984.
**BR, R**

————, comp. and ed. *Arts in Schools: State by State.* 2nd ed. Reston, Va.: Music Educators National Conference, 1988.
**A, BR**

*Teacher's Guide for Advocacy.* Reston, Va.: Music Educators National Conference, 1992.
**BR, FPA**

Tillman, Rix W. *Music Educator's Guide to Personalized Instruction.* West Nyack, N.Y.: Parker, 1975.
**BR, CI**

*Voices of Industry.* Reston, Va.: Music Educators National Conference, 1990.
**BR, CI**

Warner, Thomas E. *Periodical Literature on Music in America, 1620-1920: A Classified Bibliography with Annotations.* Bibliographies in American Music, 11. Warren, Mich.: Harmonie Park Press, 1988.
**BR, R**

Watanabe, Ruth. "Notes: The Quarterly Journal of the Music Library Association." In *International Music Journals*, ed. Linda M. Fidler and Richard S. James, 319-22. New York: Greenwood, 1990.
**BR, J, R**

Weichlein, William Jesset. *A Checklist of American Music Periodicals, 1850-1900.* Detroit, Mich.: Information Coordinators, 1970.
**BR, J**

Wenger, Harry. "Selecting Equipment for Your Performing Group." In *Voices of Industry*, 7-12. Reston, Va.: Music Educators National Conference, 1990.
**BR, CI**

Whipple, Guy Montrose, ed. *Music Education: 35th Yearbook of the National Society for the Study of Education (Part II).* Bloomington, Ill.: Public School Publishing, 1936.
**BR, CI, FPA, P**

Wilson, A. Verne, comp.  *TIPS: Retirement for Music Educators.*  Reston, Va.: Music Educators National Conference, 1993.
**BR**

Winesanker, Michael, comp.  *A List of Books on Music.*  Rev. ed.  Reston, Va.: National Association of Schools of Music, 1977.
**BR**

Winick, Steven.  *Rhythm: An Annotated Bibliography.*  Metuchen, N.J.: Scarecrow, 1974.
**BR, P, R**

Yaffe, Michael C.  *Annotated Bibliography of Publications, 1934-1976: The National Association of Schools of Music.*  Reston, Va.: National Association of Schools of Music, 1976.
**BR**

_____.  *Annotated Bibliography of Publications, 1977-1980: The National Association of Schools of Music.*  Reston, Va.: National Association of Schools of Music, 1980.
**BR**

# (CI)

## CURRICULUM AND INSTRUCTION

Abeles, Harold F., Charles R. Hoffer, and Robert H. Klotman.  *Foundations of Music Education.*  2nd ed.  New York: Schirmer Books, 1994.
**CI, FPA**

*Academic Preparation for College: What Students Need to Know and Be Able to Do.*  New York: College Entrance Examination Board, 1983.
**CI, RSC**

*Action for Excellence: A Comprehensive Plan to Improve Our Nation's Schools.*  Denver, Colo.: Education Commission of the States, 1983.
**CI, RSC**

Adler, Mortimer Jerome.  *The Paideia Proposal: An Educational Manifesto.*  New York: Macmillan, 1982.
**CI**

*Agenda for Excellence at the Middle Level: A Statement by NASSP's Council on Middle Level Education.* Reston, Va.: National Association of Secondary School Principals, 1985.
**CI, RSC**

*Agenda for Excellence in Music at the Middle Level.* Reston, Va.: Music Educators National Conference, 1994.
**CI**

Airasian, Peter. "The Impact of the Taxonomy on Testing and Evaluation." In *Bloom's Taxonomy—A Forty-Year Retrospective: 93rd Yearbook of the National Society for the Study of Education (Part II)*, ed. Lorin W. Anderson and Lauren A. Sosniak, 82-102. Chicago: University of Chicago Press, 1994.
**CI, P**

Alvarez, Barbara. "Musical Thinking and the Young Child." In *Dimensions of Musical Thinking*, ed. Eunice Boardman, 57-64. Reston, Va.: Music Educators National Conference, 1989.
**CI, P**

*America 2000 Arts Partnership.* Washington: U.S. Department of Education and the National Endowment for the Arts, 1992.
**A, CI**

*America's Culture Begins with Education.* Reston, Va.: Music Educators National Conference, 1990.
**CI, FPA**

American Council for the Arts. *Toward a New Era in Arts Education.* Reston, Va.: Music Educators National Conference, 1988.
**A, CI**

————. *Why We Need the Arts: Eight Quotable Speeches by Leaders in Education, Business, and the Arts.* Reston, Va.: Music Educators National Conference, 1989.
**A, CI, RSC**

*American Educational Research Journal.* Washington: American Educational Research Association, 1964-.
**CI, J, R**

American String Teachers Association, National School Orchestra Association, and Music Educators National Conference. *The Complete String Guide: Standards, Programs, Purchase, and Maintenance.* Reston, Va.: Music Educators National Conference, 1988.
**BR, CI**

Anderson, Jill Kuespert. *TIPS: Music in Our Schools Month (MIOSM)*. Reston, Va.: Music Educators National Conference, 1988.
**BR, CI**

Anderson, Lorin W. "Research on Teaching and Teacher Education." In *Bloom's Taxonomy—A Forty-Year Retrospective: 93rd Yearbook of the National Society for the Study of Education (Part II)*, ed. Lorin W. Anderson and Lauren A. Sosniak, 126-45. Chicago: University of Chicago Press, 1994.
**CI, R**

Anderson, Lorin W., and Lauren A. Sosniak, eds. *Bloom's Taxonomy—A Forty-Year Retrospective: 93rd Yearbook of the National Society for the Study of Education (Part II)*. Chicago: National Society for the Study of Education, 1994.
**BR, CI, FPA, P**

Anderson, Tom. *Sing Choral Music at Sight*. Reston, Va.: Music Educators National Conference, 1992.
**CI**

Anderson, William M., ed. and comp. *Teaching Music with a Multicultural Approach*. Reston, Va.: Music Educators National Conference, 1991.
**CI**

Anderson, William M., and Patricia Shehan Campbell, eds. *Multicultural Perspectives in Music Education*. 2nd ed. Reston, Va.: Music Educators National Conference, 1996.
**CI**

Andress, Barbara. *Music in Early Childhood*. Washington: Music Educators National Conference, 1973.
**CI**

————, ed. *Promising Practices: Prekindergarten Music Education*. Reston, Va.: Music Educators National Conference, 1989.
**CI**

Andress, Barbara, and Linda Miller Walker, eds. *Readings in Early Childhood Music Education*. Reston, Va.: Music Educators National Conference, 1992.
**CI**

Andrews, Frances M. *Junior High School General Music: Foundations of Music Education Series*. Englewood Cliffs, N.J.: Prentice-Hall, 1971.
**CI, FPA**

Apfelstadt, Hilary. "Musical Thinking in the Choral Rehearsal." In *Dimensions of Musical Thinking*, ed. Eunice Boardman, 73-81. Reston, Va.: Music Educators National Conference, 1989.
CI, P

Armstrong, Thomas. *Multiple Intelligences in the Classroom*. Alexandria, Va.: Association for Supervision and Curriculum Development, 1994.
CI, P

Arnstine, Donald. "The Aesthetic as a Context for General Education." In *Aesthetics and Problems of Education*, ed. Ralph A. Smith, 402-13. Urbana: University of Illinois Press, 1971.
A, CI, FPA

*Arts Education Research Agenda for the Future*. Washington: U.S. Department of Education, 1994.
A, CI, R, RSC

*Arts Go to School: An Arts-in-Education Handbook*. New York: American Council for the Arts, 1983.
A, BR, CI

*Arts in Education: Research Report*. Washington: National School Boards Association, 1978.
A, CI, R, RSC

*Arts in Rural America*. Washington: National Endowment for the Arts, 1991.
A, CI

*Arts in Schools—Perspectives from Four Nations: A Report from the National Endowment for the Arts*. Washington: National Endowment for the Arts, 1993.
A, CI, RSC

Arts, Education, and Americans Panel. *Coming to Our Senses: The Significance of the Arts for American Education*. New York: McGraw-Hill, 1977.
A, CI, FPA, RSC

Aschner, Mary Jane. "Teaching the Anatomy of Criticism." In *Aesthetics and Problems of Education*, ed. Ralph A. Smith, 425-34. Urbana: University of Illinois Press, 1971.
A, CI, FPA

Aspin, David. "Assessment and Education in the Arts." In *The Aesthetic Imperative: Relevance and Responsibility in Arts Education*, ed. Malcolm Ross, 25-52. New York: Pergamon, 1981.
A, CI, FPA, P

*Assessment of Community Education Programs in Music.* Reston, Va.: National Association of Schools of Music, 1988.
**BR, CI, P, RSC**

*Assessment of Graduate Programs in Music.* Reston, Va.: National Association of Schools of Music, 1985.
**BR, CI, P**

*Assessment of Undergraduate Programs in Music.* Reston, Va.: National Association of Schools of Music, 1991.
**BR, CI, P**

Atterbury, Betty W. "Research on the Teaching of Elementary General Music." In *Handbook of Research on Music Teaching and Learning*, ed. Richard J. Colwell, 594-601. New York: Schirmer Books, 1992.
**CI, R**

————, ed. *Elementary General Music: The Best of MEJ.* Reston, Va.: Music Educators National Conference, 1992.
**CI**

Atterbury, Betty W., and Carol P. Richardson. *The Experience of Teaching General Music.* New York: McGraw-Hill, 1995.
**CI**

Bachmann, Marie-Laure. *Dalcroze Today: An Education through and into Music.* Transl. D. Parlett. New York: Oxford University Press, 1991.
**CI**

Baird, Peggy Flanagan. *Music Books for the Elementary School Library.* Washington: Music Educators National Conference, 1972.
**BR, CI**

Baldwin, Lillian L. "Listening." In *Music Education: 35th Yearbook of the National Society for the Study of Education (Part II)*, ed. Guy Montrose Whipple, 91-98. Bloomington, Ill.: Public School Publishing, 1936.
**CI**

Balfe, Judith H., and Joni Cherbo Heine. "On the Necessity of Adult Arts Education beyond the Classroom." In *Arts Education beyond the Classroom*, ed. Judith H. Balfe and Joni Cherbo Heine, 3-6. New York: American Council for the Arts, 1988.
**A, CI**

_____, eds. *Arts Education beyond the Classroom*. New York: American Council for the Arts, 1988.

**A, CI, RSC**

Ball, Charles H. "Thoughts on Music as Aesthetic Education." In *Toward an Aesthetic Education: A Report*, 57-62. Washington: Music Educators National Conference, 1971.

**A, CI, FPA**

Bamberger, Jeanne Shapiro, et al. *The Art of Listening: Developing Musical Perception*. 5th ed. New York: Harper and Row, 1988.

**CI, P**

Barnes, Stephen H., ed. *A Cross-Section of Research in Music Education*. Washington: University Press of America, 1982.

**CI, R**

Barrett, Janet. "Core Thinking Skills in Music." In *Dimensions of Musical Thinking*, ed. Eunice Boardman, 45-56. Reston, Va.: Music Educators National Conference, 1989.

**CI, P**

Barron, John P., comp. *A Selected Bibliography of the Kodály Concept of Music Education*. Willowdale, Ontario: Avondale, 1979.

**BR, CI**

Batcheller, John M. *Music in Early Childhood*. New York: Center for Applied Research in Education, 1975.

**CI**

Baumann, Max Peter, ed. *Music in the Dialogue of Cultures: Traditional Music and Cultural Policy*. New York: C. F. Peters, 1991.

**CI, P**

Baxter, Steve, and Sandra L. Stauffer. "Music Teaching: A Review of Common Practice." In *The Crane Symposium: Toward an Understanding of the Teaching and Learning of Music Performance*, ed. Charles Fowler, 49-62. Potsdam: Potsdam College of the State University of New York, 1988.

**CI, R**

Bayless, Kathleen M., and Marjorie E. Ramsey. *Music: A Way of Life for the Young Child*. 4th ed. New York: Merrill, 1991.

**CI**

Beall, Gretchen Hieronymus. "Methodology and Music in General Education." In *Music Education in the United States: Contemporary Issues*, ed. J. Terry Gates, 202-23. Tuscaloosa: University of Alabama Press, 1988.
**CI, FPA, P**

————. "Music Education in Adolescence: A Problem in Perspectives." In *Symposium in Music Education: A Festschrift for Charles Leonhard*, ed. Richard J. Colwell, 61-92. Urbana-Champaign: University of Illinois, 1982.
**CI, P**

Beattie, John W. "The Accrediting and the Programming of School Music." In *Music Education: 35th Yearbook of the National Society for the Study of Education (Part II)*, ed. Guy Montrose Whipple, 141-45. Bloomington, Ill.: Public School Publishing, 1936.
**CI, FPA**

————. "The Selection and Training of Teachers." In *Music Education: 35th Yearbook of the National Society for the Study of Education (Part II)*, ed. Guy Montrose Whipple, 207-19. Bloomington, Ill.: Public School Publishing, 1936.
**CI**

Becknell, Arthur F. "The Timelessness of Jaques-Dalcroze's Approach." In *The Eclectic Curriculum in American Music Education*, 2nd ed., ed. Polly Carder, 31-35. Reston, Va.: Music Educators National Conference, 1990.
**CI**

Benn, Oleta A. "A Message for New Teachers." In *Basic Concepts in Music Education: 57th Yearbook of the National Society for the Study of Education*, ed. Nelson B. Henry, 339-55. Chicago: University of Chicago Press, 1958.
**CI, FPA**

Benner, Charles H. *Teaching Performing Groups: From Research to the Music Classroom No. 2*. Washington: Music Educators National Conference, 1972.
**CI, R**

Bennett, Michael. "Getting a Child Started in Instrumental Music." In *Voices of Industry*, 19-23. Reston, Va.: Music Educators National Conference, 1990.
**CI**

Benson, Warren. *Creative Projects in Musicianship: A Report of Pilot Projects Sponsored by the Contemporary Music Project at Ithaca College and Interlochen Arts Academy*. Washington: Contemporary Music Project, Music Educators National Conference, 1967.
**CI, RSC**

Bentley, Arnold. *Music in Education: A Point of View.* Atlantic Highlands, N.J.: Humanities Press, 1975.
**CI, FPA**

Bentley, Arnold, Kurt E. Eicke, and Robert G. Petzold, eds. *The Third International Seminar on Research in Music Education.* London: Bärenreiter, 1973.
**CI, R, RSC**

Bergin, Bob. "The Role of Instruments: Preschool through Third Grade." In *Voices of Industry*, 33-40. Reston, Va.: Music Educators National Conference, 1990.
**BR, CI**

Biasini, Americole, and Lenore Pogonowski. *Manhattanville Music Curriculum Program (MMCP) Interaction.* 2nd ed. Bellingham, Wash.: Americole, 1979.
**CI, RSC**

Bjorkvold, Jon Roar. *The Muse Within: Creativity and Communication, Song and Play from Childhood through Maturity.* Transl. W. H. Halverson. New York: Harper Collins, 1992.
**CI, P**

Black, Max. "Education as Art and Discipline." In *Aesthetics and Problems of Education*, ed. Ralph A. Smith, 529-36. Urbana: University of Illinois Press, 1971.
**A, CI, FPA**

Blacking, John, and Joann W. Kealiinohomoku, eds. *The Performing Arts: Music and Dance.* New York: Mouton, 1979.
**A, CI, RSC**

Bloom, Benjamin Samuel. Excerpts from the "Taxonomy of Educational Objectives, the Classification of Educational Goals, Handbook I: Cognitive Domain." In *Bloom's Taxonomy—A Forty-Year Retrospective: 93rd Yearbook of the National Society for the Study of Education (Part II)*, ed. Lorin W. Anderson and Lauren A. Sosniak, 9-27. Chicago: University of Chicago Press, 1994.
**CI, P**

————. "Reflections on the Development and Use of the Taxonomy." In *Bloom's Taxonomy—A Forty-Year Retrospective: 93rd Yearbook of the National Society for the Study of Education (Part II)*, ed. Lorin W. Anderson and Lauren A. Sosniak, 1-8. Chicago: University of Chicago Press, 1994.
**CI, P**

————, ed. *Taxonomy of Educational Objectives: The Classification of Educational Goals.* 1956. Reprint, New York: Longman, 1984.
**CI, P**

Bloom, Kathryn. "Development of Arts and Humanities Programs." In *Toward an Aesthetic Education: A Report*, 89-99. Washington: Music Educators National Conference, 1971.
**A, CI, FPA**

_____. "Research and Development Needs for Comprehensive Programs in the Arts in Education at the Precollegiate Level." In *Arts and Aesthetics: An Agenda for the Future*, ed. Stanley S. Madeja, 317-30. St. Louis, Mo.: CEMREL, 1977.
**A, CI, R**

Boardman, Eunice. "A Message for the Teacher of Teachers." In *Basic Concepts in Music Education II*, ed. Richard J. Colwell, 279-88. Niwot: University Press of Colorado, 1991.
**CI, FPA**

_____. "Music Teacher Education." In *Handbook of Research on Teacher Education*, ed. W. Robert Houston, Martin Haberman, and John P. Sikula, 730-45. New York: Macmillan, 1990.
**CI, R**

_____. "The Relation of Music Study to Thinking." In *Dimensions of Musical Thinking*, ed. Eunice Boardman, 1-7. Reston, Va.: Music Educators National Conference, 1989.
**CI, P**

_____, ed. *Dimensions of Musical Thinking*. Reston, Va.: Music Educators National Conference, 1989.
**CI, P**

Boardman, Eunice, and Carroll A. Rinehart, comps. *Individualized Instruction in Music*. Reston, Va.: Music Educators National Conference, 1975.
**CI**

Boney, Joan, and Lois Rhea. *A Guide to Student Teaching in Music*. Englewood Cliffs, N.J.: Prentice-Hall, 1970.
**BR, CI**

Bonis, Ferenc, ed. *The Selected Writings of Zoltán Kodály*. Transl. Lili Halapy and Fred Macnicol. New York: Boosey and Hawkes, 1974.
**CI, FPA**

Boston, Bruce O. *The American High School, Time for Reform: A Report for the Council for Basic Education*. Washington: Council for Basic Education, 1982.
**CI, RSC**

_____, ed. *Perspectives on Implementation: Arts Education Standards for America's Students*. Reston, Va.: Music Educators National Conference, 1994.
**A, CI, FPA**

Boswell, Jacquelyn, ed. *The Young Child and Music: Contemporary Principles in Child Development and Music Education*. Reston, Va.: Music Educators National Conference, 1985.
**CI, P, RSC**

————. "Reflections and Applications for Middle School." In *Toward Tomorrow: New Visions for General Music*, ed. Sandra L. Stauffer, 131-33. Reston, Va.: Music Educators National Conference, 1995.
**CI**

Boyer, Ernest L. *High School: A Report on Secondary Education in America - The Carnegie Foundation for the Advancement of Teaching*. New York: Harper and Row, 1983.
**CI, RSC**

————. *Ready to Learn: A Mandate for the Nation*. Princeton, N.J.: Carnegie Foundation for the Advancement of Teaching, 1991.
**CI, RSC**

Boyle, J. David, ed. *Instructional Objectives in Music*. Vienna, Va.: Music Educators National Conference, National Commission of Instruction, 1974.
**CI**

Boyle, J. David, and Rudolf E. Radocy. *Measurement and Evaluation of Musical Experiences*. New York: Schirmer Books, 1987.
**CI, P**

Brandt, Ronald S., ed. *Readings from Educational Leadership: Cooperative Learning and the Collaborative School*. Alexandria, Va.: Association for Supervision and Curriculum Development, 1991.
**CI**

————, ed. *Readings from Educational Leadership: Effective Schools and School Improvement*. Alexandria, Va.: Association for Supervision and Curriculum Development, 1989.
**CI**

————, ed. *Readings from Educational Leadership: Restructuring Schools*. Alexandria, Va.: Association for Supervision and Curriculum Development, 1993.
**CI**

————, ed. *Readings from Educational Leadership: Teaching Thinking*. Alexandria, Va.: Association for Supervision and Curriculum Development, 1989.
**CI**

*British Journal of Music Education*. Cambridge: Cambridge University Press, 1984-.
**CI, J, P, R**

Britton, Allen P. "American Music Education: Is It Better than We Think? A Discussion of the Roles of Performance and Repertory, Together with Brief Mention of Certain Other Problems." In *Basic Concepts in Music Education II*, ed. Richard J. Colwell, 175-90. Niwot: University Press of Colorado, 1991.
**CI, FPA**

Brocklehurst, J. Brian. *Response to Music: Principles of Music Education.* London: Routledge and K. Paul, 1971.
**CI, FPA**

Brookhart, Edward. *Music in American Higher Education: An Annotated Bibliography.* Bibliographies in American Music, 10. Warren, Mich.: Harmonie Park Press, 1988.
**BR, CI**

Broudy, Harry S. *Building a Philosophy of Education.* 2nd ed. Englewood Cliffs, N.J.: Prentice-Hall, 1961.
**CI, FPA**

―――――. *A Critique of Performance-Based Teacher Education.* Washington: American Association of Colleges for Teacher Education, 1972.
**CI**

―――――. *Enlightened Cherishing: An Essay on Aesthetic Education.* 1972. Reprint, Urbana: University of Illinois Press, 1994.
**A, CI, FPA**

―――――. "Enlightened Preference and Justification." In *Aesthetics and Problems of Education*, ed. Ralph A. Smith, 305-19. Urbana: University of Illinois Press, 1971.
**A, CI, FPA**

―――――. *Paradox and Promise: Essays on American Life and Education.* Englewood Cliffs, N.J.: Prentice-Hall, 1961.
**CI, FPA**

―――――. "Some Duties of a Theory of Educational Aesthetics." In *Aesthetics and Problems of Education*, ed. Ralph A. Smith, 103-16. Urbana: University of Illinois Press, 1971.
**A, CI, FPA**

―――――. "Some Reactions to a Concept of Aesthetic Education." In *Arts and Aesthetics: An Agenda for the Future*, ed. Stanley S. Madeja, 251-61. St. Louis, Mo.: CEMREL, 1977.
**A, CI, FPA**

―――――. *The Uses of Schooling.* New York: Routledge, 1988.
**CI, FPA**

_____. *The Whys and Hows of Aesthetic Education.* St. Louis, Mo.: CEMREL, 1977.
**A, CI, FPA**

Broudy, Harry S., and John R. Palmer. *Exemplars of Teaching Method.* Chicago: Rand McNally, 1965.
**CI, FPA**

Brown, Amy. "Approaches to Classroom Music for Children." In *Music and Child Development,* ed. J. Craig Peery, Irene W. Peery, and Thomas W. Draper, 184-93. New York: Springer-Verlag, 1987.
**CI**

Bruhn, Karl. "Advocacy: Getting to 'How to'." In *Perspectives on Implementation: Arts Education Standards for America's Students,* ed. Bruce O. Boston, 9-18. Reston, Va.: Music Educators National Conference, 1994.
**A, CI, FPA**

Bruner, Jerome S. *On Knowing: Essays for the Left Hand.* Exp. ed. Cambridge: Belknap Press of Harvard University Press, 1979.
**CI, P**

_____. *The Process of Education.* 1960. Reprint, Cambridge: Harvard University Press, 1977.
**CI, FPA; P**

_____. *Toward a Theory of Instruction.* New York: Norton, 1968.
**CI, FPA, P**

Burmeister, Clifton A. "The Role of Music in General Education." In *Basic Concepts in Music Education: 57th Yearbook of the National Society for the Study of Education,* ed. Nelson B. Henry, 215-35. Chicago: University of Chicago Press, 1958.
**CI, FPA**

_____. "The Role of Music in General Education." In *Basic Concepts in Music Education II,* ed. Richard J. Colwell, 191-208. Niwot: University Press of Colorado, 1991.
**CI, FPA**

Byler, Robert. "Jazz Journal International." In *International Music Journals,* ed. Linda M. Fidler and Richard S. James, 181-84. New York: Greenwood, 1990.
**CI, J**

_____. "Journal of Jazz Studies." In *International Music Journals,* ed. Linda M. Fidler and Richard S. James, 193-95. New York: Greenwood, 1990.
**CI, J**

Campbell, Patricia Shehan. "Eurhythmics, Aural Training, and Creative Thinking: The Dalcroze Pedagogy for Children." In *The Eclectic Curriculum in American Music Education*, 2nd ed., ed. Polly Carder, 43-51. Reston, Va.: Music Educators National Conference, 1990.
**CI**

_____. *Lessons from the World: A Cross-Cultural Guide to Music Teaching and Learning.* New York: Schirmer Books, 1991.
**BR, CI**

Campbell, Patricia Shehan, and Carol Scott-Kassner. *Music in Childhood: From Preschool through the Elementary Grades.* New York: Schirmer Books, 1994.
**CI**

Canada, Benjamin O. "Building Support for the Arts Standards among School Administrators." In *Perspectives on Implementation: Arts Education Standards for America's Students*, ed. Bruce O. Boston, 63-69. Reston, Va.: Music Educators National Conference, 1994.
**A, CI, FPA**

*Canadian Music Educator.* St. Catherines, Ontario: Canadian Music Educators' Association, 1959-.
**CI, J, P, R**

Carder, Polly, ed. *The Eclectic Curriculum in American Music Education.* 2nd ed. Reston, Va.: Music Educators National Conference, 1990.
**CI**

Carter, Gene R. "Schools of Tomorrow." In *Toward Tomorrow: New Visions for General Music*, ed. Sandra L. Stauffer, 11-14. Reston, Va.: Music Educators National Conference, 1995.
**CI, FPA**

Casey, Joseph L. *Teaching Techniques and Insights for Instrumental Music Educators.* Rev. ed. Chicago: G.I.A. Publications, 1993.
**CI**

Chall, Jeanne S., and Allan F. Mirsky. "The Implications for Education." In *Education and the Brain: 77th Yearbook of the National Society for the Study of Education (Part II)*, ed. Jeanne S. Chall and Allan F. Mirsky, 371-78. Chicago: University of Chicago Press, 1978.
**CI, P**

————, eds. *Education and the Brain: 77th Yearbook of the National Society for the Study of Education (Part II)*. Chicago: University of Chicago Press, 1978.
**BR, CI, P**

*Challenges in Music Education: Proceedings of the XI International Conference of the International Society for Music Education*. Ed. Frank Callaway. Perth: University of Western Australia, 1976.
**CI, R, RSC**

*Chamber Music: Performance and Study at Music Training Institutions*. Reston, Va.: National Association of Schools of Music, 1982.
**CI, RSC**

Choate, Robert A., ed. *Documentary Report of the Tanglewood Symposium*. Washington: Music Educators National Conference, 1968.
**CI, FPA, RSC**

Choksy, Lois. *The Kodály Method: Comprehensive Music Education from Infant to Adult*. 2nd ed. Englewood Cliffs, N.J.: Prentice-Hall, 1988.
**CI**

Clark, J. Bunker. *Music at KU: A History of the University of Kansas Music Department*. Lawrence: Department of Music and Dance, University of Kansas, 1986.
**BR, CI**

Coleman, Satis N. *Creative Music for Children: A Plan of Training Based on the Natural Evolution of Music*. New York: G. P. Putnam's Sons, 1931.
**CI, P**

Collins, Thomas Clark, ed. *Music Education Materials: A Selected Annotated Bibliography*. Washington: Music Educators National Conference, 1968.
**BR, CI**

Colwell, Richard J. "The Development of Continuing Education 1950-2050." In *Music Education for Tomorrow's Society*, ed. Arthur Motycka, 50-60. Jamestown, R.I.: GAMT Music, 1976.
**CI, FPA**

————. "Evaluation." In *Basic Concepts in Music Education II*, ed. Richard J. Colwell, 247-78. Niwot: University Press of Colorado, 1991.
**CI**

_____. "Evaluation in Music Education: Perspicacious or Peregrine." In *Symposium in Music Education: A Festschrift for Charles Leonhard*, ed. Richard J. Colwell, 157-95. Urbana-Champaign: University of Illinois, 1982.

**CI, FPA, P**

_____. *The Evaluation of Music Teaching and Learning.* Englewood Cliffs, N.J.: Prentice-Hall, 1970.

**CI, P**

_____, ed. *Handbook of Research on Music Teaching and Learning.* New York: Schirmer Books, 1992.

**BR, CI, P, R**

_____, ed. *Symposium in Music Education: A Festschrift for Charles Leonhard.* Urbana-Champaign: University of Illinois, 1982.

**CI, FPA, R, RSC**

*Comparative Music Education: Proceedings of the Fourth International Conference of the International Society for Music Education.* Mainz: International Society for Music Education, 1962.

**CI, R, RSC**

Conklin, Kenneth R. "The Aesthetic Dimension of Education in the Abstract Disciplines." In *Aesthetics and Problems of Education*, ed. Ralph A. Smith, 537-54. Urbana: University of Illinois Press, 1971.

**A, CI, FPA**

Consortium of National Arts Education Associations. *National Standards for Arts Education: Dance, Music, Theatre, Visual Arts. What Every Young American Should Know and Be Able to Do in the Arts.* Reston, Va.: Music Educators National Conference, 1994.

**A, CI, FPA**

Copland, Aaron. *What to Listen for in Music.* 1939. Rev. ed. San Francisco: McGraw-Hill, 1988.

**CI, FPA, P**

Costanza, Peter, and Timothy Russell. "Methodologies in Music Education." In *Handbook of Research on Music Teaching and Learning*, ed. Richard J. Colwell, 498-508. New York: Schirmer Books, 1992.

**CI, R**

Covington, Martin V. "Musical Chairs: Who Drops Out of Music Instruction and Why?" In *Documentary Report of the Ann Arbor Symposium on the Applications of Psychology to the Teaching and Learning of Music: Motivation and Creativity (Session III)*, 49-54. Reston, Va.: Music Educators National Conference, 1983.

**CI, P**

Cowden, Robert L., and Robert H. Klotman. *Administration and Supervision of Music.* 2nd ed. New York: Schirmer Books, 1991.
**CI, FPA**

Cox, Richard C., and Nancy Jordan Unks. *A Selected and Annotated Bibliography of Studies Concerning the Taxonomy of Educational Objectives: Cognitive Domain.* Pittsburgh, Pa.: University of Pittsburgh, 1967.
**BR, CI**

Crane, Julia. "Principles of Education Applied." In *The Crane Symposium: Toward an Understanding of the Teaching and Learning of Music Performance*, ed. Charles Fowler, 5-12. Potsdam: Potsdam College of the State University of New York, 1988.
**CI, FPA**

Crawford, Richard. "Music at Michigan: A Historical Perspective." In *100 Years of Music at Michigan, 1880-1980*, 9-38. Ann Arbor: University of Michigan, 1979.
**BR, CI**

Csikszentmihalyi, Mihaly, and Ulrich Schiefele. "Arts Education, Human Development, and the Quality of Experience." In *The Arts, Education, and Aesthetic Knowing: 91st Yearbook of the National Society for the Study of Education (Part II)*, ed. Bennett Reimer and Ralph A. Smith, 169-91. Chicago: University of Chicago Press, 1992.
**A, CI, P**

Curtis, Louis Woodson. "Music Theory." In *Music Education: 35th Yearbook of the National Society for the Study of Education (Part II)*, ed. Guy Montrose Whipple, 109-21. Bloomington, Ill.: Public School Publishing, 1936.
**CI**

Cutietta, Robert A., ed. *Strategies for Teaching Specialized Ensembles.* Reston, Va.: Music Educators National Conference, 1996.
**CI**

Cziko, Gary. "Implicit and Explicit Learning: Implications for and Applications to Music Teaching." In *The Crane Symposium: Toward an Understanding of the Teaching and Learning of Music Performance*, ed. Charles Fowler, 89-117. Potsdam: Potsdam College of the State University of New York, 1988.
**CI, P**

Davidson, Jennifer. *TIPS: Thinking Skills in the Music Classroom.* Reston, Va.: Music Educators National Conference, 1993.
**CI, P**

_____. "Assessment in General Music: So Where Do I Start?" In *Toward Tomorrow: New Visions for General Music*, ed. Sandra L. Stauffer, 67-69. Reston, Va.: Music Educators National Conference, 1995.
**CI**

Davidson, Lyle, and Larry Scripp. "Surveying the Coordinates of Cognitive Skills in Music." In *Handbook of Research on Music Teaching and Learning*, ed. Richard J. Colwell, 392-413. New York: Schirmer Books, 1992.
**CI, P, R**

Davis, Donald J. "Evaluation and Curriculum Development in the Arts." In *Toward an Aesthetic Education: A Report*, 117-27. Washington: Music Educators National Conference, 1971.
**A, CI, P**

Davis, Jessica, and Howard Gardner. "The Cognitive Revolution: Consequences for the Understanding and Education of the Child as Artist." In *The Arts, Education, and Aesthetic Knowing: 91st Yearbook of the National Society for the Study of Education (Part II)*, ed. Bennett Reimer and Ralph A. Smith, 92-123. Chicago: University of Chicago Press, 1992.
**A, CI, FPA, P**

Davison, Archibald Thompson. *Music Education in America: What Is Wrong with It? What Shall We Do About It?* New York: Harper and Brothers, 1926.
**CI, FPA**

Dearden, R. F. "The Aesthetic Form of Understanding." In *Aesthetics and Problems of Education*, ed. Ralph A. Smith, 285-304. Urbana: University of Illinois Press, 1971.
**A, CI, FPA**

*Design for Arts in Education*. Washington: Heldref, 1899-.
**A, CI, FPA, J**

DeTurk, Mark. "Critical and Creative Musical Thinking." In *Dimensions of Musical Thinking*, ed. Eunice Boardman, 21-32. Reston, Va.: Music Educators National Conference, 1989.
**CI, P**

Dewey, John. *Art as Experience*. 1934. Reprint, New York: Perigee Books, 1980.
**A, CI, FPA**

_____. *The Child and the Curriculum*. 1902. Reprint, Chicago: University of Chicago Press, 1971.
**CI, FPA**

_____. *Democracy and Education: An Introduction to the Philosophy of Education.* 1916. Reprint, New York: Free Press, 1966.
**CI, FPA**

_____. *Experience and Education.* 1938. Reprint, New York: Collier Books, 1974.
**CI, FPA, P**

_____. *Freedom and Culture.* 1939. Reprint, Buffalo, N.Y.: Prometheus Books, 1989.
**CI, FPA**

_____. *How We Think: A Restatement of the Relation of Reflective Thinking to the Educative Process.* 1910. Reprint, Buffalo, N.Y.: Prometheus Books, 1991.
**CI, FPA, P**

_____. *Logic: The Theory of Inquiry.* 1938. Reprint, New York: Irvington, 1982.
**CI, FPA, P**

Dewey, John and Evelyn. *Schools of Tomorrow.* 1915. Reprint, New York: Dutton, 1962.
**CI, FPA**

Dewey, John, Albert C. Barnes, and Laurence Buermeyer. *Art and Education: A Collection of Essays.* 1929. 3rd ed., rev. Merion, Pa.: Barnes Foundation, 1978.
**A, CI, FPA**

Dillon, Jacquelyn. "How to Educate Parents for a Better String Program." In *Voices of Industry*, 25-31. Reston, Va.: Music Educators National Conference, 1990.
**BR, CI**

Dillon-Krass, Jacquelyn, and Dorothy A. Straub, comp. *TIPS: Establishing a String and Orchestra Program.* Reston, Va.: Music Educators National Conference, 1991.
**CI**

Dingley, Bob. "Selecting Music for Your Performing Group." In *Voices of Industry*, 1-5. Reston, Va.: Music Educators National Conference, 1990.
**CI**

Dobbs, Jack P. B., ed. *Music Education - Facing the Future: Proceedings of the 19th World Conference of the International Society for Music Education.* Reading, England: International Society for Music Education, 1990.
**CI, R, RSC**

*Documentary Report of the Ann Arbor Symposium: National Symposium on the Applications of Psychology to the Teaching and Learning of Music (Sessions I and II).* Reston, Va.: Music Educators National Conference, 1981.
**CI, P, R, RSC**

Documentary Report of the Ann Arbor Symposium on the Applications of Psychology to the Teaching and Learning of Music: Motivation and Creativity (Session III). Reston, Va.: Music Educators National Conference, 1983.

**CI, P, R, RSC**

Doerksen, David P. *Guide to Evaluating Teachers of Music Performance Groups.* Reston, Va.: Music Educators National Conference, 1990.

**BR, CI, P**

Duerksen, George L. *Teaching Instrumental Music: From Research to the Music Classroom, No. 3.* Washington: Music Educators National Conference, 1972.

**CI, R**

Dykema, Peter W. "Significant Relationships of Music to Other Subjects." In *Music Education: 35th Yearbook of the National Society for the Study of Education (Part II)*, ed. Guy Montrose Whipple, 23-33. Bloomington, Ill.: Public School Publishing, 1936.

**A, CI, FPA**

Earhart, Will. "Creative Activities." In *Music Education: 35th Yearbook of the National Society for the Study of Education (Part II)*, ed. Guy Montrose Whipple, 123-37. Bloomington, Ill.: Public School Publishing, 1936.

**CI**

————. *The Meaning and Teaching of Music.* New York: Witmark Educational Publications, 1935.

**CI, FPA, P**

Eaton, Marcia Muelder. "Teaching through Puzzles in the Arts." In *The Arts, Education, and Aesthetic Knowing: 91st Yearbook of the National Society for the Study of Education (Part II)*, ed. Bennett Reimer and Ralph A. Smith, 151-68. Chicago: University of Chicago Press, 1992.

**A, CI, FPA**

Ecker, David W. "The Development of Qualitative Intelligence." In *Aesthetics and Problems of Education*, ed. Ralph A. Smith, 172-77. Urbana: University of Illinois Press, 1971.

**A, CI, FPA, P**

Eddy, Junius. "Beyond 'Enrichment': Developing a Comprehensive Community-School Arts Curriculum." In *Arts and the Schools*, ed. Jerome J. Hausman and Joyce Wright, 157-204. New York: McGraw-Hill, 1980.

**A, CI**

Edelfelt, Roy A. "Staff Development and Teaching in the Arts." In *The Teaching Process, Arts and Aesthetics*, ed. Gerard L. Knieter and Jane Stallings, 129-47. St. Louis, Mo.: CEMREL, 1979.
**A, CI, FPA**

Edelstein, Stefan, et al. *Creating Curriculum in Music.* Menlo Park, Calif.: Addison-Wesley, 1980.
**CI**

Eder, Terry E. "The Choral Journal." In *International Music Journals*, ed. Linda M. Fidler and Richard S. James, 83-85. New York: Greenwood, 1990.
**CI, J**

*Educating Americans for the 21st Century.* Washington: National Science Board, 1983.
**CI, RSC**

*Educational Leadership.* Washington: Association for Supervision and Curriculum Development, 1943-.
**CI, J**

Edwards, Roger H. "Model Building." In *Handbook of Research on Music Teaching and Learning*, ed. Richard J. Colwell, 38-47. New York: Schirmer Books, 1992.
**CI, P, R**

_____. "Transfer and Performance Instruction." In *The Crane Symposium: Toward an Understanding of the Teaching and Learning of Music Performance*, ed. Charles Fowler, 119-42. Potsdam: Potsdam College of the State University of New York, 1988.
**CI, P**

Edwards, Ruth. *The Compleat Music Teacher.* Los Altos, Calif.: Geron-X, 1970.
**CI**

Efland, Arthur. "Conceptions of Teaching in the Arts." In *The Teaching Process, Arts and Aesthetics*, ed. Gerard L. Knieter and Jane Stallings, 152-86. St. Louis, Mo.: CEMREL, 1979.
**A, CI, FPA, P**

Egan, Robert F. *Music and the Arts in the Community: The Community Music School in America.* Metuchen, N.J.: Scarecrow, 1989.
**A, CI, FPA**

Eggleston, John. "The Arts and the Whole Curriculum." In *The Arts and Personal Growth*, ed. Malcolm Ross, 58-68. New York: Pergamon, 1980.
**A, CI**

Eisner, Elliot W. *Cognition and Curriculum Reconsidered.* 2nd ed. New York: Teachers College, 1994.
CI

_____. "Implications of Artistic Intelligences for Education." In *Artistic Intelligences: Implications for Education*, ed. William J. Moody, 31-42. New York: Teachers College, 1990.
A, CI, P

_____. "Thoughts on an Agenda for Research and Development in Arts Education." In *Arts and Aesthetics: An Agenda for the Future*, ed. Stanley S. Madeja, 411-22. St. Louis, Mo.: CEMREL, 1977.
A, CI, R

_____, ed. *The Arts, Human Development, and Education.* Berkeley, Calif.: McCutchan, 1976.
A, CI

Elliott, Charles. "Comments on Music Education." In *Artistic Intelligences: Implications for Education*, ed. William J. Moody, 140-44. New York: Teachers College, 1990.
CI, FPA

Ellsworth, E. Victor. "American String Teacher." In *International Music Journals*, ed. Linda M. Fidler and Richard S. James, 29-31. New York: Greenwood, 1990.
CI, J

_____. "Guitar Player." In *International Music Journals*, ed. Linda M. Fidler and Richard S. James, 152-53. New York: Greenwood, 1990.
CI, J

_____. "International Society of Bassists Journal." In *International Music Journals*, ed. Linda M. Fidler and Richard S. James, 174-76. New York: Greenwood, 1990.
CI, J

_____. "Strad." In *International Music Journals*, ed. Linda M. Fidler and Richard S. James, 408-09. New York: Greenwood, 1990.
CI, J

*Encyclopedia of Adolescence.* Ed. Richard Lerner, Anne C. Petersen, and Jeanne Brooks-Gunn. New York: Garland, 1991.
BR, CI, R

*Encyclopedia of Educational Research.* Ed. Marvin C. Alkin, Michele Linden, Jana Noel, and Karen Ray. 6th ed. New York: Macmillan, 1992.
BR, CI, R

Engel, Martin. "Toward a Federal Policy for the Arts in Education." In *Arts and Aesthetics: An Agenda for the Future*, ed. Stanley S. Madeja, 202-19. St. Louis, Mo.: CEMREL, 1977.
**A, CI**

Epperson, Gordon. "E Pluribus Unum—Music Education for the One and Many: Aesthetics and the Art of Teaching." In *Music Education in the United States: Contemporary Issues*, ed. J. Terry Gates, 168-78. Tuscaloosa: University of Alabama Press, 1988.
**CI, FPA**

Erbes, Robert L. *Certification Practices and Trends in Music Teacher Education*. 4th ed. Reston, Va.: Music Educators National Conference, 1992.
**BR, CI**

————. "The Influences of Education Reform on Policy in Teacher Education." In *Policy Issues in Music Education: A Report of the Proceedings of the Robert Petzold Symposium*, ed. Gerald Olson, Anthony L. Barresi, and David Nelson, 41-57. Madison: School of Music, University of Wisconsin, 1991.
**CI, FPA**

Ernst, Karl D., and Charles L. Gary. *Music in General Education*. Washington: Music Educators National Conference Publications, 1965.
**CI**

Ernst, Roy, G. Theodore Wiprud, and Heidi Castleman. *Chamber Music in Our Schools: An Overview and Recommendations*. New York: Chamber Music America, 1990.
**CI**

*Experiments in Musical Creativity: A Report of Pilot Projects Sponsored by the Contemporary Music Project in Baltimore, San Diego, and Farmingdale*. Washington: Music Educators National Conference, 1966.
**CI, P, RSC**

*Fact and Value in Contemporary Musical Scholarship*. Boulder, Colo.: College Music Society, 1986.
**CI, RSC**

Farkas, Alexander. "Can Kodály Help My Teaching?" In *The Eclectic Curriculum in American Music Education*, 2nd ed., ed. Polly Carder, 103-06. Reston, Va.: Music Educators National Conference, 1990.
**CI**

Farnsworth, Charles Hubert. *Education through Music*. New York: American Book Company, 1909.
**CI**

Fehrs-Rampolla, Barbara. "Opportunities in the Classroom: A Teacher's Perspective." In *Perspectives on Implementation: Arts Education Standards for America's Students*, ed. Bruce O. Boston, 31-37. Reston, Va.: Music Educators National Conference, 1994.

**A, CI, FPA**

Feierabend, John M., comp. *TIPS: Music Activities in Early Childhood*. Reston, Va.: Music Educators National Conference, 1990.

**CI**

Feininger, Karl. *An Experimental Psychology of Music*. New York: A. Gemunder, 1909.

**CI, P**

Feldman, David Henry, Mihaly Csikszentmihalyi, and Howard Gardner. *Changing the World: A Framework for the Study of Creativity*. Westport, Conn.: Praeger, 1994.

**CI, P**

Ferrara, Lawrence. *Philosophy and the Analysis of Music: Bridges to Musical Sound, Form, and Reference*. New York: Greenwood, 1991.

**CI, FPA**

Fidler, Linda M., and Richard S. James. "Jazz Index." In *International Music Journals*, ed. Linda M. Fidler and Richard S. James, 474-75. New York: Greenwood, 1990.

**BR, CI, J**

*First Music Assessment: An Overview*. Washington: United States Government Printing Office, 1974.

**CI, P, RSC**

Fisher, Henry. *Psychology for Music Teachers: The Laws of Thought Applied to Sounds and Their Symbols, with Other Relevant Matter*. 3rd ed. London: Curwen, 1905.

**CI, P**

Flagg, Marion Elizabeth. *Musical Learning: A Guide to Child Growth*. Boston: C. C. Birchard, 1949.

**BR, CI, P**

Fleming, Lissa A. *Getting Started with Jazz Band*. Reston, Va.: Music Educators National Conference, 1994.

**CI**

Fletcher, Peter. *Education and Music.* New York: Oxford University Press, 1989.

**CI**

_____. *Roll over Rock: A Study of Music in Contemporary Culture.* London: Stainer and Bell, 1981.

**CI, P**

Fosburg, Linda. "Arts Councils and Arts Education." In *Arts and Aesthetics: An Agenda for the Future*, ed. Stanley S. Madeja, 170-77. St. Louis, Mo.: CEMREL, 1977.

**A, CI**

Foshay, Arthur W. "Inquiry into Aesthetics Education for Curriculum-Making." In *Arts and Aesthetics: An Agenda for the Future*, ed. Stanley S. Madeja, 243-50. St. Louis, Mo.: CEMREL, 1977.

**A, CI, FPA, R**

Foundation for College Education in Music. *Comprehensive Musicianship.* Washington: Contemporary Music Project, Music Educators National Conference, 1965.

**CI, RSC**

Fowler, Charles B. "Arts Education for Tomorrow: Straight Talk about the Future of Music Education." In *Toward Tomorrow: New Visions for General Music*, ed. Sandra L. Stauffer, 21-29. Reston, Va.: Music Educators National Conference, 1995.

**A, CI, FPA**

_____. "Toward a Democratic Art: A Reconstructionist View of Music Education." In *Music Education in the United States: Contemporary Issues*, ed. J. Terry Gates, 130-55. Tuscaloosa: University of Alabama Press, 1988.

**CI, FPA**

_____, ed. *Arts in Education, Education in Arts: Entering the Dialogue of the 80's.* Washington: Charles B. Fowler, 1984.

**A, CI, FPA**

_____, ed. *An Arts in Education Source Book.* New York: The Fund, 1980.

**A, BR, CI**

_____, ed. *The Crane Symposium: Toward an Understanding of the Teaching and Learning of Music Performance.* New York: Potsdam College of the State University of New York, 1988.

**CI, R, RSC**

_____, ed. *Summit Conference on the Arts and Education: A Report*. Washington: Alliance for Arts Education, 1980.

**A, CI, RSC**

Fowler, Charles B., Timothy Gerber, and Vincent P. Lawrence. *Music: Its Role and Importance in Our Lives*. New York: Glencoe, 1994.

**CI, FPA**

Fox, Donna Brink. "Teaching Tots and Toddlers." In *Music and Child Development: The Biology of Music Making - Proceedings of the 1987 Denver Conference*, ed. Frank R. Wilson and Franz L. Roehmann, 384-88. St. Louis, Mo.: MMB Music, 1990.

**CI, P, R**

Franklin, Erik. *Music Education: Psychology and Method*. London: Harrap, 1972.

**CI, P**

Froehlich, Hildegard C. "Issues and Characteristics Common to Research on Teaching in Instructional Settings." In *Handbook of Research on Music Teaching and Learning*, ed. Richard J. Colwell, 561-67. New York: Schirmer Books, 1992.

**CI, R**

Furst, Edward J. "Bloom's Taxonomy: Philosophical and Educational Issues." In *Bloom's Taxonomy—A Forty-Year Retrospective: 93rd Yearbook of the National Society for the Study of Education (Part II)*, ed. Lorin W. Anderson and Lauren A. Sosniak, 28-40. Chicago: University of Chicago Press, 1994.

**CI, FPA**

Gardner, Howard. *Art, Mind, and Brain: A Cognitive Approach to Creativity*. New York: Basic Books, 1982.

**A, CI, P**

_____. *The Arts and Human Development: A Psychological Study of the Artistic Process*. 1973. Reprint, New York: Basic Books, 1994.

**A, CI, P**

_____. *Creating Minds: An Anatomy of Creativity Seen through the Lives of Freud, Einstein, Picasso, Stravinsky, Eliot, Graham, and Gandhi*. New York: Basic Books, 1993.

**A, CI, P**

_____. *Frames of Mind: The Theory of Multiple Intelligences*. 10th anniv. ed. New York: Basic Books, 1993.

**CI, P**

_____. *The Mind's New Science: A History of the Cognitive Revolution.* New York: Basic Books, 1985.

**CI, P**

_____. "Multiple Intelligences: Implications for Art and Creativity." In *Artistic Intelligences: Implications for Education*, ed. William J. Moody, 11-27. New York: Teachers College, 1990.

**A, CI, P**

_____. *Multiple Intelligences: The Theory in Practice.* New York: Basic Books, 1993.

**CI, P**

_____. "Sifting the Special from the Shared: Notes toward an Agenda for Research in Arts Education." In *Arts and Aesthetics: An Agenda for the Future*, ed. Stanley S. Madeja, 267-78. St. Louis, Mo.: CEMREL, 1977.

**A, CI, R**

_____. *To Open Minds: Chinese Clues to the Dilemma of Contemporary Education.* New York: Basic Books, 1989.

**CI, P**

_____. *The Unschooled Mind: How Children Think and How Schools Should Teach.* New York: Basic Books, 1991.

**CI, P**

Gardner, Howard, and David N. Perkins, eds. *Art, Mind, and Education: Research from Project Zero.* Urbana: University of Illinois Press, 1989.

**A, CI, P, R**

Garfias, Robert. "Hispanics in Music in Higher Education." In *Racial and Ethnic Directions in American Music*, CMS Report No. 3, 33-37. Boulder, Colo.: College Music Society, 1982.

**CI**

Gary, Charles L., ed. *The Study of Music in the Elementary School: A Conceptual Approach.* Washington: Music Educators National Conference, 1967.

**CI**

Gary, Charles L., and Wade M. Robinson. "Implications of Aesthetic Education for Professional Action." In *Toward an Aesthetic Education: A Report*, 129-34. Washington: Music Educators National Conference, 1971.

**A, CI, FPA**

Gates, J. Terry, ed. *Music Education in the United States: Contemporary Issues.* Tuscaloosa: University of Alabama Press, 1988.
**CI, FPA**

Geahigan, George. "The Arts in Education: A Historical Perspective." In *The Arts, Education, and Aesthetic Knowing: 91st Yearbook of the National Society for the Study of Education (Part II)*, ed. Bennett Reimer and Ralph A. Smith, 1-19. Chicago: University of Chicago Press, 1992.
**A, CI, FPA**

Gelber, Gary. "Psychological Development of the Conservatory Student." In *The Biology of Music Making: Proceedings of the 1984 Denver Conference*, ed. Franz L. Roehmann and Frank R. Wilson, 3-15. St. Louis, Mo.: MMB Music, 1988.
**CI, P**

*General Music Today.* Reston, Va.: Music Educators National Conference, 1987-.
**CI, J**

*Generaton of Fellows: Grants to Individuals from the National Endowment for the Arts.* Washington: National Endowment for the Arts, 1993.
**A, CI, RSC**

George, Luvenia A. *Teaching the Music of Six Different Cultures.* Rev. ed. Danbury, Conn.: World Music, Multicultural Materials for Educators, 1987.
**CI**

George, Paul S., et al. *The Middle School: And Beyond.* Alexandria, Va.: Association for Supervision and Curriculum Development, 1992.
**CI**

Gerber, Linda L. "Music in Early Childhood: Postscript and Preview." In *Symposium in Music Education: A Festschrift for Charles Leonhard*, ed. Richard J. Colwell, 45-57. Urbana-Champaign: University of Illinois, 1982.
**CI, P**

Gerber, Timothy, and William O. Hughes, eds. *Music in the High School: Current Approaches to Secondary General Music Instruction.* Reston, Va.: Music Educators National Conference, 1988.
**CI, RSC**

Getz, Russell P. "Music Education in Tomorrow's Schools: A Practical Approach." In *The Future of Musical Education in America: Proceedings of the July 1983 Conference*, ed. Donald J. Shetler, 21-31. Rochester, N.Y.: Eastman School of Music Press, 1984.
**CI, FPA**

Gfeller, Kate. "Arts Education Policies for Students with Disabilities." In *Policy Issues in Music Education: A Report of the Proceedings of the Robert Petzold Symposium*, ed. Gerald Olson, Anthony L. Barresi, and David Nelson, 76-87. Madison: School of Music, University of Wisconsin, 1991.
**A, CI, FPA**

Gildersleeve, Glenn. "Standards and the Evaluation and Measurement of Achievement in Music." In *Music Education: 35th Yearbook of the National Society for the Study of Education (Part II)*, ed. Guy Montrose Whipple, 195-206. Bloomington, Ill.: Public School Publishing, 1936.
**CI, FPA, P**

Gillespie, Robert, Beth Gilbert, and Mary Lou Jones. *Getting Started with Strolling Strings.* Reston, Va.: Music Educators National Conference, 1995.
**CI**

Glenn, Mabelle. "Rhythm." In *Music Education: 35th Yearbook of the National Society for the Study of Education (Part II)*, ed. Guy Montrose Whipple, 51-58. Bloomington, Ill.: Public School Publishing, 1936.
**CI**

————. "Singing." In *Music Education: 35th Yearbook of the National Society for the Study of Education (Part II)*, ed. Guy Montrose Whipple, 59-67. Bloomington, Ill.: Public School Publishing, 1936.
**CI**

Glenn, Neal Edwin, and Edgar M. Turrentine. *Introduction to Advanced Study in Music Education.* Dubuque, Iowa: Wm. C. Brown, 1968.
**CI**

Glidden, Robert. "Music in Higher Education." In *Music Education in the United States: Contemporary Issues*, ed. J. Terry Gates, 240-58. Tuscaloosa: University of Alabama Press, 1988.
**CI**

Godfrey, James H., ed. *The Best of the Soundpost.* Reston, Va.: National School Orchestra Association, 1989.
**CI**

Golby, Michael. "The Responsive School." In *The Arts and Personal Growth*, ed. Malcolm Ross, 16-26. New York: Pergamon, 1980.
**A, CI, FPA**

Goodlad, John I. "Beyond the Rhetoric of Promise." In *Arts and the Schools*, ed. Jerome J. Hausman and Joyce Wright, 205-36. New York: McGraw-Hill, 1980.
**A, CI, P**

————. *A Place Called School: Prospects for the Future.* New York: McGraw-Hill, 1984.
**CI**

————. "Toward a Place in the Curriculum for the Arts." In *The Arts, Education, and Aesthetic Knowing: 91st Yearbook of the National Society for the Study of Education (Part II)*, ed. Bennett Reimer and Ralph A. Smith, 192-212. Chicago: University of Chicago Press, 1992.
**A, CI, FPA**

Goodlad, John I., and Jack Morrison. "The Arts and Education." In *Arts and the Schools*, ed. Jerome J. Hausman and Joyce Wright, 1-21. New York: McGraw-Hill, 1980.
**A, CI**

Goodman, A. Harold *Music Education: Perspectives and Perceptions - Including 37 Outstanding Music Educators.* Dubuque, Iowa: Kendall/Hunt, 1982.
**CI, FPA**

Gordon, Edgar B. "A Program of Music Activities Outside the School." In *Music Education: 35th Yearbook of the National Society for the Study of Education (Part II)*, ed. Guy Montrose Whipple, 187-94. Bloomington, Ill.: Public School Publishing, 1936.
**CI**

Gordon, Edwin E. *Guiding Your Child's Musical Development.* Chicago: G.I.A. Publications, 1991.
**CI, P**

————. *A Music Learning Theory for Newborn and Young Children.* Chicago: G.I.A. Publications, 1990.
**CI, P**

Gotshalk, D. W. "Aesthetic Education as a Domain." In *Aesthetics and Problems of Education*, ed. Ralph A. Smith, 117-25. Urbana: University of Illinois Press, 1971.
**A, CI, FPA**

Gottlieb, Jack, ed. *Leonard Bernstein's Young People's Concerts.* Rev. and exp. ed. New York: Anchor Books, 1992.
**CI**

Graham, C. Ray. "Music and Learning of Language in Early Childhood." In *Music and Child Development*, ed. J. Craig Perry, Irene W. Peery, and Thomas W. Draper, 177-83. New York: Springer-Verlag, 1987.
**CI, P**

Graham, Richard M. "Music Education of Exceptional Children." In *Basic Concepts in Music Education II*, ed. Richard J. Colwell, 222-36. Niwot: University Press of Colorado, 1991.
**CI, P**

————. "Music Methodology for Exceptional Children: Current View of Professional Activity in Music Education and Music Therapy." In *Music Education in the United States: Contemporary Issues*, ed. J. Terry Gates, 224-39. Tuscaloosa: University of Alabama Press, 1988.
**CI, P**

————, comp. *Music for the Exceptional Child*. Reston, Va.: Music Educators National Conference, 1975.
**CI, P**

Graham, Richard M., and Alice S. Beer. *Teaching Music to the Exceptional Child: A Handbook for Mainstreaming*. Englewood Cliffs, N.J.: Prentice-Hall, 1980.
**BR, CI, P**

Grant, Willis, ed. *Music in Education*. London: Butterworths, 1963.
**CI, FPA, RSC**

Green, Barry, and Timothy W. Gallwey. *The Inner Game of Music*. Garden City, N.Y.: Anchor, 1986.
**CI, P**

Green, Elizabeth A. H. *Teaching Stringed Instruments in Classes: Foundations of Music Education Series*. 1966. Reprint, Bloomington, Ind.: American String Teachers Association, 1987.
**CI**

Green, Lucy. *Music on Deaf Ears: Musical Meaning, Ideology, Education*. New York: Manchester University Press, 1988.
**CI, FPA, P**

Greenberg, Norman C. "Conclusion: The Influence of Cultural Forces on Music and Art." In *Racial and Ethnic Directions in American Music*, CMS Report No. 3, 61-75. Boulder, Colo.: College Music Society, 1982.
**CI, P**

Greene, Maxine. "Art, Technique, and the Indifferent Gods." In *Aesthetics and Problems of Education*, ed. Ralph A. Smith, 555-63. Urbana: University of Illinois Press, 1971.
**A, CI, FPA**

_____. "Arts Education in the Humanities: Toward a Breaking of the Boundaries." In *Artistic Intelligences: Implications for Education*, ed. William J. Moody, 147-58. New York: Teachers College, 1990.
**A, CI**

_____. "Teaching for Aesthetic Experience." In *Toward an Aesthetic Education: A Report*, 21-43. Washington: Music Educators National Conference, 1971.
**A, CI, FPA**

Greer, R. Douglas. *Design for Music Learning*. New York: Teachers College, 1980.
**CI, FPA, P**

*Growing Up Complete: The Imperative for Music Education*. Reston, Va.: Music Educators National Conference, 1991.
**CI, FPA, RSC**

Gryskiewicz, Stanley S. "Directing Creativity: Marching with Different Drummers." In *Documentary Report of the Ann Arbor Symposium on the Applications of Psychology to the Teaching and Learning of Music: Motivation and Creativity (Session III)*, 13-15. Reston, Va.: Music Educators National Conference, 1983.
**CI, P**

*Guidelines for Performances of School Music Groups: Expectations and Limitations*. Reston, Va.: Music Educators National Conference, 1986.
**BR, CI**

Gurin, Richard S. "The Arts Education Standards: A Payoff for Business." In *Perspectives on Implementation: Arts Education Standards for America's Students*, ed. Bruce O. Boston, 82-88. Reston, Va.: Music Educators National Conference, 1994.
**A, CI, FPA**

Haack, Paul. "The Acquisition of Music Listening Skills." In *Handbook of Research on Music Teaching and Learning*, ed. Richard J. Colwell, 451-65. New York: Schirmer Books, 1992.
**CI, P, R**

Hall, Louis O., ed. *Strategies for Teaching: Guide for Music Methods Courses*. Reston, Va.: Music Educators National Conference, 1996.
**CI**

Hamann, Donald L., ed. *Creativity in the Music Classroom: The Best of MEJ.* Reston, Va.: Music Educators National Conference, 1992.
CI, P

Hanshumaker, James. "The Art of Recognizing Artistic Teaching in the Arts." In *The Teaching Process, Arts and Aesthetics*, ed. Gerard L. Knieter and Jane Stallings, 223-39. St. Louis, Mo.: CEMREL, 1979.
A, CI, FPA

Hargreaves, David J., and Marilyn P. Zimmerman. "Developmental Theories of Music Learning." In *Handbook of Research on Music Teaching and Learning*, ed. Richard J. Colwell, 377-91. New York: Schirmer Books, 1992.
CI, P, R

Hargreaves, David J., and Maurice J. Galton. "Aesthetic Learning: Psychological Theory and Educational Practice." In *The Arts, Education, and Aesthetic Knowing: 91st Yearbook of the National Society for the Study of Education (Part II)*, ed. Bennett Reimer and Ralph A. Smith, 124-50. Chicago: University of Chicago Press, 1992.
A, CI, P

Hartshorn, William C. *Music for the Academically Talented Student in the Secondary School.* Washington: National Education Association and Music Educators National Conference, 1960.
CI

_____. "The Role of Listening." In *Basic Concepts in Music Education: 57th Yearbook of the National Society for the Study of Education*, ed. Nelson B. Henry, 261-91. Chicago: University of Chicago Press, 1958.
CI, P

Hausman, Jerome J. "A Contemporary Aesthetics Curriculum." In *Toward an Aesthetic Education: A Report*, 45-55. Washington: Music Educators National Conference, 1971.
A, CI, FPA

Hausman, Jerome J., and Joyce Wright, eds. *Arts and the Schools.* New York: McGraw-Hill, 1980.
A, CI, FPA

Havas, Kato. *Stage Fright: Its Causes and Cures with Special Reference to Violin Playing.* London: Bosworth Publishers, 1973.
CI, P

Healy, Jane M. "Musical Brains for the World of Tomorrow." In *Toward Tomorrow: New Visions for General Music*, ed. Sandra L. Stauffer, 15-19. Reston, Va.: Music Educators National Conference, 1995.
CI, FPA

Hedden, Steven K. "Psychomotor Skills." In *Documentary Report of the Ann Arbor Symposium: National Symposium on the Applications of Psychology to the Teaching and Learning of Music (Sessions I and II)*, 22-28. Reston, Va.: Music Educators National Conference, 1981.

**CI, P, R**

Hedden, Steven K., and David G. Woods. "Student Outcomes of Teaching Systems for General Music, Grades K-8." In *Handbook of Research on Music Teaching and Learning*, ed. Richard J. Colwell, 669-75. New York: Schirmer Books, 1992.

**CI, R**

Heller, Jack J., and Warren C. Campbell. "Auditory Perception in Music Teaching and Learning." In *Documentary Report of the Ann Arbor Symposium: National Symposium on the Applications of Psychology to the Teaching and Learning of Music (Sessions I and II)*, 8-15. Reston, Va.: Music Educators National Conference, 1981.

**CI, P, R**

Henry, Nelson B., ed. *Basic Concepts in Music Education: 57th Yearbook of the National Society for the Study of Education.* Chicago: University of Chicago Press, 1958.

**BR, CI, FPA**

Herman, Joan L., Pamela R. Aschbacher, and Lynn Winters. *A Practical Guide to Alternative Assessment.* Alexandria, Va.: Association for Supervision and Curriculum Development, 1992.

**BR, CI, P**

Herndon, Marcia, and Susanne Ziegler, eds. *Music, Gender, and Culture.* New York: C. F. Peters, 1990.

**CI, P**

Herz, Beverley, and Craig D. Northrup. "Planning a Successful Concert Tour." In *Voices of Industry*, 13-18. Reston, Va.: Music Educators National Conference, 1990.

**BR, CI**

Hicks, Charles E., James A. Standifer, and Warrick L. Carter, eds. *Methods and Perspectives in Urban Music Education.* Washington: University Press of America, 1983.

**CI, FPA**

Highet, Gilbert. *The Art of Teaching.* 1950. Reprint, New York: Vintage Books, 1989.

**CI, FPA**

Highwater, Jamake. "Music of American Indians." In *Racial and Ethnic Directions in American Music*, CMS Report No. 3, 3-8. Boulder, Colo.: College Music Society, 1982.

**CI**

Hilgard, Ernest Ropiequet, ed. *Theories of Learning and Instruction: 63rd Yearbook of the National Society for the Study of Education.* Chicago: University of Chicago Press, 1964.
**BR, CI, P**

Hilley, Martha F., and Tommie Pardue, eds. *Strategies for Teaching Middle-Level and High School Keyboard.* Reston, Va.: Music Educators National Conference, 1996.
**CI**

Hinckley, June, ed. *Music at the Middle Level: Building Strong Programs.* Reston, Va.: Music Educators National Conference, 1994.
**CI**

————. "Issues in High School General Music." In *Toward Tomorrow: New Visions for General Music*, ed. Sandra L. Stauffer, 135-38. Reston, Va.: Music Educators National Conference, 1995.
**CI**

Hindemith, Paul. *Elementary Training for Musicians.* 1946. Reprint, New York: Associated Music Publishers, 1974.
**CI**

Hodges, Donald A. "The Acquisition of Music Reading Skills." In *Handbook of Research on Music Teaching and Learning*, ed. Richard J. Colwell, 466-71. New York: Schirmer Books, 1992.
**CI, P, R**

Hodgkinson, Harold L. "Arts in the Future: A Pragmatic Analysis." In *Arts and Aesthetics: An Agenda for the Future*, ed. Stanley S. Madeja, 28-45. St. Louis, Mo.: CEMREL, 1977.
**A, CI, FPA**

Hoffa, Harlan Edward. "Implementing the National Standards: Developing Professional Resources." In *Perspectives on Implementation: Arts Education Standards for America's Students*, ed. Bruce O. Boston, 19-30. Reston, Va.: Music Educators National Conference, 1994.
**A, CI, FPA**

Hoffer, Charles R. "Artistic Intelligences and Music Education." In *Artistic Intelligences: Implications for Education*, ed. William J. Moody, 135-40. New York: Teachers College, 1990.
**A, CI, P**

————. *Introduction to Music Education.* 2nd ed. Celmont, Calif.: Wadsworth, 1993.
**CI, FPA**

Hoffman, Mary E. *Teacher Competency and the Balanced Music Curriculum.* Reston, Va.: Music Educators National Conference, 1985.
**CI**

Holz, E. A. *Teaching Band Instruments to Beginners: Foundations of Music Education Series.* Englewood Cliffs, N.J.: Prentice-Hall, 1966.
**CI**

Hood, Marguerite Vivian. "A Music Program for Rural Schools." In *Music Education: 35th Yearbook of the National Society for the Study of Education (Part II)*, ed. Guy Montrose Whipple, 173-85. Bloomington, Ill.: Public School Publishing, 1936.
**CI**

_____. *Teaching Rhythm and Using Classroom Instruments: Foundations of Music Education Series.* Englewood Cliffs, N.J.: Prentice-Hall, 1970.
**CI**

Hope, Samuel. "Making Disciplinary Connections." In *Perspectives on Implementation: Arts Education Standards for America's Students*, ed. Bruce O. Boston, 38-46. Reston, Va.: Music Educators National Conference, 1994.
**A, CI, FPA**

Horner, V. *Music Education: The Background of Research and Opinion.* Hawthorn: Australian Council for Educational Research, 1965.
**CI, R**

House, Robert William. *Administration in Music Education.* Englewood Cliffs, N.J.: Prentice-Hall, 1973.
**CI, FPA**

_____. "Curriculum Construction in Music Education." In *Basic Concepts in Music Education: 57th Yearbook of the National Society for the Study of Education*, ed. Nelson B. Henry, 236-60. Chicago: University of Chicago Press, 1958.
**CI**

_____. "The Future of Music Education in Higher Education." In *Music Education for Tomorrow's Society*, ed. Arthur Motycka, 61-72. Jamestown, R.I.: GAMT Music, 1976.
**CI, FPA**

_____. "The Professional Preparation of Music Administrators." In *Symposium in Music Education: A Festschrift for Charles Leonhard*, ed. Richard J. Colwell, 277-89. Urbana-Champaign: University of Illinois, 1982.
**CI, FPA**

Houston, W. Robert, Martin Haberman, and John P. Sikula, eds. *Handbook of Research on Teacher Education.* 2nd ed. New York: Macmillan, 1996.
**BR, CI, R**

Humphreys, Jere T., William V. May, and David Nelson. "Research on Music Ensembles." In *Handbook of Research on Music Teaching and Learning*, ed. Richard J. Colwell, 651-68. New York: Schirmer Books, 1992.
**CI, R**

Hunt, Paul B. "Brass Bulletin." In *International Music Journals*, ed. Linda M. Fidler and Richard S. James, 62-63. New York: Greenwood, 1990.
**CI, J**

————. "Brass Quarterly/Brass and Woodwind Quarterly." In *International Music Journals*, ed. Linda M. Fidler and Richard S. James, 63-65. New York: Greenwood, 1990.
**CI, J**

————. "Jazz Educators Journal." In *International Music Journals*, ed. Linda M. Fidler and Richard S. James, 177-78. New York: Greenwood, 1990.
**CI, J**

————. "Percussive Notes/The Percussionist." In *International Music Journals*, ed. Linda M. Fidler and Richard S. James, 337-39. New York: Greenwood, 1990.
**CI, J**

————. "Woodwind World—Brass and Percussion." In *International Music Journals*, ed. Linda M. Fidler and Richard S. James, 443-46. New York: Greenwood, 1990.
**CI, J**

*International Conference on the Role and Place of Music in the Education of Youth and Adults: Report of the Third International Conference.* Copenhagen, Denmark: International Society for Music Education, 1958.
**CI, RSC**

*International Journal of Music Education.* Huddersfield, England: International Society for Music Education, 1983-.
**CI, FPA, J, P, R**

Jackson, Philip W., ed. *Handbook of Research on Curriculum: A Project of the American Educational Research Association.* New York: Macmillan, 1992.
**BR, CI, R**

Jaques-Dalcroze, Emile. *Eurhythmics, Art, and Education.* Ed. Cynthia Cox, transl. Frederick Rothwell. 1930. Reprint, Salem: N.H.: Ayer, 1985.
**CI**

————. *The Eurhythmics of Jaques-Dalcroze.* 3rd rev. ed. London: Constable, 1920.
**CI**

————. *The Jaques-Dalcroze Method of Eurhythmics: Rhythmic Movement.* New York: H. W. Gray, 1920.
**CI**

————. *Rhythm, Music, and Education.* Transl. Harold F. Rubinstein. 1921. Reprint, Salem, N.H.: Ayer, 1988.
**CI**

Jenkins, Iredell. "Aesthetic Education and Moral Refinement." In *Aesthetics and Problems of Education*, ed. Ralph A. Smith, 178-99. Urbana: University of Illinois Press, 1971.
**A, CI, FPA**

Johnson, Nancy Jo. "Involving School Boards in Implementing the Arts Standards." In *Perspectives on Implementation: Arts Education Standards for America's Students*, ed. Bruce O. Boston, 70-74. Reston, Va.: Music Eduators National Conference, 1994.
**A, CI, FPA**

Johnson, Philip. "Black Music, the Arts and Education." In *The Claims of Feeling: Readings in Aesthetic Education*, ed. Malcolm Ross, 37-63. Philadelphia: Falmer, 1989.
**A, CI, FPA**

Johnston, J. Howard, and Glenn C. Markle. *What Research Says to the Middle Level Practitioner.* Columbus, Ohio: National Middle School Association, 1986.
**CI, R**

Jones, Archie Neff. *Music Education in Action: Basic Principles and Practical Methods.* Dubuque, Iowa: Wm. C. Brown, 1964.
**CI, FPA**

Jones, Elizabeth. "Applications of Research to Pedagogy." In *The Biology of Music Making: Proceedings of the 1984 Denver Conference*, ed. Franz L. Roehmann and Frank R. Wilson, 287-90. St. Louis, Mo.: MMB Music, 1988.
**CI, P**

————. "What Children Teach Us about Learning Music." In *Music and Child Development: The Biology of Music Making - Proceedings of the 1987 Denver Conference*, ed. Frank R. Wilson and Franz L. Roehmann, 366-76. St. Louis, Mo.: MMB Music, 1990.
**CI, P**

Jones, Merilyn. "Professional Methodology: Introduction." In *Music Education in the United States: Contemporary Issues*, ed. J. Terry Gates, 181-84. Tuscaloosa: University of Alabama Press, 1988.

**CI, FPA**

Jones, Sharon. "Teaching Music for Life." In *Music and Child Development: The Biology of Music Making - Proceedings of the 1987 Denver Conference*, ed. Frank R. Wilson and Franz L. Roehmann, 389-99. St. Louis, Mo.: MMB Music, 1990.

**CI, P**

Jones, William LaRue. "The Orchestra and American Education." In *Music Education in the United States: Contemporary Issues*, ed. J. Terry Gates, 277-86. Tuscaloosa: University of Alabama Press, 1988.

**CI, FPA**

Jordan, Joyce. "Multicultural Music Education in a Pluralistic Society." In *Handbook of Research on Music Teaching and Learning*, ed. Richard J. Colwell, 735-48. New York: Schirmer Books, 1992.

**CI, R**

Jorgensen, Estelle R., ed. *Philosopher, Teacher, Musician: Perspectives on Music Education.* Urbana: University of Illinois Press, 1993.

**CI, FPA**

Joseph, Annabelle S. "The Importance of Rhythmic Training in Music Education." In *The Eclectic Curriculum in American Music Education*, 2nd ed., ed. Polly Carder, 37-42. Reston, Va.: Music Educators National Conference, 1990.

**CI**

*Journal of Aesthetic Education.* Urbana: University of Illinois Press, 1966-.

**A, CI, FPA, J, R**

*Journal of Educational Psychology.* Washington: American Psychological Association, 1910-.

**CI, J, P, R**

*Journal of Educational Research.* Washington: Heldref, 1920-.

**CI, J, R**

*Journal of Music Teacher Education.* Reston, Va.: Music Educators National Conference, 1991-.

**CI, J, R**

Joyce, Bruce R., Marsha Weil, and Beverly Showers. *Models of Teaching.* 4th ed. Boston: Allyn and Bacon, 1992.

**CI, FPA**

*Juilliard Report on Teaching the Literature and Materials of Music.* 1953. Reprint, Westport, Conn.: Greenwood, 1970.

**CI, RSC**

*K-12 Arts Education in the U.S.: Present Context, Future Needs.* Reston, Va.: Music Educators National Conference, 1986.

**A, CI**

Kaagan, Stephen S. *Aesthetic Persuasion: Pressing the Cause of Arts Education in American Schools.* Los Angeles: Getty Center for Education in the Arts, 1990.

**A, CI**

Kabalevsky, Dmitri Borisovich. *Music and Education: A Composer Writes about Musical Education.* London: J. Kingsley, 1988.

**CI, FPA**

Kaelin, Eugene F. "Aesthetic Education: A Role for Aesthetics Proper." In *Aesthetics and Problems of Education*, ed. Ralph A. Smith, 144-61. Urbana: University of Illinois Press, 1971.

**A, CI, FPA**

Kaelin, Eugene F., and David W. Ecker. "The Institutional Prospects of Aesthetic Education." In *Arts and Aesthetics: An Agenda for the Future*, ed. Stanley S. Madeja, 229-42. St. Louis, Mo.: CEMREL, 1977.

**A, CI, FPA**

Kantorski, Vincent J. "The Council for Research in Music Education Bulletin." In *International Music Journals*, ed. Linda M. Fidler and Richard S. James, 100-02. New York: Greenwood, 1990.

**CI, FPA, J, P, R**

————. "Instrumentalist." In *International Music Journals*, ed. Linda M. Fidler and Richard S. James, 166-68. New York: Greenwood, 1990.

**CI, J**

————. "Journal of Band Research." In *International Music Journals*, ed. Linda M. Fidler and Richard S. James, 189-90. New York: Greenwood, 1990.

**CI, J, R**

————. "Journal of Research in Music Education." In *International Music Journals*, ed. Linda M. Fidler and Richard S. James, 203-05. New York: Greenwood, 1990.

**CI, J, P, R**

_____. "Music Educators Journal." In *International Music Journals*, ed. Linda M. Fidler and Richard S. James, 249-53. New York: Greenwood, 1990.

**CI, J**

_____. "Update: The Applications of Research in Music Education." In *International Music Journals*, ed. Linda M. Fidler and Richard S. James, 469-70. New York: Greenwood, 1990.

**CI, J, P, R**

Kapinus, Barbara, et al. "National Standards: Implications and Strategies for the States." In *Perspectives on Implementation: Arts Education Standards for America's Students*, ed. Bruce O. Boston, 89-95. Reston, Va.: Music Educators National Conference, 1994.

**A, CI, FPA**

Kaplan, Max. *Foundations and Frontiers of Music Education*. New York: Holt, Rinehart and Winston, 1966.

**CI, FPA**

_____. *Music Education in a Changing World: A Report*. Washington: Music Educators National Conference, 1958.

**CI, RSC**

_____. "Society, Sociology, and Music Education." In *Music Education in the United States: Contemporary Issues*, ed. J. Terry Gates, 3-32. Tuscaloosa: University of Alabama Press, 1988.

**CI, P**

Kaplan, Phyllis, and Judith Theiss. "Music Education and Elementary School." In *Toward Tomorrow: New Visions for General Music*, ed. Sandra L. Stauffer, 127-29. Reston, Va.: Music Educators National Conference, 1995.

**CI**

Kaplan, Phyllis, and Sandra L. Stauffer. *Cooperative Learning in Music*. Reston, Va.: Music Educators National Conference, 1994.

**CI**

Karafelis, Plato, and Robert I. Hugh. "Integrated Arts and Music Composition at Wolcott Elementary School." In *Toward Tomorrow: New Visions for General Music*, ed. Sandra L. Stauffer, 111-20. Reston, Va.: Music Educators National Conference, 1995.

**A, CI**

Katz, Jonathan, ed. *Arts and Education Handbook: A Guide to Productive Collaborations*. Washington: National Assembly of State Arts Agencies, 1988.

**A, BR, CI**

Kemp, Anthony E., and Laurence Lepherd. "Research Methods in International and Comparative Music Education." In *Handbook of Research on Music Teaching and Learning*, ed. Richard J. Colwell, 773-88. New York: Schirmer Books, 1992.
**CI, R**

Kendall, John D. *Talent, Education, and Suzuki: What the American Music Educator Should Know about Shinichi Suzuki.* Washington: Music Educators National Conference, 1966.
**CI**

Kennell, Richard P. "Contributions to Music Education." In *International Music Journals*, ed. Linda M. Fidler and Richard S. James, 98-100. New York: Greenwood, 1990.
**CI, J, P, R**

————. "Dialogue in Instrumental Music Education." In *International Music Journals*, ed. Linda M. Fidler and Richard S. James, 114-16. New York: Greenwood, 1990.
**CI, J, R**

————. "Music Teacher." In *International Music Journals*, ed. Linda M. Fidler and Richard S. James, 257-59. New York: Greenwood, 1990.
**CI, J**

————. "Musical Thinking in the Instrumental Rehearsal." In *Dimensions of Musical Thinking*, ed. Eunice Boardman, 83-89. Reston, Va.: Music Educators National Conference, 1989.
**CI, P**

————. "The School Musician." In *International Music Journals*, ed. Linda M. Fidler and Richard S. James, 389-92. New York: Greenwood, 1990.
**CI, J**

Keppel, Francis. "The Arts and Education Today Compared to the Sixties." In *Arts and Aesthetics: An Agenda for the Future*, ed. Stanley S. Madeja, 25-27. St. Louis, Mo.: CEMREL, 1977.
**A, CI, FPA**

Keyserling, Harriet. "The Politics of Mainstreaming Arts in Education." In *Artistic Intelligences: Implications for Education*, ed. William J. Moody, 63-68. New York: Teachers College, 1990.
**A, CI, FPA**

Kimpton, Jeffrey. *Public Education and the Arts: Linked by Necessity.* Reston, Va.: Music Educators National Conference, 1985.
**A, CI, FPA**

Kingsbury, Henry. *Music, Talent, and Performance: A Conservatory Cultural System.* Philadelphia: Temple University Press, 1988.
**CI, P**

Kirchhoff, Craig. "The School and College Band: Wind Band Pedagogy in the United States." In *Music Education in the United States: Contemporary Issues*, ed. J. Terry Gates, 259-76. Tuscaloosa: University of Alabama Press, 1988.
**CI, FPA**

Klotman, Robert H. "The Musician in Education: 2025 A.D." In *Music Education for Tomorrow's Society*, ed. Arthur Motycka, 12-20. Jamestown, R.I.: GAMT Music, 1976.
**CI, FPA**

————, ed. *Scheduling Music Classes.* Washington: Music Educators National Conference, 1968.
**CI**

Knapp, David. "Clavier." In *International Music Journals*, ed. Linda M. Fidler and Richard S. James, 85-87. New York: Greenwood, 1990.
**CI, J**

————. "The NATS Journal." In *International Music Journals*, ed. Linda M. Fidler and Richard S. James, 308-10. New York: Greenwood, 1990.
**CI, J**

————. "The Piano Quarterly." In *International Music Journals*, ed. Linda M. Fidler and Richard S. James, 342-46. New York: Greenwood, 1990.
**CI, J**

Knieter, Gerard L. "The Nature of Aesthetic Education." In *Toward an Aesthetic Education: A Report*, 3-19. Washington: Music Educators National Conference, 1971.
**A, CI, FPA, P**

Knieter, Gerard L., and Jane Stallings, eds. *The Teaching Process, Arts and Aesthetics.* St. Louis, Mo.: CEMREL, 1979.
**A, CI, FPA, RSC**

Knowles, Rosalind. "American Choral Review." In *International Music Journals*, ed. Linda M. Fidler and Richard S. James, 14-16. New York: Greenwood, 1990.
**CI, J, R**

Knuth, Alice Snyder, and William E. Knuth. *Basic Resources for Learning Music.* 2nd ed. Belmont, Calif.: Wadsworth, 1973.
**CI**

Kodály, Zoltán. "Folk Song in Pedagogy." In *The Eclectic Curriculum in American Music Education*, 2nd ed., ed. Polly Carder, 75-77. Reston, Va.: Music Educators National Conference, 1990.

**CI**

Kohut, Daniel L. *Musical Performance: Learning Theory and Pedagogy.* Champaign, Ill.: Stipes Publishing, 1992.

**CI, P**

Kowall, Bonnie C., ed. *Perspectives in Music Education: Source Book III.* Washington: Music Educators National Conference, 1966.

**BR, CI, FPA**

Krathwohl, David R. "Reflections on the Taxonomy: Its Past, Present, and Future." In *Bloom's Taxonomy—A Forty-Year Retrospective: 93rd Yearbook of the National Society for the Study of Education (Part II)*, ed. Lorin W. Anderson and Lauren A. Sosniak, 181-202. Chicago: University of Chicago Press, 1994.

**CI, FPA, P**

Kratus, John K. "American Music Teacher." In *International Music Journals*, ed. Linda M. Fidler and Richard S. James, 18-22. New York: Greenwood, 1990.

**CI, J**

————. "College Music Symposium." In *International Music Journals*, ed. Linda M. Fidler and Richard S. James, 90-93. New York: Greenwood, 1990.

**CI, J, P, R**

Kraus, Egon. "Zoltán Kodály's Legacy to Music Education." In *The Eclectic Curriculum in American Music Education*, 2nd ed., ed. Polly Carder, 79-92. Reston, Va.: Music Educators National Conference, 1990.

**CI**

Kreitzer, Amelia E., and George F. Madaus. "Empirical Investigations of the Hierarchical Structure of the Taxonomy." In *Bloom's Taxonomy—A Forty-Year Retrospective: 93rd Yearbook of the National Society for the Study of Education (Part II)*, ed. Lorin W. Anderson and Lauren A. Sosniak, 64-81. Chicago: University of Chicago Press, 1994.

**CI, R**

Kvet, Edward J., ed. *Instructional Literature for Middle-Level Band.* Reston, Va.: Music Educators National Conference, 1995.

**CI**

Kwalwasser, Jacob. *Problems in Public School Music.* Rev. ed. New York: M. Witmark and Sons, 1941.

**CI**

LaBerge, David. "Perceptual and Motor Schemas in the Performance of Musical Pitch." In *Documentary Report of the Ann Arbor Symposium: National Symposium on the Applications of Psychology to the Teaching and Learning of Music (Sessions I and II)*, 179-96. Reston, Va.: Music Educators National Conference, 1981.
**CI, P, R**

Labuta, Joseph A. "Curriculum Development for Music Education." In *Symposium in Music Education: A Festschrift for Charles Leonhard*, ed. Richard J. Colwell, 111-31. Urbana-Champaign: University of Illinois, 1982.
**CI**

Landers, Ray. *The Talent Education School of Shinichi Suzuki: An Analysis - Applications of Its Philosophy and Methods to All Areas of Instruction*. 3rd ed. Smithtown, N.Y.: Exposition, 1984.
**CI, FPA**

Landis, Beth, and Polly Carder. "The Dalcroze Approach." In *The Eclectic Curriculum in American Music Education*, 2nd ed., ed. Polly Carder, 7-29. Reston, Va.: Music Educators National Conference, 1990.
**CI**

_____. "The Kodály Approach." In *The Eclectic Curriculum in American Music Education*, 2nd ed., ed. Polly Carder, 55-74. Reston, Va.: Music Educators National Conference, 1990.
**CI**

_____. "The Orff Approach." In *The Eclectic Curriculum in American Music Education*, 2nd ed., ed. Polly Carder, 109-36. Reston, Va.: Music Educators National Conference, 1990.
**CI**

Landon, Joseph W. *Clinical Practice in Music Education: A Guide to Field Experiences in the Preparation of Teachers*. Fullerton, Calif.: Music Education Publications, 1988.
**BR, CI**

_____. *Leadership for Learning in Music Education*. Fullerton, Calif.: Music Education Publications, 1975.
**CI, FPA**

Lanfer, Helen. *The Music within Us: An Exploration in Creative Music Education*. New York: Hebrew Arts Music Publications, 1979.
**CI, P**

LaRue, Jan. *Guidelines for Style Analysis.* 2nd ed. Detroit Monographs in Musicology/Studies in Music, 12. Warren, Mich.: Harmonie Park Press, 1992.
**CI**

Lashley, Horace. "Arts Education, the Curriculum and the Multi-Cultural Society." In *The Arts and Personal Growth*, ed. Malcolm Ross, 27-36. New York: Pergamon, 1980.
**A, CI**

Lautzenheiser, Tim. *The Art of Successful Teaching: A Blend of Content and Context.* Chicago: G.I.A. Publications, 1992.
**CI**

Lawrence, Ian. *Composers and the Nature of Music Education.* London: Scolar, 1978.
**CI, FPA, P**

Lawrence, Vera Brodsky. *CMP Library: Contemporary Music Project for Creativity in Music Education.* 2nd ed. Washington: Music Educators National Conference, 1969.
**BR, CI, RSC**

Lehman, Paul R. "Curriculum and Program Evaluation." In *Handbook of Research on Music Teaching and Learning*, ed. Richard J. Colwell, 281-94. New York: Schirmer Books, 1992.
**CI, R**

_____. "Issues of Assessment." In *Perspectives on Implementation: Arts Education Standards for America's Students*, ed. Bruce O. Boston, 47-54. Reston, Va.: Music Educators National Conference, 1994.
**A, CI, P**

_____. *Music in Today's Schools: Rationale and Commentary.* Reston, Va.: Music Educators National Conference, 1987.
**CI, FPA**

_____. *Who Cares about Quality in Education?* Reston, Va.: Music Educators National Conference, 1986.
**CI, FPA**

_____, ed. *Teaching Examples: Ideas for Music Educators.* Reston, Va.: Music Educators National Conference, 1994.
**CI**

Leonhard, Charles. "Evaluation in Music Education." In *Basic Concepts in Music Education: 57th Yearbook of the National Society for the Study of Education*, ed. Nelson B. Henry, 310-38. Chicago: University of Chicago Press, 1958.
**CI, P**

_____. "The Future of Musical Education in America: A Pragmatist's View." In *The Future of Musical Education in America: Proceedings of the July 1983 Conference*, ed. Donald J. Shetler, 60-71. Rochester, N.Y.: Eastman School of Music Press, 1984.
**CI, FPA**

_____. "Methods Courses in Music Teacher Education." In *Music Education in the United States: Contemporary Issues*, ed. J. Terry Gates, 193-201. Tuscaloosa: University of Alabama Press, 1988.
**CI, FPA**

_____. "Music Teacher Education in the United States." In *Symposium in Music Education: A Festschrift for Charles Leonhard*, ed. Richard J. Colwell, 233-47. Urbana-Champaign: University of Illinois, 1982.
**CI, FPA**

_____. *A Realistic Rationale for Teaching Music*. Reston, Va.: Music Educators National Conference, 1985.
**CI, FPA**

_____. *Recreation through Music*. New York: A. S. Barnes, 1952.
**CI**

_____. *The Status of Arts Education in American Public Schools: Report of a Survey Conducted by the National Arts Education Research Center at the University of Illinois*. Urbana: Council for Research in Music Education, School of Music, University of Illinois, 1991.
**A, BR, CI, RSC**

Leonhard, Charles, and Robert William House. *Foundations and Principles of Music Education*. 2nd ed. New York: McGraw-Hill, 1972.
**CI, FPA**

Lieberman, Ann, ed. *The Changing Contexts of Teaching: 91st Yearbook of the National Society for the Study of Education (Part I)*. Chicago: National Society for the Study of Education, 1992.
**BR, CI**

Lieberman, Julie Lyonn. *You Are Your Instrument: The Definitive Musician's Guide to Practice and Performance*. 3rd ed. New York: Huiksi Music, 1995.
**BR, CI, P**

Lipman, Samuel. "On Adult Arts Education." In *Arts Education beyond the Classroom*, ed. Judith H. Balfe and Joni Cherbo Heine, 7-10. New York: American Council for the Arts, 1988.
**A, CI**

List, Lynne K. *Music, Art, and Drama Experiences for the Elementary Curriculum.* New York: Teachers College, Columbia University, 1982.

**A, CI**

Lynch, Robert L. "Implementing the Standards: Making Use of the Arts Community." In *Perspectives on Implementation: Arts Education Standards for America's Students*, ed. Bruce O. Boston, 75-81. Reston, Va.: Music Educators National Conference, 1994.

**A, CI, FPA**

Madeja, Stanley S., ed. *Arts and Aesthetics: An Agenda for the Future.* St. Louis, Mo.: CEMREL, 1977.

**A, CI, FPA, RSC**

_____, ed. *The Arts, Cognition and Basic Skills.* St. Louis, Mo.: CEMREL, 1978.

**A, CI, P, RSC**

Madeja, Stanley S., and Harry T. Kelly. "A Curriculum Development Model for Aesthetic Education." In *Aesthetics and Problems of Education*, ed. Ralph A. Smith, 345-56. Urbana: University of Illinois Press, 1971.

**A, CI, FPA**

_____. "The Process of Curriculum Development for Aesthetic Education." In *Toward an Aesthetic Education: A Report*, 101-15. Washington: Music Educators National Conference, 1971.

**A, CI, FPA**

Madison, Thurber H. "The Need for New Concepts in Music Education." In *Basic Concepts in Music Education: 57th Yearbook of the National Society for the Study of Education*, ed. Nelson B. Henry, 3-29. Chicago: University of Chicago Press, 1958.

**CI, FPA**

Madsen, Charles H., Jr., and Clifford K. Madsen. *Teaching/Discipline: A Positive Approach for Educational Development.* 3rd ed. Raleigh, N.C.: Contemporary Publishing, 1983.

**CI, P, R**

Madsen, Clifford K. *Music Therapy: A Behavioral Guide for the Mentally Retarded.* Lawrence, Kans.: National Association for Music Therapy, 1981.

**BR, CI, P**

Madsen, Clifford K., and Cornelia Yarbrough. *Competency-Based Music Education.* Raleigh, N.C.: Contemporary Publishing, 1985.

**CI**

Madsen, Clifford K., and Terry Lee Kuhn. *Contemporary Music Education.* 2nd ed. Raleigh, N.C.: Contemporary Publishing, 1994.

**CI, FPA**

Madsen, Clifford K., and Carol A. Prickett, eds. *Applications of Research in Music Behavior.* Tuscaloosa: University of Alabama Press, 1987.

**CI, P, R, RSC**

Madsen, Clifford K., R. Douglas Greer, and Charles H. Madsen, Jr., eds. *Research in Music Behavior: Modifying Music Behavior in the Classroom.* New York: Teachers College, 1975.

**CI, P, R**

Maehr, Martin L. "The Development of Continuing Interests in Music." In *Documentary Report of the Ann Arbor Symposium on the Applications of Psychology to the Teaching and Learning of Music: Motivation and Creativity (Session III)*, 5-11. Reston, Va.: Music Educators National Conference, 1983.

**CI, P**

*Making the Grade: Report of the Twentieth Century Fund Task Force on Federal Elementary and Secondary Education Policy.* New York: Twentieth Century Fund, 1983.

**CI, RSC**

Mark, Desmond, ed. *Stock-Taking of Musical Life - Music Sociography and Its Relevance to Music Educaton: Report on a Seminar Organized by the ISME Commission on Music in Cultural, Educational and Mass Media Policies.* Vienna, Austria: Doblinger, 1981.

**CI, R, RSC**

Mark, Michael L. "Aesthetics and Utility Reconciled: The Importance to Society of Education in Music." In *Music Education in the United States: Contemporary Issues*, ed. J. Terry Gates, 111-29. Tuscaloosa: University of Alabama Press, 1988.

**CI, FPA, P**

————. *Contemporary Music Education.* 3rd ed. New York: Schirmer Books, 1996.

**CI, FPA**

————, ed. *The Music Educator and Community Music: The Best of MEJ.* Reston, Va.: Music Educators National Conference, 1992.

**CI**

Marzano, Robert J., et al. *Dimensions of Thinking: A Framework for Curriculum and Instruction.* Alexandria, Va.: Association for Supervision and Curriculum Development, 1988.

**CI, P, R**

Mast, Paul B. "Journal of Music Theory." In *International Music Journals*, ed. Linda M. Fidler and Richard S. James, 195-98. New York: Greenwood, 1990.
**CI, J, R**

Mattern, David, and Norval L. Church. "Instrumental Activities." In *Music Education: 35th Yearbook of the National Society for the Study of Education (Part II)*, ed. Guy Montrose Whipple, 75-90. Bloomington, Ill.: Public School Publishing, 1936.
**CI**

May, William V., and Craig Tolin. *Pronunciation Guide for Choral Literature.* Reston, Va.: Music Educators National Conference, 1987.
**BR, CI**

Mayer, Frederick R., ed. *The String Orchestra Super List.* Reston, Va.: Music Educators National Conference, 1993.
**BR, CI**

McAllester, David P., ed. *Becoming Human through Music: The Wesleyan Symposium on the Perspectives of Social Anthropology in the Teaching and Learning of Music.* Reston, Va.: Music Educators National Conference, 1985.
**CI, P, RSC**

McCarthy, Marie, ed. *Winds of Change: A Colloquium in Music Education with Charles Fowler and David J. Elliott.* New York: ACA Books, University of Maryland at College Park, 1994.
**CI, FPA, RSC**

McCullough-Brabson, Ellen. "Music and Cultural Diversity: Thoughts from a World Music Cheerleader." In *Toward Tomorrow: New Visions for General Music*, ed. Sandra L. Stauffer, 75-80. Reston, Va.: Music Educators National Conference, 1995.
**CI**

McDonald, Dorothy T. *Music in Our Lives: The Early Years.* Washington: National Association for the Education of Young Children, 1989.
**CI**

McDonald, Dorothy T., and Gene M. Simons. *Musical Growth and Development: Birth through Six.* New York: Schirmer Books, 1988.
**CI, P**

McEwen, John Blackwood. *The Foundations of Musical Aesthetics.* London: K. Paul Trubner, 1917.
**CI, FPA**

McKay, George Frederick. "The Range of Musical Experience." In *Basic Concepts in Music Education: 57th Yearbook of the National Society for the Study of Education*, ed. Nelson B. Henry, 123-39. Chicago: University of Chicago Press, 1958.
**CI, FPA**

McKenna, Gerard, and William R. Schmid, eds. *The Tanglewood Symposium Revisited: Music in American Society Ten Years Later*. Milwaukee: University of Wisconsin, 1978.
**CI, FPA, RSC**

McPherson, Bruce. *Measure by Measure: A History of the New England Conservatory from 1867*. Boston: New England Conservatory, 1995.
**BR, CI**

Merrion, Margaret D. *Instructional and Classroom Management for Music Educators*. Washington: University Press of America, 1982.
**CI, P**

————, ed. *What Works: Instructional Strategies for Music Education*. Reston, Va.: Music Educators National Conference, 1989.
**CI, R**

Meske, Eunice Boardman. "Educating the Music Teacher: Participaton in a Metamorphosis." In *Symposium in Music Education: A Festschrift for Charles Leonhard*, ed. Richard J. Colwell, 249-65. Urbana-Champaign: University of Illinois, 1982.
**CI, FPA, P, R**

Metz, Donald. *Teaching General Music in Grades 6-9*. Columbus, Ohio: Merrill, 1980.
**A, CI**

Michel, Donald E. *Music Therapy: An Introduction, Including Music in Special Education*. 2nd ed. Springfield, Ill.: C. C. Thomas, 1985.
**CI, P**

Michelson, Steven K. *Getting Started with High School Choir*. Reston, Va.: Music Educators National Conference, 1994.
**CI**

Miller, Linda Bryant. "Children's Musical Behaviors in the Natural Environment." In *Music and Child Development*, ed. J. Craig Peery, Irene W. Peery, and Thomas W. Draper, 206-24. New York: Springer-Verlag, 1987.
**CI, P**

Miller, Louise. "Working with State Legislatures." In *Perspectives on Implementation: Arts Education Standards for America's Students*, ed. Bruce O. Boston, 96-100. Reston, Va.: Music Educators National Conference, 1994.

**A, CI, FPA**

Miller, Rodney E. *Institutionalizing Music: The Administration of Music Programs in Higher Education.* Springfield, Ill.: C. C. Thomas, 1993.

**CI**

Mills, Elizabeth. *In the Suzuki Style: A Manual for Raising Musical Consciousness in Children.* Berkeley, Calif.: Diablo, 1974.

**BR, CI**

*Missouri Journal of Research in Music Education.* Jefferson City: Missouri State Department of Education, 1962-.

**CI, J, P, R**

Mitchell, Ruth, ed. *Measuring Up to the Challenge: What Standards and Assessment Can Do for Arts Education.* New York: ACA Books, 1994.

**A, CI, P, RSC**

Monsour, Sally. "General Music Tomorrow." In *Toward Tomorrow: New Visions for General Music*, ed. Sandra L. Stauffer, 43-47. Reston, Va.: Music Educators National Conference, 1995.

**CI, FPA**

Moody, William J., ed. *Artistic Intelligences: Implications for Education.* New York: Teachers College, 1990.

**A, CI, FPA, P, RSC**

Moog, Helmut. *The Musical Experience of the Pre-School Child.* Transl. Claudia Clarke. London: Schott Music, 1976.

**CI, P**

Moore, Brian. "Musical Thinking Processes." In *Dimensions of Musical Thinking*, ed. Eunice Boardman, 33-44. Reston, Va.: Music Educators National Conference, 1989.

**CI, P**

Moore, Marvelene C. "Cultural Diversity and Music: Authenticity in Performance." In *Toward Tomorrow: New Visions for General Music*, ed. Sandra L. Stauffer, 71-73. Reston, Va.: Music Educators National Conference, 1995.

**CI**

Moorhead, Gladys Evelyn, and Donald Pond. *Music of Young Children.* 1941. Reprint, Santa Barbara, Calif.: Pillsbury Foundation for the Advancement of Music Education, 1978.

**CI**

Morgan, Hazel Nohavec, ed. *Music Education Source Book: A Compendium of Data, Opinion and Recommendations.* Chicago: Music Educators National Conference, 1951.

**BR, CI, FPA**

————, ed. *Music in American Education: Music Education Source Book II.* Chicago: Music Educators National Conference, 1955.

**BR, CI, FPA**

Morgan, Russell V. "Ear-Training." In *Music Education: 35th Yearbook of the National Society for the Study of Education (Part II),* ed. Guy Montrose Whipple, 69-73. Bloomington, Ill.: Public School Publishing, 1936.

**CI**

Morgan, Russell V., and Hazel Nohavec Morgan. *Music Education in Action.* Enl. and rev. ed. Park Ridge, Ill.: N. A. Kjos Music, 1960.

**CI**

Motycka, Arthur. *Musico-Aesthetic Education: A Phenomenological Proposition.* Jamestown, R.I.: GAMT Music, 1975.

**CI, FPA**

————, ed. *Music Education for Tomorrow's Society.* Jamestown, R.I.: GAMT Music, 1976.

**CI, FPA**

Mullins, Shirley. *Teaching Music: The Human Experience.* Yellow Springs, Ohio: S. Mullins, 1985.

**CI, P**

Murphy, Judith, and George Sullivan. *Music in American Society: An Interpretive Report of the Tanglewood Symposium.* Washington: Music Educators National Conference, 1968.

**CI, FPA, RSC**

Mursell, James L. *Education for Musical Growth.* Boston, Mass.: Ginn, 1948.

**CI, P**

————. "Growth Processes in Music Education." In *Basic Concepts in Music Education II,* ed. Richard J. Colwell, 111-29. Niwot: University Press of Colorado, 1991.

**CI, P**

_____. "Growth Processes in Music Education." In *Basic Concepts in Music Education: 57th Yearbook of the National Society for the Study of Education*, ed. Nelson B. Henry, 140-62. Chicago: University of Chicago Press, 1958.
**CI, P**

_____. *Human Values in Music Education.* New York: Silver Burdett, 1934.
**CI, FPA, P**

_____. *Music and the Classroom Teacher.* New York: Silver Burdett, 1951.
**CI**

_____. *Music Education: Principles and Programs.* Morristown, N.J.: Silver Burdett, 1956.
**CI, FPA**

_____. *Music in American Schools.* Rev. ed. New York: Silver Burdett, 1953.
**CI, FPA**

_____. *Principles of Democratic Education.* New York: Norton, 1955.
**CI, FPA**

_____. *Principles of Education.* New York: Norton, 1934.
**CI, FPA**

_____. "Principles of Music Education." In *Music Education: 35th Yearbook of the National Society for the Study of Education (Part II)*, ed. Guy Montrose Whipple, 3-16. Bloomington, Ill.: Public School Publishing, 1936.
**CI, FPA**

_____. *Principles of Musical Education.* New York: Macmillan, 1927.
**CI, FPA**

_____. "Reading Music." In *Music Education: 35th Yearbook of the National Society for the Study of Education (Part II)*, ed. Guy Montrose Whipple, 99-107. Bloomington, Ill.: Public School Publishing, 1936.
**CI**

Mursell, James L., and Mabelle Glenn. *The Psychology of School Music Teaching.* New York: Silver Burdett, 1938.
**CI, P**

*Music Education for Elementary School Children.* Washington: Music Educators National Conference, 1960.
**CI**

*Music Education in the Modern World: Materials of the Ninth Conference of the International Society for Music Education.*  Moscow: Progress Publishers, 1974.
**CI, P, R, RSC**

*Music Education Materials: A Selected Bibliography.*  Chicago: Music Educators National Conference, 1959.
**BR, CI**

*Music in Education: International Conference on the Role and Place of Music in the Education of Youth and Adults.*  Paris: UNESCO, 1955.
**CI, RSC**

*Music in General Studies: A Survey of National Practice in Higher Education.*  Boulder, Colo.: College Music Society, 1983.
**CI, RSC**

*Music in Special Education.*  Washington: Music Educators National Conference, 1972.
**CI, P**

*Music in the Undergraduate Curriculum, A Reassessment: A Report of the Study Group on the Content of the Undergraduate Curriculum.*  Boulder, Colo.: College Music Society, 1989.
**CI, RSC**

*Music Schools and Music Education.*  New York: Foundation Center, 1986.
**BR, CI**

*Music Teacher Education: Partnership and Process.*  Reston, Va.: Music Educators National Conference, 1987.
**CI, FPA, RSC**

Myers, David, and Chelcy Bowles.  "General Music Education: College through Adulthood." In *Toward Tomorrow: New Visions for General Music*, ed. Sandra L. Stauffer, 139-43. Reston, Va.: Music Educators National Conference, 1995.
**CI**

Myers, Rose Maree.  "The Theory Is Realized: A Creative Arts Elementary School." In *Artistic Intelligences: Implications for Education*, ed. William J. Moody, 72-76. New York: Teachers College, 1990.
**A, CI**

*Nation at Risk: The Imperative for Educational Reform.*  National Commission on Excellence in Education. Washington: U.S. Government Printing Office, 1983.
**CI, RSC**

Neiman, Marcus L., comp. *Life in the Music Classroom.* Reston, Va.: Music Educators National Conference, 1992.
**BR, CI**

Neuls-Bates, Carol, ed. *The Status of Women in College Music: Preliminary Studies - Proceedings of the Meeting on Women in the Profession.* Binghamton, N.Y.: College Music Society, 1976.
**CI, RSC**

Nickson, Noel. *Education through Music.* Brisbane, Australia: University of Queensland Press, 1967.
**CI**

Nordholm, Harriet. *Singing in the Elementary Schools: Foundations of Music Education Series.* Englewood Cliffs, N.J.: Prentice-Hall, 1966.
**CI, FPA**

O'Brien, James Patrick. *Teaching Music.* New York: Holt, Rinehart, and Winston, 1983.
**CI**

O'Connor, Joseph. *Not Pulling Strings: An Exploration of Music and Instrumental Teaching Using Neuro-Linguistic Programming.* Portland, Ore.: Metamorphous, 1989.
**CI, P**

Olson, David R. "The Arts as Basic Skills." In *The Arts, Cognition and Basic Skills*, ed. Stanley S. Madeja, 59-81. St. Louis, Mo.: CEMREL, 1978.
**A, CI**

*Opportunity-to-Learn Standards for Music Instruction: Grades Pre K-12 Curriculum and Scheduling, Staffing, Materials and Equipment, and Facilities.* Reston, Va.: Music Educators National Conference, 1994.
**CI**

Orff, Carl. "The Schulwerk - Its Origins and Aims." In *The Eclectic Curriculum in American Music Education*, 2nd ed., ed. Polly Carder, 137-44. Reston, Va.: Music Educators National Conference, 1990.
**CI**

Overby, Lynnette Young, Ann Richardson, Lillian S. Hasko, and Luke Kahlich, eds. *Early Childhood Creative Arts: Proceedings of the International Early Childhood Creative Arts Conference.* Reston, Va.: Music Educators National Conference and National Dance Association, 1991.
**A, CI, P, RSC**

Palmer, Mary J., comp. *TIPS: Getting Started with Elementary School Music.* Reston, Va.: Music Educators National Conference, 1988.

**CI**

————, ed. *Promising Practices: High School General Music.* Reston, Va.: Music Educators National Conference, 1989.

**CI**

Palmer, Mary J., and Wendy L. Sims, eds. *Music in Prekindergarten: Planning and Teaching.* Reston, Va.: Music Educators National Conference, 1993.

**CI**

Pankratz, David, and Kevin V. Mulcahy, eds. *The Challenge to Reform Arts Education: What Role Can Research Play?* New York: ACA Books, 1989.

**A, CI, FPA, R**

*Papers from the Dearborn Conference on Music in General Studies.* Boulder, Colo.: College Music Society, 1984.

**CI, RSC**

*Papers from the Forum on the Education of Music Consumers.* Reston, Va.: National Association of Schools of Music, 1974.

**CI, RSC**

Parsons, Michael J. "Cognition as Interpretation in Art Education." In *The Arts, Education, and Aesthetic Knowing: 91st Yearbook of the National Society for the Study of Education (Part II)*, ed. Bennett Reimer and Ralph A. Smith, 70-91. Chicago: University of Chicago Press, 1992.

**A, CI, P**

Paul, John B., ed. *Music Education: The Proceedings of the Workshop on Music Education.* Washington: Catholic University of America Press, 1954.

**CI, RSC**

Pautz, Mary P. "Musical Thinking in the General Music Classroom." In *Dimensions of Musical Thinking*, ed. Eunice Boardman, 65-72. Reston, Va.: Music Educators National Conference, 1989.

**CI, P**

————. "Musical Thinking in the Teacher Education Classroom." In *Dimensions of Musical Thinking*, ed. Eunice Boardman, 101-09. Reston, Va.: Music Educators National Conference, 1989.

**CI, P**

Paynter, John. *Music in the Secondary School Curriculum: Trends and Developments in Class Music Teaching.* New York: Cambridge University Press, 1982.
  **CI**

Peery, Irene Weiss, Dale Nyboer, and J. Craig Peery. "The Virtue and Vice of Musical Performance Competitions for Children." In *Music and Child Development*, ed. J. Craig Peery, Irene W. Peery, and Thomas W. Draper, 225-36. New York: Springer-Verlag, 1987.
  **CI, P**

Peery, J. Craig, and Irene Weiss Peery. "The Role of Music in Child Development." In *Music and Child Development*, ed. J. Craig Peery, Irene W. Peery, and Thomas W. Draper, 3-31. New York: Springer-Verlag, 1987.
  **CI, P**

*Performing Together: The Arts and Education.* Washington: Alliance for Arts Education, 1985.
  **A, CI**

*Perspectives on Education Reform: Arts Education as Catalyst.* Santa Monica, Calif.: Getty Center for Education in the Arts, 1993.
  **A, CI**

Peters, G. David, and Robert F. Miller. *Music Teaching and Learning.* New York: Longman, 1982.
  **CI, P**

*Phi Delta Kappan.* Bloomington, Ind.: Phi Delta Kappa, 1915-.
  **CI, J**

Phillips, Kenneth H. "Research on the Teaching of Singing." In *Handbook of Research on Music Teaching and Learning*, ed. Richard J. Colwell, 568-76. New York: Schirmer Books, 1992.
  **CI, R**

Piaget, Jean. *To Understand Is to Invent: The Future of Education.* Transl. George-Anne Roberts. 1948. Reprint, New York: Penguin, 1976.
  **CI, P**

Pierce, Anne E. "The Selection and Organization of Music Materials." In *Music Education: 35th Yearbook of the National Society for the Study of Education (Part II)*, ed. Guy Montrose Whipple, 147-65. Bloomington, Ill.: Public School Publishing, 1936.
  **CI**

Pitts, Lilla Belle. "Typical Musical Activities of the School." In *Music Education: 35th Yearbook of the National Society for the Study of Education (Part II)*, ed. Guy Montrose Whipple, 45-50. Bloomington, Ill.: Public School Publishing, 1936.
  **CI, FPA**

Plummeridge, Charles. *Music Education in Theory and Practice.* New York: Falmer, 1991.
**CI, FPA**

Pogonowski, Lenore. "Metacognition: A Dimension of Musical Thinking." In *Dimensions of Musical Thinking*, ed. Eunice Boardman, 9-19. Reston, Va.: Music Educators National Conference, 1989.
**CI, P**

_____, comp. *Readings in General Music: Selected Reprints from Soundings, a Publication of the Society for General Music, 1982 to 1987.* Reston, Va.: Music Educators National Conference, 1988.
**CI**

Potosky, Alice. *Promoting School Music: A Practical Guide.* Reston, Va.: Music Educators National Conference, 1984.
**BR, CI, FPA**

Pratt, Rosalie R., ed. *International Symposium on Music in Medicine, Education, and Therapy for the Handicapped.* Lanham, Md.: University Press of America, 1985.
**CI, P, RSC**

_____, ed. *Music Therapy and Music Education for the Handicapped: Developments and Limitations in Practice and Research.* St. Louis, Mo.: MMB Music, 1993.
**CI, P, RSC**

Probasco, Jim. *A Parent's Guide to Band and Orchestra.* White Hall, Va.: Betterway, 1991.
**BR, CI**

_____. *A Parent's Guide to Teaching Music.* White Hall, Va.: Betterway, 1992.
**BR, CI.**

*Quarterly Journal of Music Teaching and Learning.* Greeley: University of Northern Colorado School of Music, 1990-.
**CI, FPA, J, P, R**

*Racial and Ethnic Directions in American Music.* CMS Report No. 3. Boulder, Colo.: College Music Society, 1982.
**CI, RSC**

Raiman, Melvyn L., ed. *Midwest Symposium on Music Education.* Tulsa, Okla.: United States Jaycees, 1978.
**CI, RSC**

Rao, Doreen. *Choral Music for Children: An Annotated List.* Reston, Va.: Music Educators National Conference, 1990.
**BR, CI**

Ree, Henry. "Education and the Arts: Are Schools the Enemy?" In *The Aesthetic Imperative: Relevance and Responsibility in Arts Education,* ed. Malcolm Ross, 90-99. New York: Pergamon, 1981.
**A, CI, FPA**

Regelski, Thomas A. *Arts Education and Brain Research.* Reston, Va.: Music Educators National Conference, 1978.
**A, CI, P**

———. *Principles and Problems of Music Education.* Englewood Cliffs, N.J.: Prentice-Hall, 1975.
**CI, FPA**

———. *Teaching General Music: Action Learning for Middle and Secondary Schools.* New York: Schirmer Books, 1981.
**CI**

Reid, Louis Arnaud. "Assessment and Aesthetic Education." In *The Aesthetic Imperative: Relevance and Responsibility in Arts Education,* ed. Malcolm Ross, 8-24. New York: Pergamon, 1981.
**A, CI, FPA, P**

———. "Knowledge and Aesthetic Education." In *Aesthetics and Problems of Education,* ed. Ralph A. Smith, 162-71. Urbana: University of Illinois Press, 1971.
**A, CI, FPA**

———. *Meaning in the Arts.* New York: Humanities Press, 1969.
**A, CI, FPA, P**

Reimer, Bennett. "Aesthetic Behaviors in Music." In *Toward an Aesthetic Education: A Report,* 65-87. Washington: Music Educators National Conference, 1971.
**A, CI, FPA, P**

———. "Building Curricula for Music Education." In *Aesthetics and Problems of Education,* ed. Ralph A. Smith, 374-86. Urbana: University of Illinois Press, 1971.
**CI, FPA**

———. "Designing Effective Arts Programs." In *Arts and the Schools,* ed. Jerome J. Hausman and Joyce Wright, 117-56. New York: McGraw-Hill, 1980.
**A, CI, FPA, P**

_____. *Development and Trial in a Junior and Senior High School of a Two-Year Curriculum in General Music.* Washington: U.S. Department of Health, Education, and Welfare, 1967.

CI

_____. "A Radical View of the Present and Future of Music Education." In *Symposium in Music Education: A Festschrift for Charles Leonhard*, ed. Richard J. Colwell, 3-22. Urbana-Champaign: University of Illinois, 1982.

CI, FPA

_____. "What Knowledge Is of Most Worth in the Arts?" In *The Arts, Education, and Aesthetic Knowing: 91st Yearbook of the National Society for the Study of Education (Part II)*, ed. Bennett Reimer and Ralph A. Smith, 20-50. Chicago: University of Chicago Press, 1992.

A, CI, FPA, P

Reimer, Bennett, and Ralph A. Smith, eds. *The Arts, Education, and Aesthetic Knowing: 91st Yearbook of the National Society for the Study of Education (Part II).* Chicago: National Society for the Study of Education, 1992.

A, BR, CI, FPA, P

Renton, Barbara Hampton. *Status of Women in College Music, 1976-77: A Statistical Study.* Boulder, Colo.: College Music Society, 1980.

CI, RSC

Resnick, Lauren B., and Leopold E. Klopfer, eds. *Toward the Thinking Curriculum: Current Cognitive Research.* Alexandria, Va.: Association for Supervision and Curriculum Development, 1989.

CI, P, R

*Restructuring and Reform: Selected Bibliography.* Reston, Va.: Music Educators National Conference, 1993.

BR, CI, R, RSC

Reul, David G. *Getting Started with Middle Level Band.* Reston, Va.: Music Educators National Conference, 1994.

CI

*Review of Educational Research.* Washington: American Educational Research Association, 1931-.

CI, J, R

Richards, Mary Helen. *Aesthetic Foundations for Thinking Rethought.* Portola Valley, Calif.: Richards Institute, 1984.

CI, FPA

Richardson, Carol P., and Nancy L. Whitaker. "Critical Thinking and Music Education." In *Handbook of Research on Music Teaching and Learning*, ed. Richard J. Colwell, 546-57. New York: Schirmer Books, 1992.

**CI, P, R**

Rideout, Roger R. "The Role of Mental Presets in Skill Acquisition." In *Handbook of Research on Music Teaching and Learning*, ed. Richard J. Colwell, 472-79. New York: Schirmer Books, 1992.

**CI, P, R**

Ristad, Eloise. *A Soprano on Her Head: Right-Side-Up Reflections on Life and Other Performances.* Moab, Utah: Real People, 1982.

**CI, P**

Rivas, Frank W. *The First National Assessment of Musical Performance - National Assessment of Educational Progress: A Project of the Education Commission of the States.* Washington: United States Government Printing Office, 1974.

**CI, P, RSC**

Robinson, Russell L. *Getting Started With Jazz/Show Choir.* Reston, Va.: Music Educators National Conference, 1994.

**CI**

_____, ed. *Preparing to Teach Music in Today's Schools: The Best of MEJ.* Reston, Va.: Music Educators National Conference, 1993.

**CI**

Rockefeller, David, Jr. "The State of Arts Education in American Public Schools." In *Arts and Aesthetics: An Agenda for the Future*, ed. Stanley S. Madeja, 46-50. St. Louis, Mo.: CEMREL, 1977.

**A, CI**

Rohwer, William D., Jr., and Kathryn Sloane. "Psychological Perspectives." In *Bloom's Taxonomy—A Forty-Year Retrospective: 93rd Yearbook of the National Society for the Study of Education (Part II)*, ed. Lorin W. Anderson and Lauren A. Sosniak, 41-63. Chicago: University of Chicago Press, 1994.

**CI, P**

Ross, Malcolm. "The Arts and Personal Growth." In *The Arts and Personal Growth*, ed. Malcolm Ross, 96-119. New York: Pergamon, 1980.

**A, CI, FPA**

_____, ed. *The Aesthetic Imperative: Relevance and Responsibility in Arts Education.* New York: Pergamon, 1981.

**A, CI, FPA, RSC**

_____, ed. *The Aesthetic in Education.* New York: Pergamon, 1985.

**A, CI, FPA**

_____, ed. *Assessment in Arts Education: A Necessary Discipline or a Loss of Happiness?* New York: Pergamon, 1986.

**A, CI, P**

_____, ed. *The Claims of Feeling: Readings in Aesthetic Education.* Philadelphia: Falmer, 1989.

**A, CI, FPA, RSC**

_____, ed. *The Development of Aesthetic Experience.* New York: Pergamon, 1982.

**A, CI, FPA, RSC**

Rossman, R. Louis. *The Business of Administration and Supervision in Music: A Selective Annotated Bibliography.* Sioux City, Iowa: Dabec Educational Products, 1989.

**BR, CI, FPA**

_____, comp. *TIPS: Discipline in the Music Classroom.* Reston, Va.: Music Educators National Conference, 1989.

**CI, P**

Runfola, Maria, and Joanne Rutkowski. "General Music Curriculum." In *Handbook of Research on Music Teaching and Learning*, ed. Richard J. Colwell, 697-709. New York: Schirmer Books, 1992.

**CI, R**

Ryder, Georgia. "African-American Music." In *Racial and Ethnic Directions in American Music*, CMS Report No. 3, 39-47. Boulder, Colo.: College Music Society, 1982.

**CI**

Sakata, Hiromi Lorraine. "Asian-Americans and Music in Higher Education." In *Racial and Ethnic Directions in American Music*, CMS Report No. 3, 29-32. Boulder, Colo.: College Music Society, 1982.

**CI**

Saliba, Konnie. "What Is the Orff-Schulwerk Approach to Teaching?" In *The Eclectic Curriculum in American Music Education*, 2nd ed., ed. Polly Carder, 145-49. Reston, Va.: Music Educators National Conference, 1990.

**CI**

Schaberg, Gail, comp. *TIPS: Teaching Music to Special Learners.* Reston, Va.: Music Educators National Conference, 1988.

**CI, P**

Schafer, R. Murray. *Ear Cleaning: Notes for an Experimental Music Course.* Toronto: Clark and Cruickshank, 1969.
**CI, P**

————. *The Soundscape: Our Sonic Environment and the Tuning of the World.* 1977. Reprint, Rochester, Vt.: Destiny Books, 1994.
**CI, FPA, P**

————. *The Thinking Ear: Complete Writings on Music Education.* Toronto: Arcana Editions, 1986.
**CI, P**

*Scheduling Time for Music.* Reston, Va.: Music Educators National Conference, 1995.
**CI**

Scheffler, Israel. *Reason and Teaching.* 1973. Reprint, Indianapolis: Hackett, 1989.
**CI, FPA**

Schleuter, Stanley and Lois. "Teaching and Learning Music Performance: What, When, and How." In *The Crane Symposium: Toward an Understanding of the Teaching and Learning of Music Performance,* ed. Charles Fowler, 63-87. Potsdam: Potsdam College of the State University of New York, 1988.
**CI, P**

Schmid, Will. "If All, Then What? What to Teach in a Musically Diverse World." In *Toward Tomorrow: New Visions for General Music,* ed. Sandra L. Stauffer, 81-84. Reston, Va.: Music Educators National Conference, 1995.
**CI**

Schmitt, Cecilia. *Rapport and Success: Human Relations in Music Education.* Philadelphia: Dorrance, 1976.
**CI, P**

Schneider, Erwin H., and Henry L. Cady. *Evaluation and Synthesis of Research Studies Related to Music Education.* Columbus: Ohio State University, 1965.
**CI, R**

Schneiderman, Barbara. *Confident Music Performance: The Art of Preparing.* St. Louis, Mo.: MMB Music, 1991.
**CI, P**

*School Choice: A Special Report of the Carnegie Foundation for the Advancement of Teaching.* Princeton, N.J.: Carnegie Foundation for the Advancement of Teaching, 1992.
**CI, RSC**

*School Music Program: A New Vision. The K-12 National Standards, Pre K Standards, and What They Mean to Music Educators.* Reston, Va.: Music Educators National Conference, 1994.
**CI**

*School Music Program: Description and Standards.* 2nd ed. Reston, Va.: Music Educators National Conference, 1986.
**CI, FPA**

*Schools and the Fine Arts: What Should Be Taught in Art, Music, and Literature?* Washington: Council for Basic Education, 1965.
**A, CI, RSC**

Schulberg, Cecilia H. *The Music Therapy Sourcebook: A Collection of Activities Categorized and Analyzed.* New York: Human Sciences, 1981.
**BR, CI, P**

Schwadron, Abraham A. *Aesthetics: Dimensions for Music Education.* Washington: Music Educators National Conference, 1967.
**CI, FPA**

————. "Comparative Music Aesthetics and Education: Observations in Speculation." In *Music Education for Tomorrow's Society*, ed. Arthur Motycka, 21-29. Jamestown, R.I.: GAMT Music, 1976.
**CI, FPA**

Scott-Kassner, Carol. "Music, the Arts, and Other Subjects: Maintaining Musical Integrity in the Integrated Curriculum." In *Toward Tomorrow: New Visions for General Music*, ed. Sandra L. Stauffer, 103-09. Reston, Va.: Music Educators National Conference, 1995.
**A, CI**

————. "Research on Music in Early Childhood." In *Handbook of Research on Music Teaching and Learning*, ed. Richard J. Colwell, 633-50. New York: Schirmer Books, 1992.
**CI, P, R**

Serafine, Mary Louise. "Music." In *Cognition and Instruction*, ed. Ronna F. Dillon and Robert J. Sternberg, 299-341. New York: Academic Press, 1986.
**CI, P**

Shamrock, Mary. "Process and Improvisation in Orff-Schulwerk." In *The Eclectic Curriculum in American Music Education*, 2nd ed., ed. Polly Carder, 151-55. Reston, Va.: Music Educators National Conference, 1990.
**CI**

Shaw, Sir Roy. "Education and the Arts." In *The Arts and Personal Growth*, ed. Malcolm Ross, 69-78. New York: Pergamon, 1980.
**A, CI**

Shehan, Patricia K. "Movement in the Music Education of Children." In *Music and Child Development: The Biology of Music Making - Proceedings of the 1987 Denver Conference*, ed. Frank R. Wilson and Franz L. Roehmann, 354-65. St. Louis, Mo.: MMB Music, 1990.
**CI, P, R**

Shetler, Donald J., ed. *The Future of Musical Education in America: Proceedings of the July 1983 Conference*. Rochester, N.Y.: Eastman School of Music Press, 1984.
**CI, FPA, RSC**

Shuell, Thomas. "The Role of Transfer in the Learning and Teaching of Music: A Cognitive Perspective." In *The Crane Symposium: Toward an Understanding of the Teaching and Learning of Music Performance*, ed. Charles Fowler, 143-67. Potsdam: Potsdam College of the State University of New York, 1988.
**CI, P**

Shuler, Scott C. "Assessment in General Music: Trends and Innovations in Local, State, and National Assessment." In *Toward Tomorrow: New Visions for General Music*, ed. Sandra L. Stauffer, 51-66. Reston, Va.: Music Educators National Conference, 1995.
**A, CI, P**

————. *Making Arts Education Curricular*. Reston, Va.: Music Educators National Conference, 1990.
**A, CI**

Shulman, Lee S. "Research on Teaching in the Arts: Review, Analysis, Critique." In *The Teaching Process, Arts and Aesthetics*, ed. Gerard L. Knieter and Jane Stallings, 244-64. St. Louis, Mo.: CEMREL, 1979.
**A, CI, R**

Sidnell, Robert G. *Building Instructional Programs in Music Education*. Englewood Cliffs, N.J.: Prentice-Hall, 1973.
**CI**

————. "Motor Learning in Music Education." In *Documentary Report of the Ann Arbor Symposium: National Symposium on the Applications of Psychology to the Teaching and Learning of Music (Sessions I and II)*, 28-35. Reston, Va.: Music Educators National Conference, 1981.
**CI, P, R**

Silverberg, Ann L. *A Sympathy with Sounds: A Brief History of the University of Illinois School of Music to Celebrate Its Centennial*. Urbana: School of Music, University of Illinois, 1995.
**BR, CI**

Simons, Gene M. *Early Childhood Musical Development: A Bibliography of Research Abstracts, 1960-1975, with Implications and Recommendations for Teaching and Research.* Reston, Va.: Music Educators National Conference, 1978.
**BR, CI, P, R**

Simpson, Alan. "Utilitarianism, the Arts and Education." In *The Aesthetic in Education*, ed. Malcolm Ross, 187-212. New York: Pergamon, 1985.
**A, CI, FPA**

Simpson, Elizabeth Jane. *The Classification of Educational Objectives: Psychomotor Domain.* Urbana: University of Illinois, 1966.
**CI, P**

Simpson, Kenneth, ed. *Some Great Music Educators: A Collection of Essays.* Borough Green, Kent, England: Novello, 1976.
**CI, FPA**

Sims, Wendy L. "Early Childhood Discussion-Group Report." In *Toward Tomorrow: New Visions for General Music*, ed. Sandra L. Stauffer, 123-25. Reston, Va.: Music Educators National Conference, 1995.
**CI**

_____, ed. *Strategies for Teaching Prekindergarten Music.* Reston, Va.: Music Educators National Conference, 1996.
**CI**

Sink, Patricia E. "Research on Teaching Junior High and Middle School General Music." In *Handbook of Research on Music Teaching and Learning*, ed. Richard J. Colwell, 602-12. New York: Schirmer Books, 1992.
**CI, R**

Sinor, Jean. "Policy Development in Arts Education for Early Childhood Programs." In *Policy Issues in Music Education: A Report of the Proceedings of the Robert Petzold Symposium*, ed. Gerald Olson, Anthony L. Barresi, and David Nelson, 92-106. Madison: School of Music, University of Wisconsin, 1991.
**A, CI, FPA**

Sizer, Theodore R. *Horace's Compromise: The Dilemma of the American High School.* Boston: Houghton Mifflin, 1984.
**CI, RSC**

Sloboda, John A., ed. *Generative Processes in Music: The Psychology of Performance, Improvisation and Composition.* New York: Oxford University Press, 1988.
**CI, P**

Small, Christopher. *Music, Society, Education: A Radical Examination of the Prophetic Function of Music in Western, Eastern, and African Cultures with Its Impact on Society and Its Use in Education.* 2nd rev. ed. London: J. Calder, 1980.

**CI, P**

Smith, C. M. "The Aesthetics of John Dewey and Aesthetic Education." In *Aesthetics and Problems of Education*, ed. Ralph A. Smith, 64-85. Urbana: University of Illinois Press, 1971.

**A, CI, FPA**

Smith, Louis M., and Sally Schumacher. *Extended Pilot Trials of the Aesthetic Education Program: A Qualitative Analysis and Evaluation.* St. Louis, Mo.: CEMREL, 1972.

**A, CI, FPA**

Smith, Nancy R. "Classroom Practice: Creating Meaning in the Arts." In *Arts and the Schools*, ed. Jerome J. Hausman and Joyce Wright, 79-115. New York: McGraw-Hill, 1980.

**A, CI, P**

Smith, Ralph A. "Aesthetic Criticism: The Method of Aesthetic Education." In *Aesthetics and Problems of Education*, ed. Ralph A. Smith, 473-84. Urbana: University of Illinois Press, 1971.

**A, CI, FPA**

————. "Is Teaching an Art?" In *Aesthetics and Problems of Education*, ed. Ralph A. Smith, 564-69. Urbana: University of Illinois Press, 1971.

**A, CI, FPA**

————. "The Philosophical Literature of Aesthetic Education." In *Toward an Aesthetic Education: A Report*, 137-69. Washington: Music Educators National Conference, 1971.

**A, CI, FPA**

————. "Toward Percipience: A Humanities Curriculum for Arts Education." In *The Arts, Education, and Aesthetic Knowing: 91st Yearbook of the National Society for the Study of Education (Part II)*, ed. Bennett Reimer and Ralph A. Smith, 51-69. Chicago: University of Chicago Press, 1992.

**A, CI, FPA**

————. "Trends and Issues in Policy-Making for Arts Education." In *Handbook of Research on Music Teaching and Learning*, ed. Richard J. Colwell, 749-59. New York: Schirmer Books, 1992.

**A, CI, FPA, R**

_____, ed. *Aesthetics and Problems of Education.* Urbana: University of Illinois Press, 1971.
**A, CI, FPA**

Smith, Ralph A., and C. M. Smith. "Justifying Aesthetic Education." In *Aesthetics and Problems of Education*, ed. Ralph A. Smith, 126-43. Urbana: University of Illinois Press, 1971.
**A, CI, FPA**

Smith, Ralph A., and Alan Simpson, eds. *Aesthetics and Arts Education.* Urbana: University of Illinois Press, 1991.
**A, CI, FPA**

Sosniak, Lauren A. "The Taxonomy, Curriculum, and Their Relations." In *Bloom's Taxonomy—A Forty-Year Retrospective: 93rd Yearbook of the National Society for the Study of Education (Part II)*, ed. Lorin W. Anderson and Lauren A. Sosniak, 103-25. Chicago: University of Chicago Press, 1994.
**CI, P**

*Southeastern Journal of Music Education.* Athens: University of Georgia Center for Continuing Education, 1990-.
**CI, J, P, R**

Sparshott, F. E. "The Unity of Aesthetic Education." In *Aesthetics and Problems of Education*, ed. Ralph A. Smith, 243-57. Urbana: University of Illinois Press, 1971.
**A, CI, FPA**

Spector, Irwin. *Rhythm and Life: The Work of Emile Jaques-Dalcroze.* Stuyvesant, N.Y.: Pendragon, 1990.
**A, CI**

Squire, Russel N. *Introduction to Music Education.* New York: Ronald, 1952.
**CI, FPA**

Stake, Robert E., ed. *Evaluating the Arts in Education: A Responsive Approach.* Columbus, Ohio: Merrill, 1975.
**A, CI**

Standifer, James A. "Policy Development in Multicultural Arts Education." In *Policy Issues in Music Education: A Report of the Proceedings of the Robert Petzold Symposium*, ed. Gerald Olson, Anthony L. Barresi, and David Nelson, 61-71. Madison: School of Music, University of Wisconsin, 1991.
**A, CI, FPA**

Standifer, James A., and Barbara Reeder. *Source Book of African and Afro-American Materials for Music Educators.* Washington: Contemporary Music Project, 1972.
**BR, CI**

Starr, William. "The Suzuki Method." In *Music and Child Development: The Biology of Music Making - Proceedings of the 1987 Denver Conference,* ed. Frank R. Wilson and Franz L. Roehmann, 377-83. St. Louis, Mo.: MMB Music, 1990.
**CI**

Stauffer, Sandra L., ed. *Toward Tomorrow: New Visions for General Music.* Reston, Va.: Music Educators National Conference, 1995.
**CI, RSC**

Stauffer, Sandra L., and Jennifer Davidson, eds. *Strategies for Teaching K-4 General Music.* Reston, Va.: Music Educators National Conference, 1996.
**CI**

Steen, Arvida. *Exploring Orff: A Teacher's Guide.* New York: Schott Music Corporation, 1992.
**CI**

Stevens, Louise K. *Planning to Make the Arts Basic: A Report to the National Endowment for the Arts on the Impact and Results of the Arts in Schools Basic Education Grants Program.* Marion, Mass.: Artsmarket Consulting, 1991.
**A, CI, RSC**

*Strategies for Success in the Band and Orchestra.* Reston, Va.: Music Educators National Conference, 1994.
**CI**

Straub, Dorothy A., Louis Bergonzi, and Anne C. Witt, eds. *Strategies for Teaching Strings and Orchestra.* Reston, Va.: Music Educators National Conference, 1996.
**CI**

Stringham, Mary, comp. *Orff-Schulwerk, Background and Commentary: Articles from German and Austrian Periodicals.* Transl. Mary Stringham. St. Louis, Mo.: MMB Music, 1976.
**CI, P**

Sunderman, Lloyd Frederick. *Historical Foundations of Music Education in the United States.* Metuchen, N.J.: Scarecrow, 1971.
**CI, FPA**

Suzuki, Shinichi. *Nurtured by Love.* 2nd ed. New York: Exposition, 1983.
**CI, FPA**

Swanwick, Keith. *Music, Mind, and Education.* New York: Routledge, 1988.
**CI, P**

_____. *Musical Knowledge: Intuition, Analysis, and Music Education.* New York: Routledge, 1994.
**CI, FPA, P**

_____. *Popular Music and the Teacher.* New York: Pergamon, 1968.
**CI, P**

_____, ed. *The Arts and Education: Papers from the National Association for Education in the Arts, 1983-1990.* Oakham, England: National Association for Education in the Arts, 1990.
**A, CI, RSC**

Swanwick, Keith, and Dorothy Taylor. *Discovering Music: Developing the Music Curriculum in Secondary Schools.* London: Batsford, 1982.
**CI**

*Syllabi for Music Methods Courses.* Reston, Va.: Music Educators National Conference, 1992.
**CI**

Tait, Malcolm John. "Teaching Strategies and Styles." In *Handbook of Research on Music Teaching and Learning*, ed. Richard J. Colwell, 525-34. New York: Schirmer Books, 1992.
**CI, P, R**

Tait, Malcolm John, and Paul Haack. *Principles and Processes of Music Education: New Perspectives.* New York: Teachers College, 1984.
**CI, FPA**

Taubman, Dorothy. "A Teacher's Perspectives on Musicians' Injuries." In *The Biology of Music Making: Proceedings of the 1984 Denver Conference*, ed. Franz L. Roehmann and Frank R. Wilson, 144-53. St. Louis, Mo.: MMB Music, 1988.
**CI, P**

Taylor, Dale B. "Childhood Sequential Development of Rhythm, Melody and Pitch." In *Music and Child Development: The Biology of Music Making - Proceedings of the 1987 Denver Conference*, ed. Frank R. Wilson and Franz L. Roehmann, 241-53. St. Louis, Mo.: MMB Music, 1990.
**CI, P**

Taylor, Dorothy. "Aesthetic Development in Music." In *The Development of Aesthetic Experience*, ed. Malcolm Ross, 94-109. New York: Pergamon, 1982.
**A, CI, FPA**

*Teacher Education in Music: Final Report.* Washington: Music Educators National Conference, 1972.

**CI, RSC**

*Teaching Choral Music: A Course of Study.* Reston, Va.: Music Educators National Conference, 1991.

**CI**

*Teaching Stringed Instruments: A Course of Study.* Reston, Va.: Music Educators National Conference, 1991.

**CI**

*Teaching Wind and Percussion Instruments: A Course of Study.* Reston, Va.: Music Educators National Conference, 1991.

**CI**

Tedlock, Barbara. "North American Indian Musics." In *Racial and Ethnic Directions in American Music*, CMS Report No. 3, 9-27. Boulder, Colo.: College Music Society, 1982.

**CI**

Tellstrom, A. Theodore. *Music in American Education: Past and Present.* New York: Holt, Rinehart, and Winston, 1971.

**CI, FPA**

*These People Have Passed the Test of Time, Can You? A Report on Arts Education.* Washington: National Endowment for the Arts, 1988.

**A, CI, RSC**

Thomas, Ronald. *Manhattanville Music Curriculum Program (MMCP) Synthesis.* Bardonia, N.Y.: Media Materials, 1971.

**CI, RSC**

Thorpe, Louis P. "Learning Theory and Music Teaching." In *Basic Concepts in Music Education: 57th Yearbook of the National Society for the Study of Education*, ed. Nelson B. Henry, 163-94. Chicago: University of Chicago Press, 1958.

**CI, P**

Tikunoff, William J., and Beatrice A. Ward. "How the Teaching Process Affects Change in the School." In *The Teaching Process, Arts and Aesthetics*, ed. Gerard L. Knieter and Jane Stallings, 100-24. St. Louis, Mo.: CEMREL, 1979.

**A, CI**

Tillman, Rix W. *Music Educator's Guide to Personalized Instruction.* West Nyack, N.Y.: Parker, 1975.

**BR, CI**

*Toward an Aesthetic Education: A Report.* Washington: Music Educators National Conference, 1971.

**A, CI, FPA, RSC**

*Toward Civilization: A Report on Arts Education.* Washington: National Endowment for the Arts, 1988.

**A, CI, RSC**

Treffinger, Donald J. "Fostering Creativity and Problem Solving." In *Documentary Report of the Ann Arbor Symposium on the Applications of Psychology to the Teaching and Learning of Music: Motivation and Creativity (Session III)*, 55-59. Reston, Va.: Music Educators National Conference, 1983.

**CI, P**

Trotter, T. H. Yorke. *Music and Mind.* London: Methuen, 1924.

**CI, P**

Tunks, Thomas W. "Applications of Psychological Positions on Learning and Development to Musical Behavior." In *Handbook of Music Psychology*, ed. Donald A. Hodges, 275-90. Lawrence, Kans.: National Association for Music Therapy, 1980.

**CI, P**

————. "The Transfer of Music Learning." In *Handbook of Research on Music Teaching and Learning*, ed. Richard J. Colwell, 437-47. New York: Schirmer Books, 1992.

**CI, P, R**

*Turning Points - Preparing American Youth for the 21st Century: The Report of the Task Force on Education of Young Adolescents.* Washington: Carnegie Council on Adolescent Development, 1989.

**CI, RSC**

Tweddell, Paul. "The Professional Development of Arts Teachers." In *The Claims of Feeling: Readings in Aesthetic Education*, ed. Malcolm Ross, 167-99. Philadelphia: Falmer, 1989.

**A, CI, FPA**

Upitis, Rena. *Can I Play You My Song? The Compositions and Invented Notations of Children.* Portsmouth, N.H.: Heinemann, 1992.

**CI, P**

Uszler, Marienne. "Research on the Teaching of Keyboard Music." In *Handbook of Research on Music Teaching and Learning*, ed. Richard J. Colwell, 584-93. New York: Schirmer Books, 1992.

**CI, R**

Vallance, Elizabeth. "Artistic Intelligences and General Education." In *Artistic Intelligences: Implications for Education*, ed. William J. Moody, 79-84. New York: Teachers College, 1990.

**A, CI, P**

Verrastro, Ralph, and Mary Leglar. "Music Teacher Education." In *Handbook of Research on Music Teaching and Learning*, ed. Richard J. Colwell, 676-96. New York: Schirmer Books, 1992.

**CI, R**

*Vision for Arts Education in the 21st Century*. Reston, Va.: Music Educators National Conference, 1994.

**A, CI, FPA**

*Voices of Industry*. Reston, Va.: Music Educators National Conference, 1990.

**BR, CI**

Vulliamy, Graham, and Ed Lee, eds. *Pop, Rock and Ethnic Music in School*. New York: Cambridge University Press, 1982.

**CI, P**

Wagner, Christoph. "Success and Failure in Musical Performance: Biomechanics of the Hand." In *The Biology of Music Making: Proceedings of the 1984 Denver Conference*, ed. Franz L. Roehmann and Frank R. Wilson, 154-79. St. Louis, Mo.: MMB Music, 1988.

**CI, R**

Waikart, Kitty. "A Nuts-and-Bolts Plan for Parents." In *Perspectives on Implementation: Arts Education Standards for America's Students*, ed. Bruce O. Boston, 55-62. Reston, Va.: Music Educators National Conference, 1994.

**A, CI, FPA**

Walker, Darwin E. *Teaching Music: Managing the Successful Music Program*. New York: Schirmer Books, 1989.

**CI, FPA**

Walker, Robert. *Music Education: Tradition and Innovation*. Springfield, Ill.: Thomas, 1984.

**CI, FPA**

Walter, Arnold. "Carl Orff's *Music for Children*." In *The Eclectic Curriculum in American Music Education*, 2nd ed., ed. Polly Carder, 157-60. Reston, Va.: Music Educators National Conference, 1990.

**CI**

Walters, Darrel L. "Sequencing for Efficient Learning." In *Handbook of Research on Music Teaching and Learning*, ed. Richard J. Colwell, 535-45. New York: Schirmer Books, 1992.

**CI, P, R**

Walters, Darrel L., and Cynthia Crump Taggart, eds. *Readings in Music Learning Theory.* Chicago: G.I.A. Publications, 1989.

**CI, P**

Ward, David. "The Arts and Special Needs." In *The Claims of Feeling: Readings in Aesthetic Education*, ed. Malcolm Ross, 99-118. Philadelphia: Falmer, 1989.

**A, CI, P**

Warner, Brigitte. *Orff-Schulwerk: Applications for the Classroom.* Englewood Cliffs, N.J.: Prentice-Hall, 1991.

**CI**

Weerts, Richard. "Research on the Teaching of Instrumental Music." In *Handbook of Research on Music Teaching and Learning*, ed. Richard J. Colwell, 577-83. New York: Schirmer Books, 1992.

**CI, R**

Welsbacher, Betty. "Musical Thinking in the Special Education Classroom." In *Dimensions of Musical Thinking*, ed. Eunice Boardman, 91-99. Reston, Va.: Music Educators National Conference, 1989.

**CI, P**

Wenger, Harry. "Selecting Equipment for Your Performing Group." In *Voices of Industry*, 7-12. Reston, Va.: Music Educators National Conference, 1990.

**BR, CI**

Werder, Richard H., ed. *Music Education in the Secondary School.* Washington: Catholic University of America Press, 1955.

**CI, R, RSC**

_____, ed. *Music Education Today: The Proceedings of the Workshop on Music.* Washington: Catholic University of America Press, 1966.

**CI, RSC**

Wheeler, D. K. "Aesthetic Education and Curriculum." In *Aesthetics and Problems of Education*, ed. Ralph A. Smith, 320-44. Urbana: University of Illinois Press, 1971.

**A, CI, FPA**

Whipple, Guy Montrose, ed. *Music Education: 35th Yearbook of the National Society for the Study of Education (Part II)*. Bloomington, Ill.: Public School Publishing, 1936.
**BR, CI, FPA, P**

White, Chappell, ed. *A Wingspread Conference on Music in General Studies*. Racine, Wisc.: Johnson Foundation, 1981.
**CI, RSC**

Whitehead, Alfred North. *The Aims of Education, and Other Essays*. 1929. Reprint, New York: Free Press, 1967.
**CI, FPA, P**

Wiggins, Jackie. *Composition in the Classroom: A Tool for Teaching*. Reston, Va.: Music Educators National Conference, 1990.
**CI**

Willoughby, David. *Comprehensive Musicianship and Undergraduate Music Curricula*. Washington: Contemporary Music Project, 1971.
**CI**

Wilson, Frank R. *Mind, Muscle, and Music: Physiological Clues to Better Teaching*. Elkart, Ind.: Selmer, 1981.
**CI, P**

————. *Tone Deaf and All Thumbs? An Introduction to Music Making for Late Bloomers and Non-Prodigies*. New York: Viking-Penguin, 1986.
**CI, P**

Wilson, Frank R., and Franz L. Roehmann. "The Study of Biomechanical and Physiological Processes in Relation to Musical Performance." In *Handbook of Research on Music Teaching and Learning*, ed. Richard J. Colwell, 509-24. New York: Schirmer Books, 1992.
**CI, P, R**

————, eds. *Music and Child Development:The Biology of Music Making - Proceedings of the 1987 Denver Conference*. St. Louis, Mo.: MMB Music, 1990.
**CI, P, RSC**

Wilson, Margaret Bush. "The Arts and the Minorities." In *Arts and Aesthetics: An Agenda for the Future*, ed. Stanley S. Madeja, 51-56. St. Louis, Mo.: CEMREL, 1977.
**A, CI**

Wing, Lizabeth Bradford. "Curriculum and Its Study." In *Handbook of Research on Music Teaching and Learning*, ed. Richard J. Colwell, 196-217. New York: Schirmer Books, 1992.
**CI, R**

Winn, Cyril. *Teaching Music.* New York: Oxford University Press, 1954.
**CI, FPA**

Witkin, Robert W. "The Concept of 'Development' in Aesthetic Education." In *The Development of Aesthetic Experience*, ed. Malcolm Ross, 67-77. New York: Pergamon, 1982.
**A, CI, FPA**

Wolff, Janet. "Questioning the Curriculum: Arts, Education and Ideology." In *The Aesthetic in Education*, ed. Malcolm Ross, 213-30. New York: Pergamon, 1985.
**A, CI, FPA**

Yarbrough, Cornelia. "Good Teaching May Be in Sonata Form." In *Applications of Research in Music Behavior*, ed. Clifford K. Madsen and Carol A. Prickett, 3-11. Tuscaloosa: University of Alabama Press, 1987.
**CI, R**

Yardley, Alice. *Senses and Sensitivity.* New York: Citation, 1973.
**CI, P**

Zemke, Sister Lorna. "Folk Song in a Kodály-Based Curriculum." In *The Eclectic Curriculum in American Music Education*, 2nd ed., ed. Polly Carder, 93-102. Reston, Va.: Music Educators National Conference, 1990.
**CI**

Zerull, David Scott. *Getting Started with High School Band.* Reston, Va.: Music Educators National Conference, 1994.
**CI**

Zimmerman, Marilyn P. "Developmental Processes in Music Learning." In *Symposium in Music Education: A Festschrift for Charles Leonhard*, ed. Richard J. Colwell, 25-44. Urbana-Champaign: University of Illinois, 1982.
**CI, P**

————. "Psychological Theory and Music Learning." In *Basic Concepts in Music Education II*, ed. Richard J. Colwell, 157-76. Niwot: University Press of Colorado, 1991.
**CI, P**

————. *Musical Characteristics of Children: From Research to the Music Classroom No. 1.* Washington: Music Educators National Conference, 1971.
**CI, P, R**

# (FPA)

## Foundations, Philosophy, and Aesthetics

Abeles, Harold F., Charles R. Hoffer, and Robert H. Klotman. *Foundations of Music Education.* 2nd ed. New York: Schirmer Books, 1994.
   **CI, FPA**

Aiello, Rita, and John A. Sloboda, eds. *Musical Perceptions.* New York: Oxford University Press, 1994.
   **FPA, P**

Alperson, Philip, ed. *What Is Music? An Introduction to the Philosophy of Music.* New York: Haven Publications, 1987.
   **FPA**

*America's Culture Begins with Education.* Reston, Va.: Music Educators National Conference, 1990.
   **CI, FPA**

Anderson, Lorin W., and Lauren A. Sosniak, eds. *Bloom's Taxonomy—A Forty-Year Retrospective: 93rd Yearbook of the National Society for the Study of Education (Part II).* Chicago: National Society for the Study of Education, 1994.
   **BR, CI, FPA, P**

Andrews, Frances M. *Junior High School General Music: Foundations of Music Education Series.* Englewood Cliffs, N.J.: Prentice-Hall, 1971.
   **CI, FPA**

Arnheim, Rudolf. "What Is Art For?" In *Aesthetics and Problems of Education*, ed. Ralph A. Smith, 231-42. Urbana: University of Illinois Press, 1971.
   **A, FPA**

Arnstine, Donald. "The Aesthetic as a Context for General Education." In *Aesthetics and Problems of Education*, ed. Ralph A. Smith, 402-13. Urbana: University of Illinois Press, 1971.
   **A, CI, FPA**

Arts, Education, and Americans Panel. *Coming to Our Senses: The Significance of the Arts for American Education.* New York: McGraw-Hill, 1977.
   **A, CI, FPA, RSC**

Aschenbrenner, Karl. "Music Criticism: Practice and Malpractice." In *On Criticizing Music: Five Philosophical Perspectives*, ed. Kingsley Price, 99-117. Baltimore: Johns Hopkins University Press, 1981.
**FPA**

Aschner, Mary Jane. "Teaching the Anatomy of Criticism." In *Aesthetics and Problems of Education*, ed. Ralph A. Smith, 425-34. Urbana: University of Illinois Press, 1971.
**A, CI, FPA**

Aspin, David. "Assessment and Education in the Arts." In *The Aesthetic Imperative: Relevance and Responsibility in Arts Education*, ed. Malcolm Ross, 25-52. New York: Pergamon, 1981.
**A, CI, FPA, P**

Babbitt, Milton. "On Having Been and Still Being an American Composer." In *Perspectives on Musical Aesthetics*, ed. John Rahn, 145-51. New York: Norton, 1994.
**FPA**

Baker, Nancy Kovaleff, and Barbara Russano Hanning, eds. *Musical Humanism and Its Legacy: Essays in Honor of Claude V. Palisca.* Stuyvesant, N.Y.: Pendragon, 1992.
**FPA, RSC**

Ball, Charles H. "Thoughts on Music as Aesthetic Education." In *Toward an Aesthetic Education: A Report*, 57-62. Washington: Music Educators National Conference, 1971.
**A, CI, FPA**

Ballantine, Christopher John. *Music and Its Social Meanings.* New York: Gordon and Breach, 1984.
**FPA, P**

Barresi, Anthony L. "Public Policy and Music Education: Policy Analysis as a Pathway to Professional Understanding." In *Policy Issues in Music Education: A Report of the Proceedings of the Robert Petzold Symposium*, ed. Gerald Olson, Anthony L. Barresi, and David Nelson, 1-15. Madison: School of Music, University of Wisconsin, 1991.
**A, FPA**

Barresi, Anthony L., and Gerald Olson. "The Nature of Policy and Music Education." In *Handbook of Research on Music Teaching and Learning*, ed. Richard J. Colwell, 760-72. New York: Schirmer Books, 1992.
**FPA, R**

Beall, Gretchen Hieronymus. "Methodology and Music in General Education." In *Music Education in the United States: Contemporary Issues*, ed. J. Terry Gates, 202-23. Tuscaloosa: University of Alabama Press, 1988.
**CI, FPA, P**

Beardsley, Monroe C. *The Aesthetic Point of View: Selected Essays of Monroe C. Beardsley.* Ed. Michael J. Wreen and Donald M. Callen. Ithaca, N.Y.: Cornell University Press, 1982.
**A, FPA**

————. *Aesthetics from Classical Greece to the Present: A Short History.* New York: Macmillan, 1975.
**A, FPA**

————. *Aesthetics: Problems in the Philosophy of Criticism.* 2nd ed. Indianapolis, Ind.: Hackett, 1981.
**A, FPA**

————. "The Classification of Critical Reasons." In *Aesthetics and Problems of Education*, ed. Ralph A. Smith, 435-44. Urbana: University of Illinois Press, 1971.
**A, FPA**

————. "Understanding Music." In *On Criticizing Music: Five Philosophical Perspectives*, ed. Kingsley Price, 55-73. Baltimore: Johns Hopkins University Press, 1981.
**FPA**

Beardsley, Monroe C., and Herbert M. Schueller, eds. *Aesthetic Inquiry: Essays on Art Criticism and the Philosophy of Art.* Belmont, Calif.: Dickenson, 1967.
**A, FPA**

Beattie, John W. "The Accrediting and the Programming of School Music." In *Music Education: 35th Yearbook of the National Society for the Study of Education (Part II)*, ed. Guy Montrose Whipple, 141-45. Bloomington, Ill.: Public School Publishing, 1936.
**CI, FPA**

Bell, Clive. *Art.* Ed. J. B. Bullen. 1914. Reprint, New York: Oxford University Press, 1987.
**A, FPA**

Benn, Oleta A. "A Message for New Teachers." In *Basic Concepts in Music Education: 57th Yearbook of the National Society for the Study of Education*, ed. Nelson B. Henry, 339-55. Chicago: University of Chicago Press, 1958.
**CI, FPA**

Bentley, Arnold. *Music in Education: A Point of View.* Atlantic Highlands, N.J.: Humanities Press, 1975.
**CI, FPA**

Berendt, Joachim-Ernst. *The World Is Sound: Music and the Landscape of Consciousness.* Transl. H. Bredigkeit. New York: Harper and Row, 1991.
**FPA, P**

Berenson, F. M. "Interpreting the Emotional Content of Music." In *The Interpretation of Music: Philosophical Essays*, ed. Michael Krausz, 61-72. New York: Oxford University Press, 1992.
**FPA, P**

Berger, Arthur. "Music as Imitation." In *Perspectives on Musical Aesthetics*, ed. John Rahn, 302-12. New York: Norton, 1994.
**A, FPA, P**

Berlyne, D. E. *Aesthetics and Psychobiology.* New York: Appleton-Century-Crofts, 1971.
**A, FPA, P**

_____, ed. *Studies in the New Experimental Aesthetics: Steps toward an Objective Psychology of Aesthetic Appreciation.* Washington: Hemisphere, 1974.
**A, FPA, P**

Berman, Laurence. *The Musical Image: A Theory of Content.* Westport, Conn.: Greenwood, 1993.
**FPA**

Bernstein, Leonard. *The Unanswered Question: Six Talks at Harvard.* Cambridge: Harvard University Press, 1976.
**FPA, P**

*Beyond the Classroom: Informing Others.* Reston, Va.: Music Educators National Conference, 1987.
**FPA**

Birge, Edward B. *History of Public School Music in the United States.* New and aug. ed. Reston, Va.: Music Educators National Conference, 1988.
**FPA**

Black, Max. "Education as Art and Discipline." In *Aesthetics and Problems of Education*, ed. Ralph A. Smith, 529-36. Urbana: University of Illinois Press, 1971.
**A, CI, FPA**

Blacking, John. "A False Trail for the Arts?" In *The Aesthetic in Education*, ed. Malcolm Ross, 1-27. New York: Pergamon, 1985.
**A, FPA**

Blaustein, Susan. "The Survival of Aesthetics: Books by Boulez, Delio, Rochberg." In *Perspectives on Musical Aesthetics*, ed. John Rahn, 333-64. New York: Norton, 1994.
**A, FPA**

Blom, Eric. *The Limitations of Music: A Study in Aesthetics.* 1928. Reprint, New York: B. Blom, 1972.
**FPA**

Bloom, Kathryn. "Development of Arts and Humanities Programs." In *Toward an Aesthetic Education: A Report*, 89-99. Washington: Music Educators National Conference, 1971.
**A, CI, FPA**

Boardman, Eunice. "A Message for the Teacher of Teachers." In *Basic Concepts in Music Education II*, ed. Richard J. Colwell, 279-88. Niwot: University Press of Colorado, 1991.
**CI, FPA**

Bonds, Mark Evan. *Wordless Rhetoric: Musical Form and the Metaphor of the Oration.* Cambridge: Harvard University Press, 1991.
**FPA, P**

Bonis, Ferenc, ed. *The Selected Writings of Zoltán Kodály.* Transl. Lili Halapy and Fred Macnicol. New York: Boosey and Hawkes, 1974.
**CI, FPA**

Boston, Bruce O., ed. *Perspectives on Implementation: Arts Education Standards for America's Students.* Reston, Va.: Music Educators National Conference, 1994.
**A, CI, FPA**

Bowman, Wayne. "A Plea for Pluralism: Variations on a Theme by George McKay." In *Basic Concepts in Music Education II*, ed. Richard J. Colwell, 94-110. Niwot: University Press of Colorado, 1991.
**FPA**

Boyd, Willard L. "Music: Basic Education." In *The Future of Musical Education in America: Proceedings of the July 1983 Conference*, ed. Donald J. Shetler, 49-59. Rochester, N.Y.: Eastman School of Music Press, 1984.
**FPA**

Britan, Halbert Hains. *The Philosophy of Music: A Comparative Investigation into the Principles of Musical Aesthetics.* New York: Longmans, 1911.
**FPA**

*British Journal of Aesthetics.* London: Oxford University Press, 1960-.
**A, FPA, J, R**

Britton, Allen P. "American Music Education: Is It Better than We Think? A Discussion of the Roles of Performance and Repertory, Together with Brief Mention of Certain Other Problems." In *Basic Concepts in Music Education II*, ed. Richard J. Colwell, 175-90. Niwot: University Press of Colorado, 1991.
**CI, FPA**

_____. "Music in Early American Public Education: A Historical Critique." In *Basic Concepts in Music Education: 57th Yearbook of the National Society for the Study of Education*, ed. Nelson B. Henry, 195-211. Chicago: University of Chicago Press, 1958.
**FPA**

Brocklehurst, J. Brian. *Response to Music: Principles of Music Education*. London: Routledge and K. Paul, 1971.
**CI, FPA**

Broudy, Harry S. "The Aesthetic Values." In *Building a Philosophy of Education*, 2nd ed., ed. Harry S. Broudy, 202-09. Englewood Cliffs, N.J.: Prentice-Hall, 1961.
**FPA**

_____. "Arts Education - Praise May Not Be Enough." In *The Crane Symposium: Toward an Understanding of the Teaching and Learning of Music Performance*, ed. Charles Fowler, 37-43. Potsdam: Potsdam College of the State University of New York, 1988.
**A, FPA**

_____. *Building a Philosophy of Education*. 2nd ed. Englewood Cliffs, N.J.: Prentice-Hall, 1961.
**CI, FPA**

_____. *Enlightened Cherishing: An Essay on Aesthetic Education*. 1972. Reprint, Urbana: University of Illinois Press, 1994.
**A, CI, FPA**

_____. "Enlightened Preference and Justification." In *Aesthetics and Problems of Education*, ed. Ralph A. Smith, 305-19. Urbana: University of Illinois Press, 1971.
**A, CI, FPA**

_____. *Paradox and Promise: Essays on American Life and Education*. Englewood Cliffs, N.J.: Prentice-Hall, 1961.
**CI, FPA**

_____. "A Realistic Philosophy of Music Education." In *Basic Concepts in Music Education: 57th Yearbook of the National Society for the Study of Education*, ed. Nelson B. Henry, 62-87. Chicago: University of Chicago Press, 1958.
**FPA**

_____. "A Realistic Philosophy of Music Education." In *Basic Concepts in Music Education II*, ed. Richard J. Colwell, 71-93. Niwot: University Press of Colorado, 1991.
**FPA**

————. "Some Duties of a Theory of Educational Aesthetics." In *Aesthetics and Problems of Education*, ed. Ralph A. Smith, 103-16. Urbana: University of Illinois Press, 1971.
**A, CI, FPA**

————. "Some Reactions to a Concept of Aesthetic Education." In *Arts and Aesthetics: An Agenda for the Future*, ed. Stanley S. Madeja, 251-61. St. Louis, Mo.: CEMREL, 1977.
**A, CI, FPA**

————. *The Uses of Schooling.* New York: Routledge, 1988.
**CI, FPA**

————. *The Whys and Hows of Aesthetic Education.* St. Louis, Mo.: CEMREL, 1977.
**A, CI, FPA**

Broudy, Harry S., and John R. Palmer. *Exemplars of Teaching Method.* Chicago: Rand McNally, 1965.
**CI, FPA**

Bruhn, Karl. "Advocacy: Getting to 'How to'." In *Perspectives on Implementation: Arts Education Standards for America's Students*, ed. Bruce O. Boston, 9-18. Reston, Va.: Music Educators National Conference, 1994.
**A, CI, FPA**

Bruner, Jerome S. *The Process of Education.* 1960. Reprint, Cambridge: Harvard University Press, 1977.
**CI, FPA, P**

————. *Toward a Theory of Instruction.* New York: Norton, 1968.
**CI, FPA, P**

Budd, Malcolm. *Music and the Emotions: The Philosophical Theories.* Boston: Routledge and Kegan Paul, 1992.
**FPA, P**

Bujic, Bojan. "Notation and Realization: Musical Performance in Historical Perspective." In *The Interpretation of Music: Philosophical Essays*, ed. Michael Krausz, 129-40. New York: Oxford University Press, 1992.
**FPA**

*Bulletin of Historical Research in Music Education.* Lawrence: University of Kansas Department of Art and Music Education and Music Therapy, 1980-.
**FPA, J, R**

Burmeister, Clifton A. "The Role of Music in General Education." In *Basic Concepts in Music Education: 57th Yearbook of the National Society for the Study of Education*, ed. Nelson B. Henry, 215-35. Chicago: University of Chicago Press, 1958.
**CI, FPA**

_____. "The Role of Music in General Education." In *Basic Concepts in Music Education II*, ed. Richard J. Colwell, 191-208. Niwot: University Press of Colorado, 1991.
**CI, FPA**

Burrows, David L. *Sound, Speech, and Music.* Amherst, Mass.: University of Massachusetts Press, 1990.
**FPA, P**

Cady, Henry L. "Children's Processing and Remembering of Music: Some Speculations." In *Documentary Report of the Ann Arbor Symposium: National Symposium on the Applications of Psychology to the Teaching and Learning of Music (Sessions I and II)*, 81-87. Reston, Va.: Music Educators National Conference, 1981.
**FPA, P**

Cage, John. "Tokyo Lecture and Three Mesostics." In *Perspectives on Musical Aesthetics*, ed. John Rahn, 152-57. New York: Norton, 1994.
**FPA**

Canada, Benjamin O. "Building Support for the Arts Standards among School Administrators." In *Perspectives on Implementation: Arts Education Standards for America's Students*, ed. Bruce O. Boston, 63-69. Reston, Va.: Music Educators National Conference, 1994.
**A, CI, FPA**

Carter, Gene R. "Schools of Tomorrow." In *Toward Tomorrow: New Visions for General Music*, ed. Sandra L. Stauffer, 11-14. Reston, Va.: Music Educators National Conference, 1995.
**CI, FPA**

Chase, Gilbert. *America's Music: From the Pilgrims to the Present.* 3rd ed., rev. Urbana: University of Illinois Press, 1992.
**FPA**

Choate, Robert A., ed. *Documentary Report of the Tanglewood Symposium.* Washington: Music Educators National Conference, 1968.
**CI, FPA, RSC**

Chomsky, Noam. *Language and Mind.* Enl. ed. New York: Harcourt Brace Jovanovich, 1972.
**FPA, P**

————. *Reflections on Language.* New York: Pantheon Books, 1975.
  **FPA, P**

Christensen, Bruce. "A Shared Vision." In *The Crane Symposium: Toward an Understanding of the Teaching and Learning of Music Performance*, ed. Charles Fowler, 17-20. Potsdam: Potsdam College of the State University of New York, 1988.
  **FPA**

Clifford, Geraldine Joncich. "An Historical Review of Teaching and Research: Perspectives for Arts and Aesthetic Education." In *The Teaching Process, Arts and Aesthetics*, ed. Gerard L. Knieter and Jane Stallings, 11-39. St. Louis, Mo.: CEMREL, 1979.
  **A, FPA, R**

Clifton, Thomas. *Music as Heard: A Study in Applied Phenomenology.* New Haven, Conn.: Yale University Press, 1983.
  **FPA, P**

Coleman, Earle J., ed. *Varieties of Aesthetic Experience.* Lanham, Md.: University Press of America, 1983.
  **A, FPA**

Collins, Douglas. "Ritual Sacrifice and the Political Economy of Music." In *Perspectives on Musical Aesthetics*, ed. John Rahn, 9-20. New York: Norton, 1994.
  **FPA**

Colwell, Richard J. "An American School of Music Education." In *Music and Child Development: The Biology of Music Making - Proceedings of the 1987 Denver Conference*, ed. Frank R. Wilson and Franz L. Roehmann, 336-53. St. Louis, Mo.: MMB Music, 1990.
  **FPA**

————. "The Development of Continuing Education 1950-2050." In *Music Education for Tomorrow's Society*, ed. Arthur Motycka, 50-60. Jamestown, R.I.: GAMT Music, 1976.
  **CI, FPA**

————. "Evaluation in Music Education: Perspicacious or Peregrine." In *Symposium in Music Education: A Festschrift for Charles Leonhard*, ed. Richard J. Colwell, 157-95. Urbana-Champaign: University of Illinois, 1982.
  **CI, FPA, P**

————. "Music Education - 2050." In *The Ithaca Conference on American Music Education: Centennial Profiles.*, ed. Mark Fonder, 119-48. Ithaca, N.Y.: Ithaca College, 1992.
  **FPA**

_____, ed. *Basic Concepts in Music Education II.* Niwot: University Press of Colorado, 1991.
**FPA, P**

_____, ed. *Symposium in Music Education: A Festschrift for Charles Leonhard.* Urbana-Champaign: University of Illinois, 1982.
**CI, FPA, R, RSC**

Conklin, Kenneth R. "The Aesthetic Dimension of Education in the Abstract Disciplines." In *Aesthetics and Problems of Education*, ed. Ralph A. Smith, 537-54. Urbana: University of Illinois Press, 1971.
**A, CI, FPA**

Consortium of National Arts Education Associations. *National Standards for Arts Education: Dance, Music, Theatre, Visual Arts. What Every Young American Should Know and Be Able to Do in the Arts.* Reston, Va.: Music Educators National Conference, 1994.
**A, CI, FPA**

Cook, Nicholas. *Music, Imagination, and Culture.* New York: Clarendon, 1992.
**FPA, P**

Cooke, Deryck. *The Language of Music.* 1959. Reprint, New York: Oxford University Press, 1989.
**FPA, P**

Copland, Aaron. *Copland on Music.* 1960. Reprint, New York: Da Capo, 1976.
**FPA, P**

_____. *Music and Imagination: The Charles Eliot Norton Lectures, 1951-52.* 1952. Reprint, Cambridge: Harvard University Press, 1980.
**FPA, P**

_____. *The New Music, 1900-1960.* Rev. ed. New York: Norton, 1968.
**FPA, P**

_____. *What to Listen for in Music.* 1939. Rev. ed. San Francisco: McGraw-Hill, 1988.
**CI, FPA, P**

Costanza, Peter. "Approaches to the Evaluation of Policy Issues in Music Education." In *Policy Issues in Music Education: A Report of the Proceedings of the Robert Petzold Symposium*, ed. Gerald Olson, Anthony L. Barresi, and David Nelson, 153-60. Madison: School of Music, University of Wisconsin, 1991.
**FPA, P**

Cowden, Robert L., and Robert H. Klotman. *Administration and Supervision of Music.* 2nd ed. New York: Schirmer Books, 1991.
**CI, FPA**

Cox, Gordon. *A History of Music Education in England, 1872-1928.* Brookfield, Vt.: Ashgate Publishing, 1993.
**FPA**

Crane, Julia. "Principles of Education Applied." In *The Crane Symposium: Toward an Understanding of the Teaching and Learning of Music Performance*, ed. Charles Fowler, 5-12. Potsdam: Potsdam College of the State University of New York, 1988.
**CI, FPA**

Curl, G. "R. K. Elliott's 'As-If' and the Experience of Art." In *The Arts: A Way of Knowing*, ed. Malcolm Ross, 85-100. New York: Pergamon, 1983.
**A, FPA**

Dahlhaus, Carl. *Esthetics of Music.* Transl. William W. Austin. New York: Cambridge University Press, 1982.
**FPA**

Dahlhaus, Carl, and Ruth Katz, eds. *Contemplating Music: Source Readings in the Aesthetics of Music.* New York: Pendragon, 1987.
**FPA**

Davies, Stephen. *Musical Meaning and Expression.* Ithaca, N.Y.: Cornell University Press, 1994.
**FPA, P**

Davis, Jessica, and Howard Gardner. "The Cognitive Revolution: Consequences for the Understanding and Education of the Child as Artist." In *The Arts, Education, and Aesthetic Knowing: 91st Yearbook of the National Society for the Study of Education (Part II)*, ed. Bennett Reimer and Ralph A. Smith, 92-123. Chicago: University of Chicago Press, 1992.
**A, CI, FPA, P**

Davison, Archibald Thompson. *Music Education in America: What Is Wrong with It? What Shall We Do About It?* New York: Harper and Brothers, 1926.
**CI, FPA**

Dearden, R. F. "The Aesthetic Form of Understanding." In *Aesthetics and Problems of Education*, ed. Ralph A. Smith, 285-304. Urbana: University of Illinois Press, 1971.
**A, CI, FPA**

DeBellis, Mark. "Theoretically Informed Listening." In *The Interpretation of Music: Philosophical Essays*, ed. Michael Krausz, 271-81.  New York: Oxford University Press, 1992.
**FPA, P**

*Design for Arts in Education.*  Washington: Heldred, 1899-.
**A, CI, FPA, J**

Dewey, John. *Art as Experience.*  1934.  Reprint, New York: Perigee Books, 1980.
**A, CI, FPA**

_____. *The Child and the Curriculum.*  1902.  Reprint, Chicago: University of Chicago Press, 1971.
**CI, FPA**

_____. *Democracy and Education: An Introduction to the Philosophy of Education.*  1916.  Reprint, New York: Free Press, 1966.
**CI, FPA**

_____. *Experience and Education.*  1938.  Reprint, New York: Collier Books, 1974.
**CI, FPA, P**

_____. *Freedom and Culture.*  1939.  Reprint, Buffalo, N.Y.: Prometheus Books, 1989.
**CI, FPA**

_____. *How We Think: A Restatement of the Relation of Reflective Thinking to the Educative Process.*  1910.  Reprint, Buffalo, N.Y.: Prometheus Books, 1991.
**CI, FPA, P**

_____. *Logic: The Theory of Inquiry.*  1938.  Reprint, New York: Irvington, 1982.
**CI, FPA, P**

Dewey, John and Evelyn. *Schools of Tomorrow.*  1915.  Reprint, New York: Dutton, 1962.
**CI, FPA**

Dewey, John, Albert C. Barnes, and Laurence Buermeyer. *Art and Education: A Collection of Essays.*  1929.  3rd ed., rev.  Merion, Pa.: Barnes Foundation, 1978.
**A, CI, FPA**

Dunn, David. "Speculations: On the Evolutionary Continuity of Music and Animal Communication Behavior."  In *Perspective on Musical Aesthetics*, ed. John Rahn, 177-93.  New York: Norton, 1994.
**FPA, P**

Dykema, Peter W. "Significant Relationships of Music to Other Subjects." In *Music Education: 35th Yearbook of the National Society for the Study of Education (Part II)*, ed. Guy Montrose Whipple, 23-33. Bloomington, Ill.: Public School Publishing, 1936.
**A, CI, FPA**

Earhart, Will. *The Meaning and Teaching of Music*. New York: Witmark Educational Publications, 1935.
**CI, FPA, P**

————. *A Steadfast Philosophy*. Washington: Music Educators National Conference, 1962.
**FPA**

Eaton, Marcia Muelder. "Teaching through Puzzles in the Arts." In *The Arts, Education, and Aesthetic Knowing: 91st Yearbook of the National Society for the Study of Education (Part II)*, ed. Bennett Reimer and Ralph A. Smith, 151-68. Chicago: University of Chicago Press, 1992.
**A, CI, FPA**

Ecker, David W. "The Development of Qualitative Intelligence." In *Aesthetics and Problems of Education*, ed. Ralph A. Smith, 172-77. Urbana: University of Illinois Press, 1971.
**A, CI, FPA, P**

Edelfelt, Roy A. "Staff Development and Teaching in the Arts." In *The Teaching Process, Arts and Aesthetics*, ed. Gerard L. Knieter and Jane Stallings, 129-47. St. Louis, Mo.: CEMREL, 1979.
**A, CI, FPA**

Efland, Arthur. "Conceptions of Teaching in the Arts." In *The Teaching Process, Arts and Aesthetics*, ed. Gerard L. Knieter and Jane Stallings, 152-86. St. Louis, Mo.: CEMREL, 1979.
**A, CI, FPA, P**

Egan, Robert F. *Music and the Arts in the Community: The Community Music School in America*. Metuchen, N.J.: Scarecrow, 1989.
**A, CI, FPA**

Ehle, Robert. "Classicism Versus Individualism: The Case for Changing Aesthetic Goals." In *Basic Concepts in Music Education II*, ed. Richard J. Colwell, 209-21. Niwot: University Press of Colorado, 1991.
**FPA**

Elliott, Charles. "Comments on Music Education." In *Artistic Intelligences: Implications for Education*, ed. William J. Moody, 140-44. New York: Teachers College, 1990.
**FPA**

Elliott, David James. *Music Matters: A New Philosophy of Music Education.* New York: Oxford University Press, 1995.
**FPA**

Engel, Martin, and Jerome J. Hausman, eds. *Curriculum and Instruction in Arts and Aesthetic Education.* St. Louis, Mo.: CEMREL, 1981.
**A, FPA, R, RSC**

Epperson, Gordon. "E Pluribus Unum—Music Education for the One and Many: Aesthetics and the Art of Teaching." In *Music Education in the United States: Contemporary Issues*, ed. J. Terry Gates, 168-78. Tuscaloosa: University of Alabama Press, 1988.
**CI, FPA**

Erbes, Robert L. "The Influences of Education Reform on Policy in Teacher Education." In *Policy Issues in Music Education: A Report of the Proceedings of the Robert Petzold Symposium*, ed. Gerald Olson, Anthony L. Barresi, and David Nelson, 41-57. Madison: School of Music, University of Wisconsin, 1991.
**CI, FPA**

Erickson, Robert. "Composing Music." In *Perspectives on Musical Aesthetics*, ed. John Rahn, 165-74. New York: Norton, 1994.
**FPA, P**

Evans, David. "Aesthetic Development: A Psychological Viewpoint." In *The Development of Aesthetic Experience*, ed. Malcolm Ross, 48-66. New York: Pergamon, 1982.
**A, FPA**

Fehrs-Rampolla, Barbara. "Opportunities in the Classroom: A Teacher's Perspective." In *Perspectives on Implementation: Arts Education Standards for America's Students*, ed. Bruce O. Boston, 31-37. Reston, Va.: Music Educators National Conference, 1994.
**A, CI, FPA**

Ferguson, Donald Nivison. *Music as Metaphor: The Elements of Expression.* Westport, Conn.: Greenwood, 1973.
**FPA**

Ferrara, Lawrence. *Philosophy and the Analysis of Music: Bridges to Musical Sound, Form, and Reference.* New York: Greenwood, 1991.
**CI, FPA**

Fisher, Frederic I. *The Science of Music: An Essay in Prehistory.* Denton, Tex.: C/G Productions, 1981.
**FPA, P**

Fiske, Harold E. *Music and Mind: Philosophical Essays on the Cognition and Meaning of Music.* Lewiston, N.Y.: Edwin Mellen Press, 1990.
**FPA, P**

————. *Music Cognition and Aesthetic Attitudes.* Lewiston, N.Y.: Edwin Mellen Press, 1993.
**FPA, P**

Fonder, Mark, ed. *The Ithaca Conference on American Music Education: Centennial Profiles.* Ithaca, N.Y.: Ithaca College, 1992.
**FPA, RSC**

Foshay, Arthur W. "Inquiry into Aesthetics Education for Curriculum-Making." In *Arts and Aesthetics: An Agenda for the Future*, ed. Stanley S. Madeja, 243-50. St. Louis, Mo.: CEMREL, 1977.
**A, CI, FPA, R**

Foucault, Michel, and Pierre Boulez. "Contemporary Music and the Public." In *Perspectives on Musical Aesthetics*, ed. John Rahn, 83-89. New York: Norton, 1994.
**FPA**

Fowler, Charles B. *Can We Rescue the Arts for America's Children: Coming to Our Senses Ten Years Later.* New York: American Council for the Arts, 1988.
**A, FPA**

————. "Arts Education for Tomorrow: Straight Talk about the Future of Music Education." In *Toward Tomorrow: New Visions for General Music*, ed. Sandra L. Stauffer, 21-29. Reston, Va.: Music Educators National Conference, 1995.
**A, CI, FPA**

————. "Finding the Way to Be Basic: Music Education in the 1990s and Beyond." In *Basic Concepts in Music Education II*, ed. Richard J. Colwell, 3-26. Niwot: University Press of Colorado, 1991.
**FPA**

————. "One Nation, Undercultured and Underqualified." In *Artistic Intelligences: Implications for Education*, ed. William J. Moody, 159-69. New York: Teachers College, 1990.
**A, FPA**

————. "Toward a Democratic Art: A Reconstructionist View of Music Education." In *Music Education in the United States: Contemporary Issues*, ed. J. Terry Gates, 130-55. Tuscaloosa: University of Alabama Press, 1988.
**CI, FPA**

_____, ed. *Arts in Education, Education in Arts: Entering the Dialogue of the 80's.* Washington: Charles B. Fowler, 1984.
**A, CI, FPA**

Fowler, Charles B., Timothy Gerber, and Vincent P. Lawrence. *Music: Its Role and Importance in Our Lives.* New York: Glencoe, 1994.
**CI, FPA**

Frances, Robert. *The Perception of Music.* Transl. W. Jay Dowling. Hillsdale, N.J.: L. Erlbaum, 1988.
**FPA, P**

Freeman, Robert. "On the Need for Bridging Music's Islands." In *The Future of Musical Education in America: Proceedings of the July 1983 Conference,* ed. Donald J. Shetler, 72-85. Rochester, N.Y.: Eastman School of Music Press, 1984.
**FPA**

Frith, Simon. "Towards an Aesthetic of Popular Music." In *Music and Society: The Politics of Composition, Performance, and Reception,* ed. Richard D. Leppert and Susan McClary, 133-49. New York: Cambridge University Press, 1987.
**FPA, P**

Furst, Edward J. "Bloom's Taxonomy: Philosophical and Educational Issues." In *Bloom's Taxonomy—A Forty-Year Retrospective: 93rd Yearbook of the National Society for the Study of Education (Part II),* ed. Lorin W. Anderson and Lauren A. Sosniak, 28-40. Chicago: University of Chicago Press, 1994.
**CI, FPA**

Gans, Eric. "Art and Entertainment." In *Perspectives on Musical Aesthetics,* ed. John Rahn, 40-53. New York: Norton, 1994.
**A, FPA**

_____. "The Beginning and End of Esthetic Form." In *Perspectives on Musical Aesthetics,* ed. John Rahn, 66-79. New York: Norton, 1994.
**FPA**

Gary, Charles L., and Wade M. Robinson. "Implications of Aesthetic Education for Professional Action." In *Toward an Aesthetic Education: A Report,* 129-34. Washington: Music Educators National Conference, 1971.
**A, CI, FPA**

Gates, J. Terry, ed. *Music Education in the United States: Contemporary Issues.* Tuscaloosa: University of Alabama Press, 1988.
**CI, FPA**

Geahigan, George. "The Arts in Education: A Historical Perspective." In *The Arts, Education, and Aesthetic Knowing: 91st Yearbook of the National Society for the Study of Education (Part II)*, ed. Bennett Reimer and Ralph A. Smith, 1-19. Chicago: University of Chicago Press, 1992.
**A, CI, FPA**

Getto, Elissa O., comp. *TIPS: Public Relations.* Reston, Va.: Music Educators National Conference, 1988.
**FPA**

Getz, Russell P. "Music Education in Tomorrow's Schools: A Practical Approach." In *The Future of Musical Education in America: Proceedings of the July 1983 Conference*, ed. Donald J. Shetler, 21-31. Rochester, N.Y.: Eastman School of Music Press, 1984.
**CI, FPA**

Gfeller, Kate. "Arts Education Policies for Students with Disabilities." In *Policy Issues in Music Education: A Report of the Proceedings of the Robert Petzold Symposium*, ed. Gerald Olson, Anthony L. Barresi, and David Nelson, 76-87. Madison: School of Music, University of Wisconsin, 1991.
**A, CI, FPA**

*Gifts of Music.* Reston, Va.: Music Educators National Conference, 1994.
**FPA**

Gildersleeve, Glenn. "Standards and the Evaluation and Measurement of Achievement in Music." In *Music Education: 35th Yearbook of the National Society for the Study of Education (Part II)*, ed. Guy Montrose Whipple, 195-206. Bloomington, Ill.: Public School Publishing, 1936.
**CI, FPA, P**

Godwin, Joscelyn, ed. *The Harmony of the Spheres: A Sourcebook of the Pythagorean Tradition in Music.* Rochester, Vt.: Inner Traditions International, 1993.
**FPA, P**

————, ed. *Music, Mysticism, and Magic: A Sourcebook.* New York: Arkana, 1987.
**BR, FPA, P**

Goehr, Lydia. *The Imaginary Museum of Musical Works: An Essay in the Philosophy of Music.* New York: Oxford University Press, 1992.
**FPA**

————. "'Music Has No Meaning to Speak Of': On the Politics of Musical Interpretation." In *The Interpretation of Music: Philosophical Essays*, ed. Michael Krausz, 177-90. New York: Oxford University Press, 1992.
**FPA, P**

Golby, Michael. "The Responsive School." In *The Arts and Personal Growth*, ed. Malcolm Ross, 16-26. New York: Pergamon, 1980.
**A, CI, FPA**

Gonzo, Carroll. "Toward a Rational Critical Process." In *Handbook of Research on Music Teaching and Learning*, ed. Richard J. Colwell, 218-26. New York: Schirmer Book, 1992.
**FPA, R**

Goodlad, John I. "Toward a Place in the Curriculum for the Arts." In *The Arts, Education, and Aesthetic Knowing: 91st Yearbook of the National Society for the Study of Education (Part II)*, ed. Bennett Reimer and Ralph A. Smith, 192-212. Chicago: University of Chicago Press, 1992.
**A, CI, FPA**

Goodman, A. Harold. *Music Education: Perspectives and Perceptions - Including 37 Outstanding Music Educators.* Dubuque, Iowa: Kendall/Hunt, 1982.
**CI, FPA**

Goodman, Nelson. *Of Mind and Other Matters.* Cambridge: Harvard University Press, 1984.
**FPA**

Gotshalk, D. W. "Aesthetic Education as a Domain." In *Aesthetics and Problems of Education*, ed. Ralph A. Smith, 117-25. Urbana: University of Illinois Press, 1971.
**A, CI, FPA**

Grant, Willis, ed. *Music in Education.* London: Butterworths, 1963.
**CI, FPA, RSC**

Green, Lucy. *Music on Deaf Ears: Musical Meaning, Ideology, Education.* New York: Manchester University Press, 1988.
**CI, FPA, P**

Greene, Maxine. "Art, Technique, and the Indifferent Gods." In *Aesthetics and Problems of Education*, ed. Ralph A. Smith, 555-63. Urbana: University of Illinois Press, 1971.
**A, CI, FPA**

_____. "Teaching for Aesthetic Experience." In *Toward an Aesthetic Education: A Report*, 21-43. Washington: Music Educators National Conference, 1971.
**A, CI, FPA**

Greer, R. Douglas. *Design for Music Learning.* New York: Teachers College, 1980.
**CI, FPA, P**

*Growing Up Complete: The Imperative for Music Education.* Reston, Va.: Music Educators National Conference, 1991.
**CI, FPA, RSC**

Gurin, Richard S. "The Arts Education Standards: A Payoff for Business." In *Perspectives on Implementation: Arts Education Standards for America's Students*, ed. Bruce O. Boston, 82-88. Reston, Va.: Music Educators National Conference, 1994.
**A, CI, FPA**

Gurney, Edmund. *The Power of Sound.* 1880. Reprint, New York: Basic Books, 1966.
**FPA, P**

Haack, Paul. "Advocacy and Policy Development: Broadening the Rationale for Music Education." In *Policy Issues in Music Education: A Report of the Proceedings of the Robert Petzold Symposium*, ed. Gerald Olson, Anthony L. Barresi, and David Nelson, 16-31. Madison: School of Music, University of Wisconsin, 1991.
**FPA**

Hall, Manly Palmer. *The Therapeutic Value of Music Including the Philosophy of Music.* Los Angeles: Philosophical Research Society, 1982.
**FPA, P**

Hanshumaker, James. "The Art of Recognizing Artistic Teaching in the Arts." In *The Teaching Process, Arts and Aesthetics*, ed. Gerard L. Knieter and Jane Stallings, 223-39. St. Louis, Mo.: CEMREL, 1979.
**A, CI, FPA**

Hanslick, Eduard. *On the Musically Beautiful: A Contribution towards the Revision of the Aesthetics of Music.* Transl. and ed. Geoffrey Payzant from 8th ed., 1891. Reprint, Indianapolis: Ind.: Hackett, 1986.
**A, FPA, P**

Hargreaves, D. H. "Dr. Brunel and Mr. Denning: Reflections on Aesthetic Knowing." In *The Arts: A Way of Knowing*, ed. Malcolm Ross, 127-60. New York: Pergamon, 1983.
**A, FPA**

Harre, Rom. "Is There a Semantics for Music? In *The Interpretation of Music: Philosophical Essays*, ed. Michael Krausz, 203-13. New York: Oxford University Press, 1992.
**FPA, P**

Harrell, Jean Gabbert. *Soundtracks: A Study of Auditory Perception, Memory, and Valuation.* Buffalo: Prometheus Books, 1986.
**FPA, P**

Hausman, Jerome J. "A Contemporary Aesthetics Curriculum." In *Toward an Aesthetic Education: A Report*, 45-55. Washington: Music Educators National Conference, 1971.
**A, CI, FPA**

————. "The Domain of the Arts." In *Arts and the Schools*, ed. Jerome J. Hausman and Joyce Wright, 23-45. New York: McGraw-Hill, 1980.
**A, FPA**

Hausman, Jerome J., and Joyce Wright, eds. *Arts and the Schools*. New York: McGraw-Hill, 1980.
**A, CI, FPA**

Heller, George N. *Historical Research in Music Educaton: A Bibliography*. 2nd ed. Lawrence: University of Kansas Department of Art and Music Education and Music Therapy, 1992.
**BR, FPA, R**

————. *Music and Music Education History: A Chronology*. 2nd ed. Lawrence: University of Kansas Department of Art and Music Education and Music Therapy, 1993.
**BR, FPA**

Heller, Jack J., and Warren C. Campbell. "Models of Language and Intellect in Music Research." In *Music Education for Tomorrow's Society*, ed. Arthur Motycka, 40-49. Jamestown, R.I.: GAMT Music, 1976.
**FPA, P, R**

Hemmeren, Goran. "The Full Voic'd Quire: Types of Interpretation of Music." In *The Interpretation of Music: Philosophical Essays*, ed. Michael Krausz, 9-31. New York: Oxford University Press, 1992.
**FPA**

Henry, Nelson B., ed. *Basic Concepts in Music Education: 57th Yearbook of the National Society for the Study of Education*. Chicago: University of Chicago Press, 1958.
**BR, CI, FPA**

Heyfron, Victor. "Artistic Creativity." In *The Aesthetic in Education*, ed. Malcolm Ross, 29-53. New York: Pergamon, 1985.
**A, FPA**

————. "The Concept of Art." In *The Arts and Personal Growth*, ed. Malcolm Ross, 79-95. New York: Pergamon, 1980.
**A, FPA**

————. "The Objective Status of Aesthetic Knowing." In *The Arts: A Way of Knowing*, ed. Malcolm Ross, 43-72. New York: Pergamon, 1983.
**A, FPA, P**

Hicks, Charles E., James A. Standifer, and Warrick L. Carter, eds. *Methods and Perspectives in Urban Music Education.* Washington: University Press of America, 1983.
**CI, FPA**

Higgins, Kathleen Marie. *The Music of Our Lives.* Philadelphia: Temple University Press, 1991.
**FPA, P**

Highet, Gilbert. *The Art of Teaching.* 1950. Reprint, New York: Vintage Books, 1989.
**CI, FPA**

Hobbs, Jack A., and Robert L. Duncan. *Arts, Ideas and Civilization.* 2nd ed. Englewood Cliffs, N.J.: Prentice-Hall, 1992.
**A, FPA**

Hodge, Joanna. "Aesthetic Decomposition: Music, Identity, and Time." In *The Interpretation of Music: Philosophical Essays*, ed. Michael Krausz, 247-58. New York: Oxford University Press, 1992.
**FPA**

Hodgkinson, Harold L. "Arts in the Future: A Pragmatic Analysis." In *Arts and Aesthetics: An Agenda for the Future*, ed. Stanley S. Madeja, 28-45. St. Louis, Mo.: CEMREL, 1977.
**A, CI, FPA**

Hodkinson, Sydney. "The Phoenix Revisited: An Etude in Musicomythology." In *The Future of Musical Education in America: Proceedings of the July 1983 Conference*, ed. Donald J. Shetler, 32-48. Rochester, N.Y.: Eastman School of Music Press, 1984.
**FPA**

Hoffa, Harlan Edward. "Implementing the National Standards: Developing Professional Resources." In *Perspectives on Implementation: Arts Education Standards for America's Students*, ed. Bruce O. Boston, 19-30. Reston, Va.: Music Educators National Conference, 1994.
**A, CI, FPA**

Hoffer, Charles R. *Introduction to Music Education.* 2nd ed. Celmont, Calif.: Wadsworth, 1993.
**CI, FPA**

Hoffman, Mary E. "The Potential for MENC as a Leader in Arts Education Policy." In *Policy Issues in Music Education: A Report of the Proceedings of the Robert Petzold Symposium*, ed. Gerald Olson, Anthony L. Barresi, and David Nelson, 172-84. Madison: School of Music, University of Wisconsin, 1991.

**A, FPA**

Hope, Samuel. "Making Disciplinary Connections." In *Perspectives on Implementation: Arts Education Standards for America's Students*, ed. Bruce O. Boston, 38-46. Reston, Va.: Music Educators National Conference, 1994.

**A, CI, FPA**

————. *Policy Questions in Music Education: Opportunity, Content, Partnership, Funding, and Politics.* Reston, Va.: Music Educators National Conference, 1985.

**FPA**

House, Robert William. *Administration in Music Education.* Englewood Cliffs, N.J.: Prentice-Hall, 1973.

**CI, FPA**

————. "The Future of Music Education in Higher Education." In *Music Education for Tomorrow's Society*, ed. Arthur Motycka, 61-72. Jamestown, R.I.: GAMT Music, 1976.

**CI, FPA**

————. "The Professional Preparation of Music Administrators." In *Symposium in Music Education: A Festschrift for Charles Leonhard*, ed. Richard J. Colwell, 277-89. Urbana-Champaign: University of Illinois, 1982.

**CI, FPA**

Howard, Vernon A. "Music as Educating Imagination." In *The Crane Symposium: Toward an Understanding of the Teaching and Learning of Music Performance*, ed. Charles Fowler, 25-35. Potsdam: College of the State University of New York, 1988.

**FPA, P**

Howe, Sondra Wieland. *Luther Whiting Mason, International Music Educator.* Warren, Mich.: Harmonie Park Press, 1997.

**FPA**

Howes, Frank Stewart. *Man, Mind and Music.* 1948. Reprint, Freeport, N.Y.: Books for Libraries, 1970.

**FPA, P**

Humphreys, Jere T. "Instrumental Music in American Education: In Service of Many Masters." In *The Ithaca Conference on American Music Education: Centennial Profiles*, ed. Mark Fonder, 25-51. Ithaca, N.Y.: Ithaca College, 1992.

**FPA**

Inglefield, Ruth K. "International Review of the Aesthetics and Sociology of Music." In *International Music Journals*, ed. Linda M. Fidler and Richard S. James, 172-74. New York: Greenwood, 1990.
**A, FPA, J, P, R**

————. "Journal of Aesthetics and Art Criticism." In *International Music Journals*, ed. Linda M. Fidler and Richard S. James, 187-88. New York: Greenwood, 1990.
**A, FPA, J, R**

*International Journal of Music Education*. Huddersfield, England: International Society for Music Education, 1983-.
**CI, FPA, J, P, R**

Jackendoff, Ray S., and Fred Lerdahl. *A Deep Parallel between Music and Language*. Bloomington: Indiana University Linguistics Club, 1980.
**FPA, P**

James, Jamie. *The Music of the Spheres: Music, Science, and the Natural Order of the Universe*. New York: Grove, 1993.
**FPA, P**

Jenkins, Iredell. "Aesthetic Education and Moral Refinement." In *Aesthetics and Problems of Education*, ed. Ralph A. Smith, 178-99. Urbana: University of Illinois Press, 1971.
**A, CI, FPA**

Johnson, Nancy Jo. "Involving School Boards in Implementing the Arts Standards." In *Perspectives on Implementation: Arts Education Standards for America's Students*, ed. Bruce O. Boston, 70-74. Reston, Va.: Music Educators National Conference, 1994.
**A, CI, FPA**

Johnson, Philip. "Black Music, the Arts and Education." In *The Claims of Feeling: Readings in Aesthetic Education*, ed. Malcolm Ross, 37-63. Philadelphia: Falmer, 1989.
**A, CI, FPA**

Jones, Archie Neff. *Music Education in Action: Basic Principles and Practical Methods*. Dubuque, Iowa: Wm. C. Brown, 1964.
**CI, FPA**

Jones, Merilyn. "Professional Methodology: Introduction." In *Music Education in the United States: Contemporary Issues*, ed. J. Terry Gates, 181-84. Tuscaloosa: University of Alabama Press, 1988.
**CI, FPA**

Jones, William LaRue. "The Orchestra and American Education." In *Music Education in the United States: Contemporary Issues*, ed. J. Terry Gates, 277-86. Tuscaloosa: University of Alabama Press, 1988.
**CI, FPA**

Jorgensen, Estelle R. "On Philosophical Method." In *Handbook of Research on Music Teaching and Learning*, ed. Richard J. Colwell, 91-101. New York: Schirmer Books, 1992.
**FPA, R**

_____, ed. *Philosopher, Teacher, Musician: Perspectives on Music Education*. Urbana: University of Illinois Press, 1993.
**CI, FPA**

*Journal of Aesthetic Education*. Urbana: University of Illinois Press, 1966-.
**A, CI, FPA, J, R**

Joyce, Bruce R., Marsha Weil, and Beverly Showers. *Models of Teaching*. 4th ed. Boston: Allyn and Bacon, 1992.
**CI, FPA**

Kabalevsky, Dmitri Borisovich. *Music and Education: A Composer Writes about Musical Education*. London: J. Kingsley, 1988.
**CI, FPA**

Kaelin, Eugene F. "Aesthetic Education: A Role for Aesthetics Proper." In *Aesthetics and Problems of Education*, ed. Ralph A. Smith, 144-61. Urbana: University of Illinois Press, 1971.
**A, CI, FPA**

Kaelin, Eugene F., and David W. Ecker. "The Institutional Prospects of Aesthetic Education." In *Arts and Aesthetics: An Agenda for the Future*, ed. Stanley S. Madeja, 229-42. St. Louis, Mo.: CEMREL, 1977.
**A, CI, FPA**

Kantorski, Vincent J. "The Council for Research in Music Education Bulletin." In *International Music Journals*, ed. Linda M. Fidler and Richard S. James, 100-02. New York: Greenwood, 1990.
**CI, FPA, J, P, R**

Kapinus, Barbara, et al. "National Standards: Implications and Strategies for the States." In *Perspectives on Implementation: Arts Education Standards for America's Students*, ed. Bruce O. Boston, 89-95. Reston, Va.: Music Educators National Conference, 1994.
**A, CI, FPA**

Kaplan, Max. *Foundations and Frontiers of Music Education.* New York: Holt, Rinehart and Winston, 1966.

**CI, FPA**

Keene, James A. *A History of Music Education in the United States.* Hanover, N.H.: University Press of New England, 1982.

**FPA**

Keppel, Francis. "The Arts and Education Today Compared to the Sixties." In *Arts and Aesthetics: An Agenda for the Future*, ed. Stanley S. Madeja, 25-27. St. Louis, Mo.: CEMREL, 1977.

**A, CI, FPA**

Kerman, Joseph. "The State of Academic Music Criticism." In *On Criticizing Music: Five Philosophical Perspectives*, ed. Kingsley Price, 38-54. Baltimore: Johns Hopkins University Press, 1981.

**FPA**

Kessen, William. "Encounters: The American Child's Meeting with Music." In *Documentary Report of the Ann Arbor Symposium: National Symposium on the Applications of Psychology to the Teaching and Learning of Music (Sessions I and II)*, 353-61. Reston, Va.: Music Educators National Conference, 1981.

**FPA, P, R**

Keyserling, Harriet. "The Politics of Mainstreaming Arts in Education." In *Artistic Intelligences: Implications for Education*, ed. William J. Moody, 63-68. New York: Teachers College, 1990.

**A, CI, FPA**

Kimpton, Jeffrey. *Public Education and the Arts: Linked by Necessity.* Reston, Va.: Music Educators National Conference, 1985.

**A, CI, FPA**

Kirchhoff, Craig. "The School and College Band: Wind Band Pedagogy in the United States." In *Music Education in the United States: Contemporary Issues*, ed. J. Terry Gates, 259-76. Tuscaloosa: University of Alabama Press, 1988.

**CI, FPA**

Kirk, Colleen Jean. "Choral Music Education in America, 1892-1992." In *The Ithaca Conference on American Music Education: Centennial Profiles*, ed. Mark Fonder, 53-84. Ithaca, N.Y.: Ithaca College, 1992.

**FPA**

Kivy, Peter. *The Fine Art of Repetition: Essays in the Philosophy of Music.* New York: Cambridge University Press, 1993.

**FPA**

_____. *Music Alone: Philosophical Reflections on the Purely Musical Experience.* Ithaca, N.Y.: Cornell University Press, 1990.
**FPA**

_____. *Sound and Semblance: Reflections on Musical Representation.* 1984. Reprint, Ithaca, N.Y.: Cornell University Press, 1991.
**FPA, P**

Klotman, Robert H. "The Musician in Education: 2025 A.D." In *Music Education for Tomorrow's Society*, ed. Arthur Motycka, 12-20. Jamestown, R.I.: GAMT Music, 1976.
**CI, FPA**

Knieter, Gerard L. "Humanistic Dimensions of Aesthetic Education." In *Music Education for Tomorrow's Society*, ed. Arthur Motycka, 1-11. Jamestown, R.I.: GAMT Music, 1976.
**FPA, P**

_____. "The Nature of Aesthetic Education." In *Toward an Aesthetic Education: A Report*, 3-19. Washington: Music Educators National Conference, 1971.
**A, CI, FPA, P**

Knieter, Gerard L., and Jane Stallings, eds. *The Teaching Process, Arts and Aesthetics.* St. Louis, Mo.: CEMREL, 1979.
**A, CI, FPA, RSC**

Kowall, Bonnie C., ed. *Perspectives in Music Education: Source Book III.* Washington: Music Educators National Conference, 1966.
**BR, CI, FPA**

Koza, Julia Eklund. "Sex Equity and Policy in Music Education: A Change of Vision, A Change of Values." In *Policy Issues in Music Education: A Report of the Proceedings of the Robert Petzold Symposium*, ed. Gerald Olson, Anthony L. Barresi, and David Nelson, 135-45. Madison: School of Music, University of Wisconsin, 1991.
**FPA, P**

Krathwohl, David R. "Reflections on the Taxonomy: Its Past, Present, and Future." In *Bloom's Taxonomy—A Forty-Year Retrospective: 93rd Yearbook of the National Society for the Study of Education (Part II)*, ed. Lorin W. Anderson and Lauren A. Sosniak, 181-202. Chicago: University of Chicago Press, 1994.
**CI, FPA, P**

Krausz, Michael. "Rightness and Reasons in Musical Interpretation." In *The Interpretation of Music: Philosophical Essays*, ed. Michael Krausz, 75-87. New York: Oxford University Press, 1992.
**FPA**

_____, ed. *The Intrepretation of Music: Philosophical Essays.* New York: Oxford University Press, 1992.

**FPA, P**

Kraut, Robert. "Perceiving the Music Correctly." In *The Interpretation of Music: Philosophical Essays*, ed. Michael Krausz, 103-16. New York: Oxford University Press, 1992.

**FPA**

Landers, Ray. *The Talent Education School of Shinichi Suzuki: An Analysis - Application of Its Philosophy and Methods to All Areas of Instruction.* 3rd ed. Smithtown, N.Y.: Exposition, 1984.

**CI, FPA**

Landon, Joseph W. *Leadership for Learning in Music Education.* Fullerton, Calif.: Music Education Publications, 1975.

**CI, FPA**

Lang, Berel, ed. *The Concept of Style.* Rev. and exp. ed. Ithaca, N.Y.: Cornell University Press, 1987.

**FPA**

Langer, Susanne Katherina. "The Cultural Importance of the Arts." In *Aesthetics and Problems of Education*, ed. Ralph A. Smith, 86-94. Urbana: University of Illinois Press, 1971.

**A, FPA**

_____. *Feeling and Form: A Theory of Art Developed from "Philosophy in a New Key."* New York: Scribner, 1953.

**A, FPA**

_____. *Philosophy in a New Key: A Study in the Symbolism of Reason, Rite, and Art.* 3rd ed. Cambridge: Harvard University Press, 1976.

**A, FPA**

_____. *Problems of Art: Ten Philosophical Lectures.* New York: Charles Scribner's Sons, 1957.

**A, FPA**

_____, ed. *Reflections on Art: A Source Book of Writings by Artists, Critics, and Philosophers.* 1958. Reprint, New York: Arno, 1979.

**A, BR, FPA**

Lasch, Christopher. "The Degradation of Work and the Apotheosis of Art." In *The Future of Musical Education in America: Proceedings of the July 1983 Conference*, ed. Donald J. Shetler, 11-20. Rochester, N.Y.: Eastman School of Music Press, 1984.
**A, FPA**

Lawrence, Ian. *Composers and the Nature of Music Education.* London: Scolar, 1978.
**CI, FPA, P**

Lehman, Paul R. *Music in Today's Schools: Rationale and Commentary.* Reston, Va.: Music Educators National Conference, 1987.
**CI, FPA**

————. *Who Cares about Quality in Education?* Reston, Va.: Music Educators National Conference, 1986.
**CI, FPA**

Leonhard, Charles. "The Future of Musical Education in America: A Pragmatist's View." In *The Future of Musical Education in America: Proceedings of the July 1983 Conference*, ed. Donald J. Shetler, 60-71. Rochester, N.Y.: Eastman School of Music Press, 1984.
**CI, FPA**

————. "The Human Values of Music Education." In *Music Education in the United States: Contemporary Issues*, ed. J. Terry Gates, 185-92. Tuscaloosa: University of Alabama Press, 1988.
**FPA**

————. "Methods Courses in Music Teacher Education." In *Music Education in the United States: Contemporary Issues*, ed. J. Terry Gates, 193-201. Tuscaloosa: University of Alabama Press, 1988.
**CI, FPA**

————. "Music Teacher Education in the United States." In *Symposium in Music Education: A Festschrift for Charles Leonhard*, ed. Richard J. Colwell, 233-47. Urbana-Champaign: University of Illinois, 1982.
**CI, FPA**

————. *A Realistic Rationale for Teaching Music.* Reston, Va.: Music Educators National Conference, 1985.
**CI, FPA**

Leonhard, Charles, and Robert William House. *Foundations and Principles of Music Education.* 2nd ed. New York: McGraw-Hill, 1972.
**CI, FPA**

Leppert, Richard D. *The Sight of Sound: Music, Representation, and the History of the Body.* Berkeley: University of California Press, 1993.
**FPA, P**

Leppert, Richard D., and Susan McClary, eds. *Music and Society: The Politics of Composition, Performance, and Reception.* New York: Cambridge University Press, 1987.
**FPA, P**

Levinson, Jerrold. "Performative vs. Critical Interpretation in Music." In *The Interpretation of Music: Philosophical Essays*, ed. Michael Krausz, 33-60. New York: Oxford University Press, 1992.
**FPA**

Lippman, Edward A. *A History of Western Musical Aesthetics.* Lincoln: University of Nebraska Press, 1992.
**FPA**

————. *A Humanistic Philosophy of Music.* New York: New York University Press, 1977.
**FPA**

Lynch, Robert L. "Implementing the Standards: Making Use of the Arts Community." In *Perspectives on Implementation: Arts Education Standards for America's Students*, ed. Bruce O. Boston, 75-81. Reston, Va.: Music Educators National Conference, 1994.
**A, CI, FPA**

Madeja, Stanley S. "Structuring a Research Agenda for the Arts and Aesthetics." In *Arts and Aesthetics: An Agenda for the Future*, ed. Stanley S. Madeja, 374-91. St. Louis, Mo.: CEMREL, 1977.
**A, FPA, R**

————, ed. *Arts and Aesthetics: An Agenda for the Future.* St. Louis, Mo.: CEMREL, 1977.
**A, CI, FPA, RSC**

Madeja, Stanley S., and Harry T. Kelly. "A Curriculum Development Model for Aesthetic Education." In *Aesthetics and Problems of Education*, ed. Ralph A. Smith, 345-56. Urbana: University of Illinois Press, 1971.
**A, CI, FPA**

————. "The Process of Curriculum Development for Aesthetic Education." In *Toward an Aesthetic Education: A Report*, 101-15. Washington: Music Educators National Conference, 1971.
**A, CI, FPA**

Madison, Thurber H. "The Need for New Concepts in Music Education." In *Basic Concepts in Music Education: 57th Yearbook of the National Society for the Study of Education*, ed. Nelson B. Henry, 3-29. Chicago: University of Chicago Press, 1958.
**CI, FPA**

Madsen, Clifford K., and Terry Lee Kuhn. *Contemporary Music Education.* 2nd ed. Raleigh, N.C.: Contemporary Publishing, 1994.
**CI, FPA**

Margolis, Joseph. "Music as Ordered Sound: Sound Complications Affecting Description and Interpretation." In *The Interpretation of Music: Philosophical Essays*, ed. Michael Krausz, 141-53. New York: Oxford University Press, 1992.
**FPA**

Mark, Michael L. "Aesthetics and Utility Reconciled: The Importance to Society of Education in Music." In *Music Education in the United States: Contemporary Issues*, ed. J. Terry Gates, 111-29. Tuscaloosa: University of Alabama Press, 1988.
**CI, FPA, P**

————. "American Music Education in the National Context, 1892 to 1992." In *The Ithaca Conference on American Music Education: Centennial Profiles*, ed. Mark Fonder, 1-23. Ithaca, N.Y.: Ithaca College, 1992.
**FPA**

————. *Contemporary Music Education.* 3rd ed. New York: Schirmer Books, 1996.
**CI, FPA**

————. "A History of Music Education Research." In *Handbook of Research on Music Teaching and Learning*, ed. Richard J. Colwell, 48-59. New York: Schirmer Books, 1992.
**FPA, R**

————. *Source Readings in Music Education History.* 1982. Reprint, Charlottesville, Va.: Lincoln-Rembrandt, 1994.
**BR, FPA**

Mark, Michael L., and Charles L. Gary. *A History of American Music Education.* New York: Schirmer Books, 1992.
**FPA**

Martin, Robert L. "Musical Works in the Worlds of Performers and Listeners." In *The Intepretation of Music: Philosophical Essays*, ed. Michael Krausz, 119-27. New York: Oxford University Press, 1992.
**FPA**

Mathieu, W. A. *The Musical Life: Reflections on What It Is and How to Live It.* Boston: Shambhala, 1994.

**FPA**

Maus, Fred Everett. "Recent Ideas and Activities of James K. Randall and Benjamin Boretz: A New Social Role for Music." In *Perspectives on Musical Aesthetics*, ed. John Rahn, 107-15. New York: Norton, 1994.

**A, FPA, P**

McCarthy, Marie, ed. *Winds of Change: A Colloquium in Music Education with Charles Fowler and David J. Elliott.* New York: ACA Books, University of Maryland at College Park, 1994.

**CI, FPA, RSC**

McEwen, John Blackwood. *The Foundations of Musical Aesthetics.* London: K. Paul Trubner, 1917.

**CI, FPA**

McKay, George Frederick. "The Range of Musical Experience." In *Basic Concepts in Music Education: 57th Yearbook of the National Society for the Study of Education*, ed. Nelson B. Henry, 123-39. Chicago: University of Chicago Press, 1958.

**CI, FPA**

McKenna, Gerard, and William R. Schmid, eds. *The Tanglewood Symposium Revisited: Music in American Society Ten Years Later.* Milwaukee: University of Wisconsin, 1978.

**CI, FPA, RSC**

McMullen, Patrick T. "Music as a Perceived Stimulus Object and Affective Responses: An Alternative Theoretical Framework." In *Handbook of Music Psychology*, ed. Donald A. Hodges, 183-94. Lawrence, Kans.: National Association for Music Therapy, 1980.

**FPA, P**

McMurray, Foster. "Part I: Pragmatism in Music." In *Basic Concepts in Music Education II*, ed. Richard J. Colwell, 27-53. Niwot: University Press of Colorado, 1991.

**FPA**

————. "Part II: Variations on a Pragmatic Theme." In *Basic Concepts in Music Education II*, ed. Richard J. Colwell, 54-70. Niwot: University Press of Colorado, 1991.

**FPA**

————. "Pragmatism in Music Education." In *Basic Concepts in Music Education: 57th Yearbook of the National Society for the Study of Education*, ed. Nelson B. Henry, 30-61. Chicago: University of Chicago Press, 1958.

**FPA**

Meske, Eunice Boardman. "Educating the Music Teacher: Participation in a Metamorphosis." In *Symposium in Music Education: A Festschrift for Charles Leonhard*, ed. Richard J. Colwell, 249-65. Urbana-Champaign: University of Illinois, 1982.
CI, FPA, P, R

Meyer, Leonard B. *Emotion and Meaning in Music.* Chicago: University of Chicago Press, 1956.
FPA, P

————. *Explaining Music: Essays and Explorations.* Chicago: University of Chicago Press, 1978.
FPA, P

————. *Music, the Arts, and Ideas.* 1967. Reprint, Chicago: University of Chicago Press, 1994.
A, FPA, P

————. "Some Remarks on Value and Greatness in Music." In *Aesthetic Inquiry: Essays on Art Criticism and the Philosophy of Art*, ed. Monroe C. Beardsley and Herbert M. Schueller, 260-73. Belmont, Calif.: Dickenson, 1967.
FPA

————. *Style and Music: Theory, History, and Ideology.* Philadelphia: University of Pennsylvania Press, 1989.
FPA, P

Miller, Louise. "Working with State Legislatures." In *Perspectives on Implementation: Arts Education Standards for America's Students*, ed. Bruce O. Boston, 96-100. Reston, Va.: Music Educators National Conference, 1994.
A, CI, FPA

Moles, Abraham A. *Information Theory and Esthetic Perception.* Transl. Joel F. Cohen. Urbana-Champaign: University of Illinois, 1966.
FPA, P

Monelle, Raymond. *Linguistics and Semiotics in Music.* Philadelphia: Harwood Academic Press, 1992.
FPA, P

Monsour, Sally. "General Music Tomorrow." In *Toward Tomorrow: New Visions for General Music*, ed. Sandra L. Stauffer, 43-47. Reston, Va.: Music Educators National Conference, 1995.
CI, FPA

Moody, William J. "Summary and Coda." In *Artistic Intelligences: Implications for Education*, ed. William J. Moody, 170-79. New York: Teachers College, 1990.
**A, FPA**

_____, ed. *Artistic Intelligences: Implications for Education.* New York: Teachers College, 1990.
**A, CI, FPA, P, RSC**

Morgan, Hazel Nohavec, ed. *Music Education Source Book: A Compendium of Data, Opinion and Recommendations.* Chicago: Music Educators National Conference, 1951.
**BR, CI, FPA**

_____, ed. *Music in American Education: Music Education Source Book II.* Chicago: Music Educators National Conference, 1955.
**BR, CI, FPA**

Motycka, Arthur. *Musico-Aesthetic Education: A Phenomenological Proposition.* Jamestown, R.I.: GAMT Music, 1975.
**CI, FPA**

_____, ed. *Music Education for Tomorrow's Society.* Jamestown, R.I.: GAMT Music, 1976.
**CI, FPA**

Murphy, Judith, and George Sullivan. *Music in American Society: An Interpretive Report of the Tanglewood Symposium.* Washington: Music Educators National Conference, 1968.
**CI, FPA, RSC**

Mursell, James L. *Human Values in Music Education.* New York: Silver Burdett, 1934.
**CI, FPA, P**

_____. *Music Education: Principles and Programs.* Morristown, N.J.: Silver Burdett, 1956.
**CI, FPA**

_____. *Music in American Schools.* Rev. ed. New York: Silver Burdett, 1953.
**CI, FPA**

_____. *Principles of Democratic Education.* New York: Norton, 1955.
**CI, FPA**

_____. *Principles of Education.* New York: Norton, 1934.
**CI, FPA**

_____. "Principles of Music Education." In *Music Education: 35th Yearbook of the National Society for the Study of Education (Part II)*, ed. Guy Montrose Whipple, 3-16. Bloomington, Ill.: Public School Publishing, 1936.
**CI, FPA**

_____. *Principles of Musical Education.* New York: Macmillan, 1927.
**CI, FPA**

*Music Teacher Education: Partnership and Process.* Reston, Va.: Music Educators National Conference, 1987.
**CI, FPA, RSC**

Narmour, Eugene, and Ruth A. Solie, eds. *Explorations in Music, the Arts, and Ideas: Essays in Honor of Leonard B. Meyer.* Stuyvesant, N.Y.: Pendragon, 1988.
**A, BR, FPA, RSC**

*NASM Futureswork: Executive Summaries, 1989-1992.* Reston, Va.: National Association of Schools of Music, 1992.
**FPA, RSC**

National Coalition for Music Education. *Building Support for School Music: A Practical Guide.* Reston, Va.: Music Educators National Conference, 1991.
**BR, FPA**

Nestrovski, Arthur. "Joyce's Critique of Music." In *Perspectives on Musical Aesthetics*, ed. John Rahn, 249-89. New York: Norton, 1994.
**FPA**

Nettl, Bruno. *The Western Impact on World Music: Change, Adaptation, and Survival.* New York: Schirmer Books, 1985.
**FPA, P**

Newman, William S. "Musical Form as a Generative Process." In *Aesthetic Inquiry: Essays on Art Criticism and the Philosophy of Art*, ed. Monroe C. Beardsley and Herbert M. Schueller, 67-75. Belmont, Calif.: Dickenson, 1967.
**FPA**

Nordholm, Harriet. *Singing in the Elementary Schools: Foundations of Music Education Series.* Englewood Cliffs, N.J.: Prentice-Hall, 1966.
**CI, FPA**

Norris, Christopher, ed. *Music and the Politics of Culture.* New York: St. Martin's, 1989.
**FPA, P**

Olson, Gerald, Anthony L. Barresi, and David Nelson, eds. *Policy Issues in Music Education: A Report of the Proceedings of the Robert Petzold Research Symposium.* Madison: School of Music, University of Wisconsin, 1991.
**FPA, R, RSC**

Osborne, Harold. "Appreciation as Percipience." In *Aesthetics and Problems of Education*, ed. Ralph A. Smith, 445-72. Urbana: University of Illinois Press, 1971.
**A, FPA**

Paddison, Max. *Adorno's Aesthetics of Music.* New York: Cambridge University Press, 1993.
**FPA, P**

Pankratz, David, and Kevin V. Mulcahy, eds. *The Challenge to Reform Arts Education: What Role Can Research Play?* New York: ACA Books, 1989.
**A, CI, FPA, R**

Pankratz, David, and Valerie B. Morris, eds. *The Future of the Arts: Public Policy and Arts Research.* New York: Praeger, 1990.
**A, FPA**

Perris, Arnold. *Music as Propaganda: Art to Persuade, Art to Control.* Westport, Conn.: Greenwood, 1985.
**FPA, P**

Phenix, Philip H. "The Aesthetic Realm of Meaning." In *Aesthetics and Problems of Education*, ed. Ralph A. Smith, 265-84. Urbana: University of Illinois Press, 1971.
**A, FPA**

*Philosophy of Music Education Review.* Bloomington: Indiana University School of Music, 1993-.
**FPA, J, R**

Pike, Alfred John. *A Phenomenological Analysis of Musical Experience and Other Related Essays.* New York: St. John's, 1970.
**FPA, P**

Pitts, Lilla Belle. "The Place of Music in a System of Education." In *Music Education: 35th Yearbook of the National Society for the Study of Education (Part II)*, ed. Guy Montrose Whipple, 17-21. Bloomington, Ill.: Public School Publishing, 1936.
**FPA**

————. "Typical Musical Activities of the School." In *Music Education: 35th Yearbook of the National Society for the Study of Education (Part II)*, ed. Guy Montrose Whipple, 45-50. Bloomington, Ill.: Public School Publishing, 1936.
**CI, FPA**

Plummeridge, Charles. *Music Education in Theory and Practice.* New York: Falmer, 1991.
**CI, FPA**

Pole, William. *The Philosophy of Music.* 6th ed. 1879. New York: Harcourt, Brace, 1924.
**FPA**

Portnoy, Julius. *The Philosopher and Music: A Historical Outline.* 1954. Reprint, New York: Da Capo, 1980.
**FPA**

Potosky, Alice. *Promoting School Music: A Practical Guide.* Reston, Va.: Music Educators National Conference, 1984.
**BR, CI, FPA**

Pratt, Carroll C. "The Form and Function of Music." In *Aesthetic Inquiry: Essays on Art Criticism and the Philosophy of Art,* ed. Monroe C. Beardsley and Herbert M. Schueller, 219-28. Belmont, Calif.: Dickenson, 1967.
**FPA**

————. *The Meaning of Music: A Study in Psychological Aesthetics.* 1931. Reprint, Ann Arbor, Mich.: University Microfilms International, 1979.
**FPA, P**

Price, Kingsley, ed. *On Criticizing Music: Five Philosophical Perspectives.* Baltimore: Johns Hopkins University Press, 1981.
**FPA, RSC**

*Quarterly Journal of Music Teaching and Learning.* Greeley: University of Northern Colorado School of Music, 1990-.
**CI, FPA, J, P, R**

Raffman, Diana. "Goodman, Density, and the Limits of Sense Perception." In *The Interpretation of Music: Philosophical Essays,* ed. Michael Krausz, 215-27. New York: Oxford University Press, 1992.
**FPA, P**

————. *Language, Music, and Mind.* Cambridge, Mass.: MIT, 1993.
**FPA, P**

Rahn, John. "What Is Valuable in Art, and Can Music Still Achieve It?" In *Perspectives on Musical Aesthetics,* ed. John Rahn, 54-65. New York: Norton, 1994.
**A, FPA**

————, ed. *Perspectives on Musical Aesthetics.* New York: Norton, 1994.
**FPA**

Rantala, Veikko, Lewis Eugene Rowell, and Eero Tarasti, eds. *Essays on the Philosophy of Music.* Helsinki: Philosophical Society of Finland, 1988.
**FPA, RSC**

Redfield, John. *Music: A Science and an Art.* New ed. New York: Tudor Publishing, 1935.
**FPA, P**

Ree, Henry. "Education and the Arts: Are Schools the Enemy?" In *The Aesthetic Imperative: Relevance and Responsibility in Arts Education,* ed. Malcolm Ross, 90-99. New York: Pergamon, 1981.
**A, CI, FPA**

Regelski, Thomas A. *Principles and Problems of Music Education.* Englewood Cliffs, N.J.: Prentice-Hall, 1975.
**CI, FPA**

Reid, Louis Arnaud. "Aesthetic Knowledge in the Arts." In *The Arts: A Way of Knowing,* ed. Malcolm Ross, 19-41. New York: Pergamon, 1983.
**A, FPA, P**

————. "Assessment and Aesthetic Education." In *The Aesthetic Imperative: Relevance and Responsibility in Arts Education,* ed. Malcolm Ross, 8-24. New York: Pergamon, 1981.
**A, CI, FPA, P**

————. "The Concept of Aesthetic Development." In *The Development of Aesthetic Experience,* ed. Malcolm Ross, 2-26. New York: Pergamon, 1982.
**A, FPA**

————. "Knowledge and Aesthetic Education." In *Aesthetics and Problems of Education,* ed. Ralph A. Smith, 162-71. Urbana: University of Illinois Press, 1971.
**A, CI, FPA**

————. "Meaning in the Arts." In *The Arts and Personal Growth,* ed. Malcolm Ross, 1-15. New York: Pergamon, 1980.
**A, FPA**

————. *Meaning in the Arts.* New York: Humanities Press, 1969.
**A, CI, FPA, P**

————. *A Study in Aesthetics.* Westport, Conn.: Greenwood, 1973.
**FPA**

Reimer, Bennett. "Aesthetic Behaviors in Music." In *Toward an Aesthetic Education: A Report,* 65-87. Washington: Music Educators National Conference, 1971.
**A, CI, FPA, P**

————. "Building Curricula for Music Education." In *Aesthetics and Problems of Education*, ed. Ralph A. Smith, 374-86. Urbana: University of Illinois Press, 1971.
**CI, FPA**

————. "Designing Effective Arts Programs." In *Arts and the Schools*, ed. Jerome J. Hausman and Joyce Wright, 117-56. New York: McGraw-Hill, 1980.
**A, CI, FPA, P**

————. "Music Education Philosophy and Psychology after Mursell." In *Basic Concepts in Music Education II*, ed. Richard J. Colwell, 130-56. Niwot: University Press of Colorado, 1991.
**FPA, P**

————. *A Philosophy of Music Education*. 2nd ed. Englewood Cliffs, N.J.: Prentice-Hall, 1989.
**FPA**

————. "A Radical View of the Present and Future of Music Education." In *Symposium in Music Education: A Festschrift for Charles Leonhard*, ed. Richard J. Colwell, 3-22. Urbana-Champaign: University of Illinois, 1982.
**CI, FPA**

————. "Toward a Philosophical Foundation for Music Education Research." In *Handbook of Research on Music Teaching and Learning*, ed. Richard J. Colwell, 21-37. New York: Schirmer Books, 1992.
**FPA, R**

————. "What Knowledge Is of Most Worth in the Arts?" In *The Arts, Education, and Aesthetic Knowing: 91st Yearbook of the National Society for the Study of Education (Part II)*, ed. Bennett Reimer and Ralph A. Smith, 20-50. Chicago: University of Chicago Press, 1992.
**A, CI, FPA, P**

Reimer, Bennett, and Jeffrey E. Wright, eds. *On the Nature of Musical Experience*. Niwot: University Press of Colorado, 1992.
**FPA**

Reimer, Bennett, and Ralph A. Smith, eds. *The Arts, Education, and Aesthetic Knowing: 91st Yearbook of the National Society for the Study of Education (Part II)*. Chicago: National Society for the Study of Education, 1992.
**A, BR, CI, FPA, P**

Richards, Mary Helen. *Aesthetic Foundations for Thinking Rethought*. Portola Valley, Calif.: Richards Institute, 1984.
**CI, FPA**

Richardson, Carol, and Peter R. Webster. "Thoughts About Children's Thinking in Music: Implications for Policy." In *Policy Issues in Music Education: A Report of the Proceedings of the Robert Petzold Symposium*, ed. Gerald Olson, Anthony L. Barresi, and David Nelson, 114-28. Madison: School of Music, University of Wisconsin, 1991.
**FPA**

Rochlitz, Rainer. "Language for One, Language for All: Adorno and Modernism." In *Perspectives on Musical Aesthetics*, ed. John Rahn, 21-39. New York: Norton, 1994.
**FPA, P**

Ross, James. "Musical Standards as Function of Musical Accomplishment." In *The Interpretation of Music: Philosophical Essays*, ed. Michael Krausz, 89-102. New York: Oxford University Press, 1992.
**FPA**

Ross, Malcolm. "The Arts and Personal Growth." In *The Arts and Personal Growth*, ed. Malcolm Ross, 96-119. New York: Pergamon, 1980.
**A, CI, FPA**

————. "Knowing Face to Face: Towards Mature Aesthetic Encountering." In *The Development of Aesthetic Experience*, ed. Malcolm Ross, 78-91. New York: Pergamon, 1982.
**A, FPA**

————. "The Last Twenty-Five Years: The Arts in Education, 1963-1988." In *The Claims of Feeling: Readings in Aesthetic Education*, ed. Malcolm Ross, 3-23. Philadelphia: Falmer, 1989.
**A, FPA**

————. "You Are the Music." In *The Aesthetic Imperative: Relevance and Responsibility in Arts Education*, ed. Malcolm Ross, 147-72. New York: Pergamon, 1981.
**A, FPA**

————, ed. *The Aesthetic Imperative: Relevance and Responsibility in Arts Education.* New York: Pergamon, 1981.
**A, CI, FPA, RSC**

————, ed. *The Aesthetic in Education.* New York: Pergamon, 1985.
**A, CI, FPA**

————, ed. *The Arts and Personal Growth.* New York: Pergamon, 1980.
**A, FPA, RSC**

_____, ed. *The Arts: A Way of Knowing.* New York: Pergamon, 1983.
**A, FPA, RSC**

_____, ed. *The Claims of Feeling: Readings in Aesthetic Education.* Philadelphia: Falmer, 1989.
**A, CI, FPA, RSC**

_____, ed. *The Development of Aesthetic Experience.* New York: Pergamon, 1982.
**A, CI, FPA, RSC**

Rossman, R. Louis. *The Business of Administration and Supervision in Music: A Selective Annotated Bibliography.* Sioux City, Iowa: Dabec Educational Products, 1989.
**BR, CI, FPA**

Rowell, Lewis Eugene. *Thinking about Music: An Introduction to the Philosophy of Music.* Amherst: University of Massachusetts Press, 1983.
**FPA**

Rubinstein, Michael. *Music to My Ear: Reflections on Music and Digressions on Metaphysics.* London: Quartet, 1985.
**FPA, P**

Said, Edward W. *Musical Elaborations.* New York: Columbia University Press, 1991.
**FPA**

Schafer, R. Murray. *The Soundscape: Our Sonic Environment and the Tuning of the World.* 1977. Reprint, Rochester, Vt.: Destiny Books, 1994.
**CI, FPA, P**

Scheffler, Israel. *Reason and Teaching.* 1973. Reprint, Indianapolis: Hackett, 1989.
**CI, FPA**

Schoen, Max. *Art and Beauty.* New York: Macmillan, 1932.
**A, FPA**

_____. *The Beautiful in Music.* London: K. Paul Trubner, 1928.
**FPA**

_____. *The Enjoyment of the Arts.* 1944. Reprint, Freeport, N.Y.: Books for Libraries, 1971.
**A, FPA**

_____. *The Understanding of Music.* 1945. Reprint, Ann Arbor, Mich.: University Microfilms, 1962.
**FPA, P**

*School Music Program: Description and Standards.* 2nd ed. Reston, Va.: Music Educators National Conference, 1986.
**CI, FPA**

Schwadron, Abraham A. *Aesthetics: Dimensions for Music Education.* Washington: Music Educators National Conference, 1967.
**CI, FPA**

————. "Comparative Music Aesthetics and Education: Observations in Speculation." In *Music Education for Tomorrow's Society*, ed. Arthur Motycka, 21-29. Jamestown, R.I.: GAMT Music, 1976.
**CI, FPA**

————. "Of Conceptions, Misconceptions, and Aesthetic Commitment." In *Music Education in the United States: Contemporary Issues*, ed. J. Terry Gates, 85-110. Tuscaloosa: University of Alabama Press, 1988.
**FPA**

Schwartz, Delmore. "Poetry as Imitation." In *Perspectives on Musical Aesthetics*, ed. John Rahn, 297-301. New York: Norton, 1994.
**A, FPA**

Schwartz, Herbert. "Music and Emotion." In *Perspectives on Musical Aesthetics*, ed. John Rahn, 293-96. New York: Norton, 1994.
**FPA, P**

Scruton, Roger. "Notes on the Meaning of Music." In *The Interpretation of Music: Philosophical Essays*, ed. Michael Krausz, 193-202. New York: Oxford University Press, 1992.
**FPA**

Seashore, Carl Emil. *In Search of Beauty in Music: A Scientific Approach to Music Esthetics.* 1947. Reprint, Westport, Conn.: Greenwood, 1981.
**FPA, P**

————. *Why We Love Music.* Philadelphia: Oliver Ditson, 1941.
**FPA, P**

Sesonske, Alexander. *What Is Art? Aesthetic Theory from Plato to Tolstoy.* New York: Oxford University Press, 1965.
**A, FPA**

Sessions, Roger. *The Musical Experience of Composer, Performer, Listener.* Princeton, N.J.: Princeton University Press, 1950, 1974.
**FPA, P**

Shepherd, John. "The 'Meaning' of Music." In *Whose Music? A Sociology of Musical Languages*, ed. John Shepherd, Phil Virden, Graham Vulliamy, and Trevor Wishart, 53-68. London: Latimer, 1977.
**FPA**

————. "Media, Social Process and Music." In *Whose Music? A Sociology of Musical Languages*, ed. John Shepherd, Phil Virden, Graham Vulliamy, and Trevor Wishart, 7-51. London: Latimer, 1977.
**FPA, P**

————. "Music and Male Hegemony." In *Music and Society: The Politics of Composition, Performance, and Reception*, ed. Richard D. Leppert and Susan McClary, 151-72. New York: Cambridge University Press, 1987.
**FPA, P**

————. "The Musical Coding of Ideologies." In *Whose Music? A Sociology of Musical Languages*, ed. John Shepherd, Phil Virden, Graham Vulliamy, and Trevor Wishart, 69-124. London: Latimer, 1977.
**FPA, P**

Shepherd, John, Phil Virden, Graham Vulliamy, and Trevor Wishart, eds. *Whose Music? A Sociology of Musical Languages.* London: Latimer, 1977.
**FPA, P**

Shetler, Donald J. "This Trip Was Really Necessary." In *Music Education for Tomorrow's Society*, ed. Arthur Motycka, 30-39. Jamestown, R.I.: GAMT Music, 1976.
**FPA**

————, ed. *The Future of Musical Education in America: Proceedings of the July 1983 Conference.* Rochester, N.Y.: Eastman School of Music Press, 1984.
**CI, FPA, RSC**

Sibley, Frank. "Making Music Our Own." In *The Interpretation of Music: Philosophical Essays*, ed. Michael Krausz, 165-76. New York: Oxford University Press, 1992.
**FPA, P**

Siegmeister, Elie. *Music and Society.* 1938. Reprint, New York: Haskell House, 1974.
**FPA, P**

Simonton, Dean Keith. "Aesthetics, Biography, and History in Musical Creativity." In *Documentary Report of the Ann Arbor Symposium on the Applications of Psychology to the Teaching and Learning of Music: Motivation and Creativity (Session III)*, 41-48. Reston, Va.: Music Educators National Conference, 1983.
**FPA, P**

Simpson, Alan. "Utilitarianism, the Arts and Education." In *The Aesthetic in Education*, ed. Malcolm Ross, 187-212. New York: Pergamon, 1985.
**A, CI, FPA**

Simpson, Kenneth, ed. *Some Great Music Educators: A Collection of Essays.* Borough Green, Kent, England: Novello, 1976.
**CI, FPA**

Sinor, Jean. "Policy Development in Arts Education for Early Childhood Programs." In *Policy Issues in Music Education: A Report of the Proceedings of the Robert Petzold Symposium*, ed. Gerald Olson, Anthony L. Barresi, and David Nelson, 92-106. Madison: School of Music, University of Wisconsin, 1991.
**A, CI, FPA**

Sloboda, John A. "Music as a Language." In *Music and Child Development: The Biology of Music Making - Proceedings of the 1987 Denver Conference*, ed. Frank R. Wilson and Franz L. Roehmann, 28-43. St. Louis, Mo.: MMB Music, 1990.
**FPA, P**

Smith, C. M. "The Aesthetics of John Dewey and Aesthetic Education." In *Aesthetics and Problems of Education*, ed. Ralph A. Smith, 64-85. Urbana: University of Illinois Press, 1971.
**A, CI, FPA**

Smith, F. Joseph. "Music Educating as Phenomenologist: An Overview." In *Music Education for Tomorrow's Society*, ed. Arthur Motycka, 73-83. Jamestown, R.I.: GAMT Music, 1976.
**FPA, P**

Smith, Louis M., and Sally Schumacher. *Extended Pilot Trials of the Aesthetic Education Program: A Qualitative Analysis and Evaluation.* St. Louis, Mo.: CEMREL, 1972.
**A, CI, FPA**

Smith, Ralph A. "Aesthetic Criticism: The Method of Aesthetic Education." In *Aesthetics and Problems of Education*, ed. Ralph A. Smith, 473-84. Urbana: University of Illinois Press, 1971.
**A, CI, FPA**

————. "Is Teaching an Art?" In *Aesthetics and Problems of Education*, ed. Ralph A. Smith, 564-69. Urbana: University of Illinois Press, 1971.
**A, CI, FPA**

————. "The Philosophical Literature of Aesthetic Education." In *Toward an Aesthetic Education: A Report*, 137-69. Washington: Music Educators National Conference, 1971.
**A, CI, FPA**

_____. "Toward Percipience: A Humanities Curriculum for Arts Education." In *The Arts, Education, and Aesthetic Knowing: 91st Yearbook of the National Society for the Study of Education (Part II)*, ed. Bennett Reimer and Ralph A. Smith, 51-69. Chicago: University of Chicago Press, 1992.
**A, CI, FPA**

_____. "Trends and Issues in Policy-Making for Arts Education." In *Handbook of Research on Music Teaching and Learning*, ed. Richard J. Colwell, 749-59. New York: Schirmer Books, 1992.
**A, CI, FPA, R**

_____, ed. *Aesthetics and Problems of Education*. Urbana: University of Illinois Press, 1971.
**A, CI, FPA**

Smith, Ralph A., and C. M. Smith. "Justifying Aesthetic Education." In *Aesthetics and Problems of Education*, ed. Ralph A. Smith, 126-43. Urbana: University of Illinois Press, 1971.
**A, CI, FPA**

Smith, Ralph A., and Alan Simpson, eds. *Aesthetics and Arts Education*. Urbana: University of Illinois Press, 1991.
**A, CI, FPA**

*Sourcebook for Futures Planning*. Reston, Va.: National Association of Schools of Music, 1990.
**BR, FPA**

Sparshott, F. E. "The Unity of Aesthetic Education." In *Aesthetics and Problems of Education*, ed. Ralph A. Smith, 243-57. Urbana: University of Illinois Press, 1971.
**A, CI, FPA**

Squire, Russel N. *Introduction to Music Education*. New York: Ronald, 1952.
**CI, FPA**

Standifer, James A. "Policy Development in Multicultural Arts Education." In *Policy Issues in Music Education: A Report of the Proceedings of the Robert Petzold Symposium*, ed. Gerald Olson, Anthony L. Barresi, and David Nelson, 61-71. Madison: School of Music, University of Wisconsin, 1991.
**A, CI, FPA**

Storr, Anthony. *Music and the Mind*. New York: Maxwell Macmillan International, 1992.
**FPA, P**

Stubley, Eleanor V. "Philosophical Foundations." In *Handbook of Research on Music Teaching and Learning*, ed. Richard J. Colwell, 3-20. New York: Schirmer Books, 1992.
**FPA, R**

Subotnick, Morton. "The Music and Musicians of the Future." In *Toward Tomorrow: New Visions for General Music*, ed. Sandra L. Stauffer, 31-42. Reston, Va.: Music Educators National Conference, 1995.
**FPA**

Sullivan, Anita. *The Seventh Dragon: The Riddle of Equal Temperament.* Lake Oswego, Ore.: Metamorphous, 1985.
**FPA, P**

Sunderman, Lloyd Frederick. *Historical Foundations of Music Education in the United States.* Metuchen, N.J.: Scarecrow, 1971.
**CI, FPA**

Suzuki, Shinichi. *Nurtured by Love.* 2nd ed. New York: Exposition, 1983.
**CI, FPA**

Swanwick, Keith. *A Basis for Music Education.* Windsor, Ontario: NFER, 1979.
**FPA**

————. *Musical Knowledge: Intuition, Analysis, and Music Education.* New York: Routledge, 1994.
**CI, FPA, P**

Tait, Malcolm John. "Further Reflections on the Language Connection." In *Music Education in the United States: Contemporary Issues*, ed. J. Terry Gates, 156-67. Tuscaloosa: University of Alabama Press, 1988.
**FPA, P**

Tait, Malcolm John, and Paul Haack. *Principles and Processes of Music Education: New Perspectives.* New York: Teachers College, 1984.
**CI, FPA**

Tame, David. *The Secret Power of Music.* New York: Destiny Books, 1984.
**FPA, P**

Taylor, Dorothy. "Aesthetic Development in Music." In *The Development of Aesthetic Experience*, ed. Malcolm Ross, 94-109. New York: Pergamon, 1982.
**A, CI, FPA**

Taylor, Fannie, and Anthony L. Barresi. *The Arts at a New Frontier: The National Endowment for the Arts.* New York: Plenum, 1984.
**A, FPA**

Taylor, Harold. "The Arts in a Democracy." In *Artistic Intelligences: Implications for Education*, ed. William J. Moody, 3-10. New York: Teachers College, 1990.
**A, FPA**

*Teacher's Guide for Advocacy.* Reston, Va.: Music Educators National Conference, 1992.
**BR, FPA**

Tellstrom, A. Theodore. *Music in American Education: Past and Present.* New York: Holt, Rinehart, and Winston, 1971.
**CI, FPA**

Tenney, James. *A History of* "Consonance" and "Dissonance." New York: Excelsior, 1988.
**FPA, P**

Tolstoy, Leo. *What Is Art?* Ed. W. Gareth Jones, transl. Aylmer Maude. 1898. Reprint, London: Bristol Classical, 1994.
**A, FPA**

Tonkin, Humphrey. "Sound, Meaning, and Sanity." In *The Crane Symposium: Toward an Understanding of the Teaching and Learning of Music Performance*, ed. Charles Fowler, 21-24. Potsdam: Potsdam College of the State University of New York, 1988.
**FPA, P**

*Toward an Aesthetic Education: A Report.* Washington: Music Educators National Conference, 1971.
**A, CI, FPA, RSC**

Tweddell, Paul. "The Professional Development of Arts Teachers." In *The Claims of Feeling: Readings in Aesthetic Education*, ed. Malcolm Ross, 167-99. Philadelphia: Falmer, 1989.
**A, CI, FPA**

Urmson, J. O. "The Ethics of Musical Performance." In *The Interpretation of Music: Philosophical Essays*, ed. Michael Krausz, 157-64. New York: Oxford University Press, 1992.
**FPA**

Virden, Phil, and Trevor Wishart. "Some Observations on the Social Stratification of Twentieth-Century Music." In *Whose Music? A Sociology of Musical Languages*, ed. John Shepherd, Phil Virden, Graham Vulliamy, and Trevor Wishart, 155-77. London: Latimer, 1977.
**FPA, P**

*Vision for Arts Education in the 21st Century.* Reston, Va.: Music Educators National Conference, 1994.

**A, CI, FPA**

Vulliamy, Graham. "Music and the Mass Culture Debate." In *Whose Music? A Sociology of Musical Languages*, ed. John Shepherd, Phil Virden, Graham Vulliamy, and Trevor Wishart, 179-200. London: Latimer, 1977.

**FPA, P**

————. "Music as a Case Study in the 'New Sociology of Education'." In *Whose Music? A Sociology of Musical Languages*, ed. John Shepherd, Phil Virden, Graham Vulliamy, and Trevor Wishart, 201-32. London: Latimer, 1977.

**FPA, P**

Waikart, Kitty. "A Nuts-and-Bolts Plan for Parents." In *Perspectives on Implementation: Arts Education Standards for America's Students*, ed. Bruce O. Boston, 55-62. Reston, Va.: Music Educators National Conference, 1994.

**A, CI, FPA**

Walker, Darwin E. *Teaching Music: Managing the Successful Music Program.* New York: Schirmer Books, 1989.

**CI, FPA**

Walker, Robert. *Music Education: Tradition and Innovation.* Springfield, Ill.: Thomas, 1984.

**CI, FPA**

————. *Musical Beliefs: Psychoacoustic, Mythical, and Educational Perspectives.* New York: Teachers College, 1990.

**FPA, P**

Walton, Kendall. "Understanding Humour and Understanding Music." In *The Interpretation of Music: Philosophical Essays*, ed. Michael Krausz, 259-69. New York: Oxford University Press, 1992.

**FPA, P**

Warnock, M. "Imagination." In *The Arts: A Way of Knowing*, ed. Malcolm Ross, 73-83. New York: Pergamon, 1983.

**A, FPA**

Weitz, Morris. "Research on the Arts and in Aesthetics: Some Pitfalls, Some Possibilities." In *Arts and Aesthetics: An Agenda for the Future*, ed. Stanley S. Madeja, 223-28. St. Louis, Mo.: CEMREL, 1977.

**A, FPA, R**

Wheeler, D. K. "Aesthetic Education and Curriculum." In *Aesthetics and Problems of Education*, ed. Ralph A. Smith, 320-44. Urbana: University of Illinois Press, 1971.
**A, CI, FPA**

Whipple, Guy Montrose, ed. *Music Education: 35th Yearbook of the National Society for the Study of Education (Part II)*. Bloomington, Ill.: Public School Publishing, 1936.
**BR, CI, FPA, P**

Whitehead, Alfred North. *The Aims of Education, and Other Essays*. 1929. Reprint, New York: Free Press, 1967.
**CI, FPA, P**

Winn, Cyril. *Teaching Music*. New York: Oxford Univerity Press, 1954.
**CI, FPA**

Wishart, Trevor. "Musical Writing, Musical Speaking." In *Whose Music? A Sociology of Musical Languages*, ed. John Shepherd, Phil Virden, Graham Vulliamy, and Trevor Wishart, 125-53. London: Latimer, 1977.
**FPA, P**

————. "On Radical Culture." In *Whose Music? A Sociology of Musical Languages*, ed. John Shepherd, Phil Virden, Graham Vulliamy, and Trevor Wishart, 233-56. London: Latimer, 1977.
**FPA**

Witkin, Robert W. "The Concept of 'Development' in Aesthetic Education." In *The Development of Aesthetic Experience*, ed. Malcolm Ross, 67-77. New York: Pergamon, 1982.
**A, CI, FPA**

————. "Expressivist Theories of Art and Ideologies of Arts Education." In *The Claims of Feeling: Readings in Aesthetic Education*, ed. Malcolm Ross, 24-36. Philadelphia: Falmer, 1989.
**A, FPA**

Wolff, Janet. "Questioning the Curriculum: Arts, Education and Ideology." In *The Aesthetic in Education*, ed. Malcolm Ross, 213-30. New York: Pergamon, 1985.
**A, CI, FPA**

Xenakis, Iannis. "Creativity." In *Perspectives on Musical Aesthetics*, ed. John Rahn, 158-64. New York: Norton, 1994.
**FPA, P**

Zuckerkandl, Victor. *Sound and Symbol: Music and the External World.* Transl. Willard R. Trask. Princeton, N.J.: Princeton University Press, 1969.
  **FPA**

# (J)

## JOURNALS

*American Educational Research Journal.* Washington: American Educational Research Association, 1964-.
  **CI, J, R**

Arneson, Arne Jon. *Music Educators Journal: Cumulative Index 1914-1987: Including Music Supervisors' Bulletin and Music Supervisors' Journal.* Stevens Point, Wisc.: Index House, 1987.
  **BR, J**

*British Journal of Aesthetics.* London: Oxford University Press, 1960-.
  **A, FPA, J, R**

*British Journal of Music Education.* Cambridge: Cambridge University Press, 1984-.
  **CI, J, P, R**

Buckwell, Patricia J. "Journal of Music Therapy." In *International Music Journals*, ed. Linda M. Fidler and Richard S. James, 198-200. New York: Greenwood, 1990.
  **J, P, R**

*Bulletin of Historical Research in Music Education.* Lawrence: University of Kansas Department of Art and Music Education and Music Therapy, 1980-.
  **FPA, J, R**

Byler, Robert. "Coda." In *International Music Journals*, ed. Linda M. Fidler and Richard S. James, 87-90. New York: Greenwood, 1990.
  **J**

————. "Jazz Journal International." In *International Music Journals*, ed. Linda M. Fidler and Richard S. James, 181-84. New York: Greenwood, 1990.
  **CI, J**

_____. "Journal of Jazz Studies." In *International Music Journals*, ed. Linda M. Fidler and Richard S. James, 193-95. New York: Greenwood, 1990.

**CI, J**

*Canadian Music Educator.* St. Catherines, Ontario: Canadian Music Educators' Association, 1959-.

**CI, J, P, R**

*Cognition and Emotion.* Hove, East Sussex, England: Erlbaum Associates, 1987-.

**J, P, R**

*Cognition: International Journal of Cognitive Psychology.* New York: Elsevier Science, 1972-.

**J, P, R**

Corrigan, Vincent J. "The Opera Quarterly." In *International Music Journals*, ed. Linda M. Fidler and Richard S. James, 465-66. New York: Greenwood, 1990.

**J, R**

*Design for Arts in Education.* Washington: Heldref, 1899-.

**A, CI, FPA, J**

Eder, Terry E. "The Choral Journal." In *International Music Journals*, ed. Linda M. Fidler and Richard S. James, 83-85. New York: Greenwood, 1990.

**CI, J**

*Educational Leaderhip.* Washington: Association for Supervision and Curriculum Development, 1943-.

**CI, J**

Ellsworth, E. Victor. "American String Teacher." In *International Music Journals*, ed. Linda M. Fidler and Richard S. James, 29-31. New York: Greenwood, 1990.

**CI, J**

_____. "Guitar Player." In *International Music Journals*, ed. Linda M. Fidler and Richard S. James, 152-53. New York: Greenwood, 1990.

**CI, J**

_____. "International Society of Bassists Journal." In *International Music Journals*, ed. Linda M. Fidler and Richard S. James, 174-76. New York: Greenwood, 1990.

**CI, J**

————. "Strad." In *International Music Journals*, ed. Linda M. Fidler and Richard S. James, 408-09. New York: Greenwood, 1990.
**CI, J**

Fidler, Linda M. "Black Music Research Journal." In *International Music Journals*, ed. Linda M. Fidler and Richard S. James, 55-57. New York: Greenwood, 1990.
**J, R**

Fidler, Linda M., and Richard S. James. "Jazz Index." In *International Music Journals*, ed. Linda M. Fidler and Richard S. James, 474-75. New York: Greenwood, 1990.
**BR, CI, J**

————. "Music Article Guide." In *International Music Journals*, ed. Linda M. Fidler and Richard S. James, 476. New York: Greenwood, 1990.
**BR, J**

————. "Music Index." In *International Music Journals*, ed. Linda M. Fidler and Richard S. James, 477-78. New York: Greenwood, 1990.
**BR, J**

————. "Popular Music Periodicals Index." In *International Music Journals*, ed. Linda M. Fidler and Richard S. James, 479. New York: Greenwood, 1990.
**BR, J**

————. "RILM Abstracts." In *International Music Journals*, ed. Linda M. Fidler and Richard S. James, 480. New York: Greenwood, 1990.
**BR, J**

————, eds. *International Music Journals*. New York: Greenwood, 1990.
**BR, J**

*General Music Today*. Reston, Va.: Music Educators National Conference, 1987-.
**CI, J**

Ginsburg, David D. "Popular Music and Society." In *International Music Journals*, ed. Linda M. Fidler and Richard S. James, 346-48. New York: Greenwood, 1990.
**J, P, R**

Hunt, Paul B. "Brass Bulletin." In *International Music Journals*, ed. Linda M. Fidler and Richard S. James, 62-63. New York: Greenwood, 1990.
**CI, J**

————. "Brass Quarterly/Brass and Woodwind Quarterly." In *International Music Journals*, ed. Linda M. Fidler and Richard S. James, 63-65. New York: Greenwood, 1990.
**CI, J**

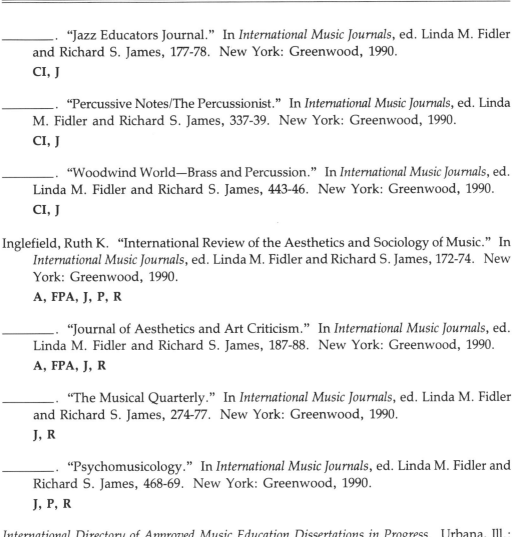

_____. "Jazz Educators Journal." In *International Music Journals*, ed. Linda M. Fidler and Richard S. James, 177-78. New York: Greenwood, 1990.
**CI, J**

_____. "Percussive Notes/The Percussionist." In *International Music Journals*, ed. Linda M. Fidler and Richard S. James, 337-39. New York: Greenwood, 1990.
**CI, J**

_____. "Woodwind World—Brass and Percussion." In *International Music Journals*, ed. Linda M. Fidler and Richard S. James, 443-46. New York: Greenwood, 1990.
**CI, J**

Inglefield, Ruth K. "International Review of the Aesthetics and Sociology of Music." In *International Music Journals*, ed. Linda M. Fidler and Richard S. James, 172-74. New York: Greenwood, 1990.
**A, FPA, J, P, R**

_____. "Journal of Aesthetics and Art Criticism." In *International Music Journals*, ed. Linda M. Fidler and Richard S. James, 187-88. New York: Greenwood, 1990.
**A, FPA, J, R**

_____. "The Musical Quarterly." In *International Music Journals*, ed. Linda M. Fidler and Richard S. James, 274-77. New York: Greenwood, 1990.
**J, R**

_____. "Psychomusicology." In *International Music Journals*, ed. Linda M. Fidler and Richard S. James, 468-69. New York: Greenwood, 1990.
**J, P, R**

*International Directory of Approved Music Education Dissertations in Progress.* Urbana, Ill.: Council for Research in Music Education, 1989-.
**BR, J, R**

*International Journal of Behavioral Development.* London, England: Erlbaum Associates, 1978-.
**J, P, R**

*International Journal of Music Education.* Huddersfield, England: International Society for Music Education, 1983-.
**CI, FPA, J, P, R**

James, Richard S. "American Music." In *International Music Journals*, ed. Linda M. Fidler and Richard S. James, 458-60. New York: Greenwood, 1990.
**J, R**

Jones, L. JaFran. "Yearbook for Traditional Music." In *International Music Journals*, ed. Linda M. Fidler and Richard S. James, 449-51. New York: Greenwood, 1990.
**J, R**

*Journal of Aesthetic Education.* Urbana: University of Illinois Press, 1966-.
**A, CI, FPA, J, R**

*Journal of Educational Psychology.* Washington: American Psychological Association, 1910-.
**CI, J, P, R**

*Journal of Educational Research.* Washington: Heldref, 1920-.
**CI, J, R**

*Journal of Experimental Psychology: General.* Washington: American Psychological Association, 1975-.
**J, P, R**

*Journal of Experimental Psychology: Human Perception and Performance.* Washington: American Psychological Association, 1975-.
**J, P, R**

*Journal of Experimental Psychology: Learning, Memory and Cognition.* Washington: American Psychological Association, 1975-.
**J, P, R**

*Journal of Music Teacher Education.* Reston, Va.: Music Educators National Conference, 1991-.
**CI, J, R**

*Journal of the Acoustical Society of America.* New York: American Institute of Physics for the Acoustical Society of America, 1929-.
**J, P, R**

Kantorski, Vincent J. "The Council for Research in Music Education Bulletin." In *International Music Journals*, ed. Linda M. Fidler and Richard S. James, 100-02. New York: Greenwood, 1990.
**CI, FPA, J, P, R**

————. "Instrumentalist." In *International Music Journals*, ed. Linda M. Fidler and Richard S. James, 166-68. New York: Greenwood, 1990.
**CI, J**

————. "Journal of Band Research." In *International Music Journals*, ed. Linda M. Fidler and Richard S. James, 189-90. New York: Greenwood, 1990.
**CI, J, R**

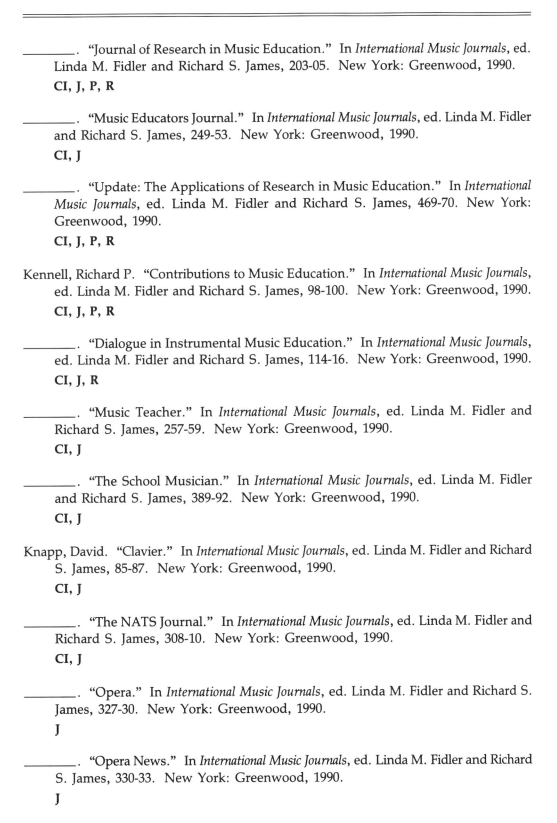

————. "Journal of Research in Music Education." In *International Music Journals*, ed. Linda M. Fidler and Richard S. James, 203-05. New York: Greenwood, 1990.

**CI, J, P, R**

————. "Music Educators Journal." In *International Music Journals*, ed. Linda M. Fidler and Richard S. James, 249-53. New York: Greenwood, 1990.

**CI, J**

————. "Update: The Applications of Research in Music Education." In *International Music Journals*, ed. Linda M. Fidler and Richard S. James, 469-70. New York: Greenwood, 1990.

**CI, J, P, R**

Kennell, Richard P. "Contributions to Music Education." In *International Music Journals*, ed. Linda M. Fidler and Richard S. James, 98-100. New York: Greenwood, 1990.

**CI, J, P, R**

————. "Dialogue in Instrumental Music Education." In *International Music Journals*, ed. Linda M. Fidler and Richard S. James, 114-16. New York: Greenwood, 1990.

**CI, J, R**

————. "Music Teacher." In *International Music Journals*, ed. Linda M. Fidler and Richard S. James, 257-59. New York: Greenwood, 1990.

**CI, J**

————. "The School Musician." In *International Music Journals*, ed. Linda M. Fidler and Richard S. James, 389-92. New York: Greenwood, 1990.

**CI, J**

Knapp, David. "Clavier." In *International Music Journals*, ed. Linda M. Fidler and Richard S. James, 85-87. New York: Greenwood, 1990.

**CI, J**

————. "The NATS Journal." In *International Music Journals*, ed. Linda M. Fidler and Richard S. James, 308-10. New York: Greenwood, 1990.

**CI, J**

————. "Opera." In *International Music Journals*, ed. Linda M. Fidler and Richard S. James, 327-30. New York: Greenwood, 1990.

**J**

————. "Opera News." In *International Music Journals*, ed. Linda M. Fidler and Richard S. James, 330-33. New York: Greenwood, 1990.

**J**

_____. "The Piano Quarterly." In *International Music Journals*, ed. Linda M. Fidler and Richard S. James, 342-46. New York: Greenwood, 1990.

**CI, J**

Knowles, Rosalind. "American Choral Review." In *International Music Journals*, ed. Linda M. Fidler and Richard S. James, 14-16. New York: Greenwood, 1990.

**CI, J, R**

Kratus, John K. "American Music Teacher." In *International Music Journals*, ed. Linda M. Fidler and Richard S. James, 18-22. New York: Greenwood, 1990.

**CI, J**

_____. "College Music Symposium." In *International Music Journals*, ed. Linda M. Fidler and Richard S. James, 90-93. New York: Greenwood, 1990.

**CI, J, P, R**

_____. "Music Perception." In *International Music Journals*, ed. Linda M. Fidler and Richard S. James, 464-65. New York: Greenwood, 1990.

**J, P, R**

_____. "The Musician." In *International Music Journals*, ed. Linda M. Fidler and Richard S. James, 281-84. New York: Greenwood, 1990.

**J**

_____. "Psychology of Music." In *International Music Journals*, ed. Linda M. Fidler and Richard S. James, 348-51. New York: Greenwood, 1990.

**J, P, R**

Mast, Paul B. "Journal of Music Theory." In *International Music Journals*, ed. Linda M. Fidler and Richard S. James, 195-98. New York: Greenwood, 1990.

**CI, J, R**

_____. "Perspectives of New Music." In *International Music Journals*, ed. Linda M. Fidler and Richard S. James, 339-42. New York: Greenwood, 1990.

**J, R**

*Missouri Journal of Research in Music Education.* Jefferson City: Missouri State Department of Education, 1962-.

**CI, J, P, R**

*Music Psychology Index.* Vol. 2. Ed. Charles T. Eagle, Jr. Denton, Tex.: Institute for Therapeutics Research, 1978.

**BR, J, P, R**

*Music Psychology Index.* Vol. 3. Ed. Charles T. Eagle, Jr., and John J. Miniter. Phoenix, Ariz.: Oryx, 1984.

**BR, J, P, R**

*Music Therapy Index.* Vol. 1. Ed. Charles T. Eagle, Jr. Lawrence, Kans.: National Association for Music Therapy, 1976.

**BR, J, P, R**

*Phi Delta Kappan.* Bloomington, Ind.: Phi Delta Kappa, 1915-.

**CI, J**

*Philosophy of Music Education Review.* Bloomington: Indiana University School of Music, 1993-.

**FPA, J, R**

*Quarterly Journal of Music Teaching and Learning.* Greeley: University of Northern Colorado School of Music, 1990-.

**CI, FPA, J, P, R**

*Review of Educational Research.* Washington: American Educational Research Association, 1931-.

**CI, J, R**

Riis, Thomas L. "Black Perspective in Music." In *International Music Journals*, ed. Linda M. Fidler and Richard S. James, 57-59. New York: Greenwood, 1990.

**J, R**

Robinson, Doris. *Music and Dance Periodicals: An International Directory and Guidebook.* Voorheesville, N.Y.: Peri, 1989.

**A, BR, J**

Schurk, William L. "Recorded Sound." In *International Music Journals*, ed. Linda M. Fidler and Richard S. James, 360-62. New York: Greenwood, 1990.

**BR, J, R**

Shrude, Marilyn. "Source: Music of the Avant Garde." In *International Music Journals*, ed. Linda M. Fidler and Richard S. James, 401-03. New York: Greenwood, 1990.

**BR, J**

*Southeastern Journal of Music Education.* Athens: University of Georgia Center for Continuing Education, 1990-.

**CI, J, P, R**

Steel, Matthew. "Symphony News/Symphony Magazine." In *International Music Journals*, ed. Linda M. Fidler and Richard S. James, 422-25. New York: Greenwood, 1990.
**J**

Watanabe, Ruth. "Notes: The Quarterly Journal of the Music Library Association." In *International Music Journals*, ed. Linda M. Fidler and Richard S. James, 319-22. New York: Greenwood, 1990.
**BR, J, R**

Weichlein, William Jesset. *A Checklist of American Music Periodicals, 1850-1900.* Detroit, Mich.: Information Coordinators, 1970.
**BR, J**

# (P)

## PSYCHOLOGY

Abeles, Harold F. "Responses to Music." In *Handbook of Music Psychology*, ed. Donald A. Hodges, 105-40. Lawrence, Kans.: National Association for Music Therapy, 1980.
**P**

Aiello, Rita, and John A. Sloboda, eds. *Musical Perceptions.* New York: Oxford University Press, 1994.
**FPA, P**

Airasian, Peter. "The Impact of the Taxonomy on Testing and Evaluation." In *Bloom's Taxonomy—A Forty-Year Retrospective: 93rd Yearbook of the National Society for the Study of Education (Part II)*, ed. Lorin W. Anderson and Lauren A. Sosniak, 82-102. Chicago: University of Chicago Press, 1994.
**CI, P**

Alvarez, Barbara. "Musical Thinking and the Young Child." In *Dimensions of Musical Thinking*, ed. Eunice Boardman, 57-64. Reston, Va.: Music Educators National Conference, 1989.
**CI, P**

Alvin, Juliette. *Music Therapy.* Rev. ed. London: John Clare Books, 1983.
**P**

Anderson, Lorin W., and Lauren A. Sosniak, eds. *Bloom's Taxonomy—A Forty-Year Retrospective: 93rd Yearbook of the National Society for the Study of Education (Part II).* Chicago: National Society for the Study of Education, 1994.
**BR, CI, FPA, P**

Apfelstadt, Hilary. "Musical Thinking in the Choral Rehearsal." In *Dimensions of Musical Thinking*, ed. Eunice Boardman, 73-81. Reston, Va.: Music Educators National Conference, 1989.
**CI, P**

Armstrong, Thomas. *Multiple Intelligences in the Classroom.* Alexandria, Va.: Association for Supervision and Curriculum Development, 1994.
**CI, P**

Askill, John. *Physics of Musical Sounds.* New York: D. Van Nostrand, 1979.
**P**

Asmus, Edward P., Jr., ed. *Proceedings of the Research Symposium on the Psychology and Acoustics of Music, 1978.* Lawrence: University of Kansas Department of Art and Music Education and Music Therapy, 1978.
**P, R**

_____, ed. *Psychology and Acoustics of Music: A Collection of Papers.* Lawrence: University of Kansas Department of Art and Music Education and Music Therapy, 1977.
**P, R, RSC**

Aspin, David. "Assessment and Education in the Arts." In *The Aesthetic Imperative: Relevance and Responsibility in Arts Education*, ed. Malcolm Ross, 25-52. New York: Pergamon, 1981.
**A, CI, FPA, P**

*Assessment of Community Education Programs in Music.* Reston, Va.: National Association of Schools of Music, 1988.
**BR, CI, P, RSC**

*Assessment of Graduate Programs in Music.* Reston, Va.: National Association of Schools of Music, 1985.
**BR, CI, P**

*Assessment of Undergraduate Programs in Music.* Reston, Va.: National Association of Schools of Music, 1991.
**BR, CI, P**

Backus, John W. *The Acoustical Foundations of Music.* 2nd ed. New York: Norton, 1977.
P

Baily, John. "Music Structure and Human Movement." In *Musical Structure and Cognition*, ed. Peter Howell, Ian Cross, and Robert West, 237-58. London: Academic Press, 1985.
P

————. "The Role of a Motor Grammar in Musical Performance." In *Music and Child Development: The Biology of Music Making - Proceedings of the 1987 Denver Conference*, ed. Frank R. Wilson and Franz L. Roehmann, 202-13. St. Louis, Mo.: MMB Music, 1990.
P

Ballantine, Christopher John. *Music and Its Social Meanings.* New York: Gordon and Breach, 1984.
FPA, P

Bamberger, Jeanne Shapiro. "Intuitive and Formal Musical Knowing: Parables of Cognitive Dissonance." In *The Arts, Cognition and Basic Skills*, ed. Stanley S. Madeja, 173-209. St. Louis, Mo.: CEMREL, 1978.
P

————. "The Mind Behind the Musical Ear." In *Music and Child Development: The Biology of Music Making - Proceedings of the 1987 Denver Conference*, ed. Frank R. Wilson and Franz L. Roehmann, 291-305. St. Louis, Mo.: MMB Music, 1990.
P

————, et al. *The Art of Listening: Developing Musical Perception.* 5th ed. New York: Harper and Row, 1988.
CI, P

Barbour, James Murray. *Tuning and Temperament: A Historical Survey.* 1951. Reprint, New York: Da Capo, 1972.
P

Barrett, Janet. "Core Thinking Skills in Music." In *Dimensions of Musical Thinking*, ed. Eunice Boardman, 45-56. Reston, Va.: Music Educators National Conference, 1989.
CI, P

Bartlett, Dale L. "Tonal and Musical Memory." In *Handbook of Music Psychology*, ed. Donald A. Hodges, 225-34. Lawrence, Kans.: National Association for Music Therapy, 1980.
P

*Basic Musical Functions and Musical Ability: Papers Given at a Seminar Arranged by the Royal Swedish Academy of Music.* 2nd ed. Stockholm: Royal Swedish Academy of Music, 1982.
P, RSC

Baumann, Max Peter, ed. *Music in the Dialogue of Cultures: Traditional Music and Cultural Policy.* New York: C. F. Peters, 1991.
CI, P

Beall, Gretchen Hieronymus. "Methodology and Music in General Education." In *Music Education in the United States: Contemporary Issues*, ed. J. Terry Gates, 202-23. Tuscaloosa: University of Alabama Press, 1988.
CI, FPA, P

————. "Music Education in Adolescence: A Problem in Perspectives." In *Symposium in Music Education: A Festschrift for Charles Leonhard*, ed. Richard J. Colwell, 61-92. Urbana-Champaign: University of Illinois, 1982.
CI, P

Benade, Arthur H. *Fundamentals of Musical Acoustics.* 1976. Reprint, New York: Dover, 1990.
P

Bentley, Arnold. *Measures of Musical Abilities.* London: Harrap, 1966.
P

————. *Musical Ability in Children and Its Measurement.* New York: October House, 1966.
P

Beranek, Leo Leroy. *Music, Acoustics, and Architecture.* 1962. Reprint, Huntington, N.Y.: R. E. Krieger, 1979.
P

Berendt, Joachim-Ernst. *The World Is Sound: Music and the Landscape of Consciousness.* Transl. H. Bredigkeit. New York: Harper and Row, 1991.
FPA, P

Berenson, F. M. "Interpreting the Emotional Content of Music." In *The Interpretation of Music: Philosophical Essays*, ed. Michael Krausz, 61-72. New York: Oxford University Press, 1992.
FPA, P

Berger, Arthur. "Music as Imitation." In *Perspectives on Musical Aesthetics*, ed. John Rahn, 302-12. New York: Norton, 1994.
A, FPA, P

Berlyne, D. E. *Aesthetics and Psychobiology*. New York: Appleton-Century-Crofts, 1971.
**A, FPA, P**

————, ed. *Studies in the New Experimental Aesthetics: Steps toward an Objective Psychology of Aesthetic Appreciation*. Washington: Hemisphere, 1974.
**A, FPA, P**

Bernstein, Leonard. *The Unanswered Question: Six Talks at Harvard*. Cambridge: Harvard University Press, 1976.
**FPA, P**

Bjorkvold, Jon Roar. "Canto - Ergo Sum: Musical Child Cultures in the United States, the Soviet Union, and Norway." In *Music and Child Development: The Biology of Music Making - Proceedings of the 1987 Denver Conference*, ed. Frank R. Wilson and Franz L. Roehmann, 117-35. St. Louis, Mo.: MMB Music, 1990.
**P**

————. *The Muse Within: Creativity and Communication, Song and Play from Childhood through Maturity*. Transl. W. H. Halverson. New York: Harper Collins, 1992.
**CI, P**

Blacking, John. *How Musical Is Man?* Seattle: University of Washington Press, 1973.
**P**

————. *Music, Culture, and Experience: Selected Papers of John Blacking*. Ed. Reginald Byron. Chicago: University of Chicago Press, 1995.
**P**

————. "Music in Children's Cognitive and Affective Development." In *Music and Child Development: The Biology of Music Making - Proceedings of the 1987 Denver Conference*, ed. Frank R. Wilson and Franz L. Roehmann, 68-78. St. Louis, Mo.: MMB Music, 1990.
**P**

Blaukopf, Kurt. *Musical Life in a Changing Society: Aspects of Music Sociology*. Transl. D. Marinelli. Portland, Ore.: Amadeus, 1992.
**P**

Bloom, Benjamin Samuel. Excerpts from the "Taxonomy of Educational Objectives, the Classification of Educational Goals, Handbook I: Cognitive Domain." In *Bloom's Taxonomy—A Forty-Year Retrospective: 93rd Yearbook of the National Society for the Study of Education (Part II)*, ed. Lorin W. Anderson and Lauren A. Sosniak, 9-27. Chicago: University of Chicago Press, 1994.
**CI, P**

————. "Reflections on the Development and Use of the Taxonomy." In *Bloom's Taxonomy—A Forty-Year Retrospective: 93rd Yearbook of the National Society for the Study of Education (Part II)*, ed. Lorin W. Anderson and Lauren A. Sosniak, 1-8. Chicago: University of Chicago Press, 1994.
**CI, P**

————, ed. *Developing Talent in Young People.* New York: Ballantine Books, 1985.
**P**

————, ed. *Taxonomy of Educational Objectives: The Classification of Educational Goals.* 1956. Reprint, New York: Longman, 1984.
**CI, P**

Bloom, Benjamin Samuel, J. Thomas Hastings, and George F. Madaus. *Handbook on Formative and Summative Evaluation of Student Learning.* New York: McGraw-Hill, 1971.
**BR, P**

Boardman, Eunice. "The Relation of Music Study to Thinking." In *Dimensions of Musical Thinking*, ed. Eunice Boardman, 1-7. Reston, Va.: Music Educators National Conference, 1989.
**CI, P**

————, ed. *Dimensions of Musical Thinking.* Reston, Va.: Music Educators National Conference, 1989.
**CI, P**

Bonds, Mark Evan. *Wordless Rhetoric: Musical Form and the Metaphor of the Oration.* Cambridge: Harvard University Press, 1991.
**FPA, P**

Bonny, Helen L., and Louis M. Savary. *Music and Your Mind: Listening with a New Consciousness.* Rev. ed. Barrytown, N.Y.: Station Hill, 1990.
**P**

Boswell, Jacquelyn, ed. *The Young Child and Music: Contemporary Principles in Child Development and Music Education.* Reston, Va.: Music Educators National Conference, 1985.
**CI, P, RSC**

Bower, Gordon, H., and Ernest Ropiequet Hilgard. *Theories of Learning.* 5th ed. Englewood Cliffs, N.J.: Prentice-Hall, 1981.
**P**

Boyd, Jenny, and Holly George-Warren. *Musicians in Tune: Seventy-Five Contemporary Musicians Discuss the Creative Process.* New York: Simon and Schuster, 1992.
**P**

Boyle, J. David. "Evaluation of Music Ability." In *Handbook of Research on Music Teaching and Learning*, ed. Richard J. Colwell, 247-65. New York: Schirmer Books, 1992.
**P, R**

Boyle, J. David, and Rudolf E. Radocy. *Measurement and Evaluation of Musical Experiences.* New York: Schirmer Books, 1987.
**CI, P**

*British Journal of Music Education.* Cambridge: Cambridge University Press, 1984-.
**CI, J, P, R**

Broudy, Harry S. "On Cognition and Emotion in the Arts." In *The Arts, Cognition and Basic Skills*, ed. Stanley S. Madeja, 18-22. St. Louis, Mo.: CEMREL, 1978.
**A, P**

Brown, Roger. "Music and Language." In *Documentary Report of the Ann Arbor Symposium: National Symposium on the Applications of Psychology to the Teaching and Learning of Music (Sessions I and II)*, 233-65. Reston, Va.: Music Educators National Conference, 1981.
**P, R**

Bruner, Jerome S. *On Knowing: Essays for the Left Hand.* Exp. ed. Cambridge: Balknap Press of Harvard University Press, 1979.
**CI, P**

————. *The Process of Education.* 1960. Reprint, Cambridge: Harvard University Press, 1977.
**CI, FPA, P**

————. *Toward a Theory of Instruction.* New York: Norton, 1968.
**CI, FPA, P**

Buck, Percy Carter. *Psychology for Musicians.* 1944. Reprint, New York: Oxford University Press, 1974.
**P**

Buckwell, Patricia J. "Journal of Music Therapy." In *International Music Journals*, ed. Linda M. Fidler and Richard S. James, 198-200. New York: Greenwood, 1990.
**J, P, R**

Budd, Malcolm. *Music and the Emotions: The Philosophical Theories.* Boston: Routledge and Kegan Paul, 1992.
**FPA, P**

Bunt, Leslie. *Music Therapy: An Art beyond Words.* New York: Routledge, 1994.
**P**

Burrows, David L. *Sound, Speech, and Music.* Amherst, Mass.: University of Massachusetts Press, 1990.
**FPA, P**

Butler, David. *The Musician's Guide to Perception and Cognition.* New York: Schirmer Books, 1992.
**BR, P**

Buttram, Joe B. "An Overview of Learning Theory and Related Developments." In *Handbook of Music Psychology*, ed. Donald A. Hodges, 235-74. Lawrence, Kans.: National Association for Music Therapy, 1980.
**P, R**

Cady, Henry L. "Children's Processing and Remembering of Music: Some Speculations." In *Documentary Report of the Ann Arbor Symposium: National Symposium on the Applications of Psychology to the Teaching and Learning of Music (Sessions I and II)*, 81-87. Reston, Va.: Music Educators National Conference, 1981.
**FPA, P**

Camp, Max W. "Rhythmic Control and Musical Understanding." In *Music and Child Development: The Biology of Music Making - Proceedings of the 1987 Denver Conference*, ed. Frank R. Wilson and Franz L. Roehmann, 191-201. St. Louis, Mo.: MMB Music, 1990.
**P**

Campbell, Don G. *Introduction to the Musical Brain.* 2nd ed. St. Louis, Mo.: MMB Music, 1992.
**P**

————, comp. *Music Physician for Times to Come: An Anthology.* Wheaton, Ill.: Theosophical Publishing House, 1991.
**BR, P**

Campbell, Warren C., and Jack J. Heller. "An Orientation for Considering Models of Musical Behavior." In *Handbook of Music Psychology*, ed. Donald A. Hodges, 29-36. Lawrence, Kans.: National Association for Music Therapy, 1980.
**P**

*Canadian Music Educator.* St. Catherines, Ontario: Canadian Music Educators' Association, 1959-.
**CI, J, P, R**

Capurso, Alexander, ed. *Music and Your Emotions: A Practical Guide to Music Selections Associated with Desired Emotional Responses.* 1952. Reprint, New York: Liveright, 1970.
**BR, P, R**

Carlsen, James C. "Auditory Perception: Concerns for Musical Learning." In *Documentary Report of the Ann Arbor Symposium: National Symposium on the Applications of Psychology to the Teaching and Learning of Music (Sessions I and II)*, 2-8. Reston, Va.: Music Educators National Conference, 1981.

P, R

Chall, Jeanne S., and Allan F. Mirsky. "The Implications for Education." In *Education and the Brain: 77th Yearbook of the National Society for the Study of Education (Part II)*, ed. Jeanne S. Chall and Allan F. Mirsky, 371-78. Chicago: University of Chicago Press, 1978.

CI, P

————, eds. *Education and the Brain: 77th Yearbook of the National Society for the Study of Education (Part II)*. Chicago: University of Chicago Press, 1978.

BR, CI, P

Chomsky, Noam. *Language and Mind*. Enl. ed. New York: Harcourt Brace Jovanovich, 1972.

FPA, P

————. *Reflections on Language*. New York: Pantheon Books, 1975.

FPA, P

Clarke, Eric. "Structure and Expression in Rhythmic Performance." In *Musical Structure and Cognition*, ed. Peter Howell, Ian Cross, and Robert West, 209-36. London: Academic Press, 1985.

P

Clarke, Eric, and Simon Emmerson, eds. *Music, Mind and Structure*. New York: Harwood Academic Publishers, 1989.

P, RSC

Clifton, Thomas. *Music as Heard: A Study in Applied Phenomenology*. New Haven, Conn.: Yale University Press, 1983.

FPA, P

Clynes, Manfred, ed. *Music, Mind, and Brain: The Neuropsychology of Music*. New York: Plenum, 1982.

P, RSC

*Cognition and Emotion*. Hove, East Sussex, England: Erlbaum Associates, 1987-.

J, P, R

*Cognition: International Journal of Cognitive Psychology.* New York: Elsevier Science, 1972-.
**J, P, R**

Coleman, Satis N. *Creative Music for Children: A Plan of Training Based on the Natural Evolution of Music.* New York: G. P. Putnam's Sons, 1931.
**CI, P**

Colwell, Richard J. "Evaluation in Music Education: Perspicacious or Peregrine." In *Symposium in Music Education: A Festschrift for Charles Leonhard*, ed. Richard J. Colwell, 157-95. Urbana-Champaign: University of Illinois, 1982.
**CI, FPA, P**

_____. *The Evaluation of Music Teaching and Learning.* Englewood Cliffs, N.J.: Prentice-Hall, 1970.
**CI, P**

_____. *Music Achievement Tests.* Chicago: Follett Educational Corporation, 1969.
**P**

_____. *Silver Burdett Music Competency Tests.* Morristown, N.J.: Silver Burdett, 1979.
**P**

_____, ed. *Basic Concepts in Music Education II.* Niwot: University Press of Colorado, 1991.
**FPA, P**

_____, ed. *Handbook of Research on Music Teaching and Learning.* New York: Schirmer Books, 1992.
**BR, CI, P, R**

Cook, Nicholas. *Music, Imagination, and Culture.* New York: Clarendon, 1992.
**FPA, P**

Cooke, Deryck. *The Language of Music.* 1959. Reprint, New York: Oxford University Press, 1989.
**FPA, P**

Cooksey, J. M. "Developing an Objective Approach to Evaluating Music Performance." In *Symposium in Music Education: A Festschrift for Charles Leonhard*, ed. Richard J. Colwell, 197-229. Urbana-Champaign: University of Illinois, 1982.
**P**

Cooper, Grosvenor W., and Leonard B. Meyer. *The Rhythmic Structure of Music.* Chicago: University of Chicago Press, 1963.
**P**

Copland, Aaron. *Copland on Music.* 1960. Reprint, New York: Da Capo, 1976.
**FPA, P**

_____. *Music and Imagination: The Charles Eliot Norton Lectures, 1951-52.* 1952. Reprint, Cambridge: Harvard University Press, 1980.
**FPA, P**

_____. *The New Music, 1900-1960.* Rev. ed. New York: Norton, 1968.
**FPA, P**

_____. *What to Listen for in Music.* 1939. Rev. ed. San Francisco: McGraw-Hill, 1988.
**CI, FPA, P**

Costall, Alan. "The Relativity of Absolute Pitch." In *Musical Structure and Cognition*, ed. Peter Howell, Ian Cross, and Robert West, 189-208. London: Academic Press, 1985.
**P**

Costanza, Peter. "Approaches to the Evaluation of Policy Issues in Music Education." In *Policy Issues in Music Education: A Report of the Proceedings of the Robert Petzold Symposium*, ed. Gerald Olson, Anthony L. Barresi, and David Nelson, 153-60. Madison: School of Music, University of Wisconsin, 1991.
**FPA, P**

Covington, Martin V. "Musical Chairs: Who Drops Out of Music Instruction and Why?" In *Documentary Report of the Ann Arbor Symposium on the Applications of Psychology to the Teaching and Learning of Music: Motivation and Creativity (Sesson III)*, 49-54. Reston, Va.: Music Educators National Conference, 1983.
**CI, P**

Critchley, MacDonald, and R. A. Henson, eds. *Music and the Brain: Studies in the Neurology of Music.* Springfield, Ill.: C. C. Thomas, 1977.
**P**

Cross, Ian. "Music and Change: On the Establishment of Rules." In *Musical Structure and Cognition*, ed. Peter Howell, Ian Cross, and Robert West, 1-20. London: Academic Press, 1985.
**P**

Cross, Ian, Peter Howell, and Robert West. "Structural Relationships in the Perception of Musical Pitch." In *Musical Structure and Cognition*, ed. Peter Howell, Ian Cross, and Robert West, 121-42. London: Academic Press, 1985.
**P**

Csikszentmihalyi, Mihaly, and Ulrich Schiefele. "Arts Education, Human Development, and the Quality of Experience." In *The Arts, Education, and Aesthetic Knowing: 91st Yearbook of the National Society for the Study of Education (Part II)*, ed. Bennett Reimer and Ralph A. Smith, 169-91. Chicago: University of Chicago Press, 1992.
**A, CI, P**

Cuddy, Lola L., and Rena Upitis. "Aural Perception." In *Handbook of Research on Music Teaching and Learning*, ed. Richard J. Colwell, 333-43. New York: Schirmer Books, 1992.
**P, R**

Cutietta, Robert A. "The Measurement of Attitudes and Preferences in Music Education." In *Handbook of Research on Music Teaching and Learning*, ed. Richard J. Colwell, 295-309. New York: Schirmer Books, 1992.
**P, R**

Cziko, Gary. "Implicit and Explicit Learning: Implications for and Applications to Music Teaching." In *The Crane Symposium: Toward an Understanding of the Teaching and Learning of Music Performance*, ed. Charles Fowler, 89-117. Potsdam: Potsdam College of the State University of New York, 1988.
**CI, P**

Dasilva, Fabio B., Anthony Blasi, and David Dees. *The Sociology of Music*. Notre Dame, Ind.: University of Notre Dame Press, 1984.
**P**

Davidson, Jennifer. *TIPS: Thinking Skills in the Music Classroom*. Reston, Va.: Music Educators National Conference, 1993.
**CI, P**

Davidson, Lyle, and Larry Scripp. "Education and Development in Music from a Cognitive Perspective." In *Children and the Arts*, ed. David J. Hargreaves, 59-86. Philadelphia: Open University Press, 1989.
**P**

————. "Surveying the Coordinates of Cognitive Skills in Music." In *Handbook of Research on Music Teaching and Learning*, ed. Richard J. Colwell, 392-413. New York: Schirmer Books, 1992.
**CI, P, R**

Davidson, Lyle, and Patricia Welsh. "From Collections to Structure: The Developmental Path of Tonal Thinking." In *Generative Processes in Music: The Psychology of Performance, Improvisation and Composition*, ed. John A. Sloboda, 260-85. New York: Oxford, 1988.
**P**

Davidson, Lyle, Patricia McKernon, and Howard Gardner. "The Acquisition of Song: A Developmental Approach." In *Documentary Report of the Ann Arbor Symposium: National Symposium on the Applications of Psychology to the Teaching and Learning of Music (Sessions I and II)*, 301-14. Reston, Va.: Music Educators National Conference, 1981.
**P**

Davies, John Booth. *The Psychology of Music.* Stanford, Calif.: Stanford University Press, 1978.
**P**

Davies, Stephen. *Musical Meaning and Expression.* Ithaca, N.Y.: Cornell University Press, 1994.
**FPA, P**

Davis, Donald J. "Evaluation and Curriculum Development in the Arts." In *Toward an Aesthetic Education: A Report*, 117-27. Washington: Music Educators National Conference, 1971.
**A, CI, P**

Davis, Jessica, and Howard Gardner. "The Cognitive Revolution: Consequences for the Understanding and Education of the Child as Artist." In *The Arts, Education, and Aesthetic Knowing: 91st Yearbook of the National Society for the Study of Education (Part II)*, ed. Bennett Reimer and Ralph A. Smith, 92-123. Chicago: University of Chicago Press, 1992.
**A, CI, FPA, P**

Davis, William B., Kate Gfeller, and Michael H. Thaut. *An Introduction to Music Therapy: Theory and Practice.* Dubuque, Iowa: William C. Brown, 1992.
**P**

Day, Ruth S. "Music Ability and Patterns of Cognition." In *Documentary Report of the Ann Arbor Symposium: National Symposium on the Applications of Psychology to the Teaching and Learning of Music (Sessions I and II)*, 270-84. Reston, Va.: Music Educators National Conference, 1981.
**P, R**

DeBellis, Mark. "Theoretically Informed Listening." In *The Interpretation of Music: Philosophical Essays*, ed. Michael Krausz, 271-81. New York: Oxford University Press, 1992.
**FPA, P**

Denckla, Martha B. "Minimal Brain Dysfunction." In *Education and the Brain: 77th Yearbook of the National Society for the Study of Education (Part II)*, ed. Jeanne S. Chall and Allan F. Mirsky, 223-68. Chicago: University of Chicago Press, 1978.
**P**

_____. "The Paradox of the Gifted/Impaired Child." In *Music and Child Development: The Biology of Music Making - Proceedings of the 1987 Denver Conference*, ed. Frank R. Wilson and Franz L. Roehmann, 227-40. St. Louis, Mo.: MMB Music, 1990.
**P**

DeTurk, Mark. "Critical and Creative Musical Thinking." In *Dimensions of Musical Thinking*, ed. Eunice Boardman, 21-32. Reston, Va.: Music Educators National Conference, 1989.
**CI, P**

Deutsch, Diana. "Musical Illusions and Handedness." In *Documentary Report of the Ann Arbor Symposium: National Symposium on the Applications of Psychology to the Teaching and Learning of Music (Sessions I and II)*, 218-31. Reston, Va.: Music Educators National Conference, 1981.
**P, R**

_____. "The Perception of Musical Configurations." In *The Biology of Music Making: Proceedings of the 1984 Denver Conference*, ed. Franz L. Roehmann and Frank R. Wilson, 112-30. St. Louis, Mo.: MMB Music, 1988.
**P, R**

_____, ed. *The Psychology of Music*. New York: Academic Press, 1982.
**P**

Dewey, John. *Experience and Education*. 1938. Reprint, New York: Collier Books, 1974.
**CI, FPA, P**

_____. *How We Think: A Restatement of the Relation of Reflective Thinking to the Educative Process*. 1910. Reprint, Buffalo, N.Y.: Prometheus Books, 1991.
**CI, FPA, P**

_____. *Logic: The Theory of Inquiry*. 1938. Reprint, New York: Irvington, 1982.
**CI, FPA, P**

Diserens, Charles M., and Harry Fine. *A Psychology of Music: The Influence of Music on Behavior*. Cincinnati, Ohio: College of Music, 1939.
**P**

*Documentary Report of the Ann Arbor Symposium: National Symposium on the Applications of Psychology to the Teaching and Learning of Music (Sessions I and II)*. Reston, Va.: Music Educators National Conference, 1981.
**CI, P, R, RSC**

*Documentary Report of the Ann Arbor Symposium on the Applications of Psychology to the Teaching and Learning of Music: Motivation and Creativity (Session III)*. Reston, Va.: Music Educators National Conference, 1983.

**CI, P, R, RSC**

Doerksen, David P. *Guide to Evaluating Teachers of Music Performance Groups*. Reston, Va.: Music Educators National Conference,1990.

**BR, CI, P**

Dowling, W. Jay. "Mental Structures through Which Music Is Perceived." In *Documentary Report of the Ann Arbor Symposium: National Symposium on the Applications of Psychology to the Teaching and Learning of Music (Sessions I and II)*, 144-49. Reston, Va.: Music Educators National Conference, 1981.

**P, R**

————. "Tonal Structure and Children's Early Tonal Learning of Music." In *Generative Processes in Music: The Psychology of Performance, Improvisation, and Composition*, ed. John A. Sloboda, 113-28. Oxford: Clarendon, 1988.

**P**

Dowling, W. Jay, and Dane L. Harwood. *Music Cognition*. New York: Academic Press, 1986.

**P**

Drake, Raleigh Moseley. *Drake Musical Aptitude Tests*. Chicago: Science Research Associates, 1957.

**P**

Dunn, David. "Speculations: On the Evolutionary Continuity of Music and Animal Communication Behavior." In *Perspectives on Musical Aesthetics*, ed. John Rahn, 177-93. New York: Norton, 1994.

**FPA, P**

Eagle, Charles T., Jr. "An Introductory Perspective on Music Psychology." In *Handbook of Music Psychology*, ed. Donald A. Hodges, 1-28. Lawrence, Kans.: National Association for Music Therapy, 1980.

**P, R**

Earhart, Will. *The Meaning and Teaching of Music*. New York: Witmark Educational Publications, 1935.

**CI, FPA, P**

Eccles Parsons, Jacquelynne. "Children's Motivation to Study Music." In *Documentary Report of the Ann Arbor Symposium on the Applications of Psychology to the Teaching and Learning of Music: Motivation and Creativity (Sessions III)*, 31-39. Reston, Va.: Music Educators National Conference, 1983.

**P**

Ecker, David W. "The Development of Qualitative Intelligence." In *Aesthetics and Problems of Education*, ed. Ralph A. Smith, 172-77. Urbana: University of Illinois Press, 1971.

**A, CI, FPA, P**

Edwards, Eleanor M. *Music Education for the Deaf.* South Waterford, Me.: Merriam-Eddy, 1974.

**P**

Edwards, Roger H. "Model Building." In *Handbook of Research on Music Teaching and Learning*, ed. Richard J. Colwell, 38-47. New York: Schirmer Books, 1992.

**CI, P, R**

_____. "Transfer and Performance Instruction." In *The Crane Symposium: Toward an Understanding of the Teaching and Learning of Music Performance*, ed. Charles Fowler, 119-42. Potsdam: Potsdam College of the State University of New York, 1988.

**CI, P**

Efland, Arthur. "Conceptions of Teaching in the Arts." In *The Teaching Process, Arts and Aesthetics*, ed. Gerard L. Knieter and Jane Stallings, 152-86. St. Louis, Mo.: CEMREL, 1979.

**A, CI, FPA, P**

Eisner, Elliot W. "Implications of Artistic Intelligences for Education." In *Artistic Intelligences: Implications for Education*, ed. William J. Moody, 31-42. New York: Teachers College, 1990.

**A, CI, P**

Engel, Martin. "An Informal Framework for Cognitive Research in Arts Education." In *The Arts, Cognition and Basic Skills*, ed. Stanley S. Madeja, 23-30. St. Louis, Mo.: CEMREL, 1978.

**A, P, R**

Epstein, Herman T. "Growth Spurts during Brain Development: Implications for Educational Policy and Practice." In *Education and the Brain: 77th Yearbook of the National Society for the Study of Education (Part II)*, ed. Jeanne S. Chall and Allan F. Mirsky, 343-70. Chicago: University of Chicago Press, 1978.

**P**

Erickson, Robert. "Composing Music." In *Perspectives on Musical Aesthetics*, ed. John Rahn, 165-74. New York: Norton, 1994.
**FPA, P**

Evans, James R., and Manfred Clynes, eds. *Rhythm in Psychological, Linguistic and Musical Processes*. Springfield, Ill.: Charles C. Thomas, 1986.
**P**

*Experiments in Musical Creativity: A Report of Pilot Projects Sponsored by the Contemporary Music Project in Baltimore, San Diego, and Farmingdale*. Washington: Music Educators National Conference, 1966.
**CI, P, RSC**

Farnsworth, Paul R. *Musical Taste: Its Measurement and Cultural Nature*. Stanford, Calif.: Stanford University Press, 1950.
**P**

————. *The Social Psychology of Music*. 2nd ed. Ames: Iowa State University Press, 1969.
**P**

Farnum, Stephen E. *Farnum Music Test*. Riverside, R.I.: Bond Publishing, 1969.
**P**

————. *The Farnum String Scale: A Performance Scale for All String Instruments*. Winona, Minn.: Hal Leonard, 1969.
**P**

Feder, Stuart, Richard L. Karmel, and George H. Pollock, eds. *Psychoanalytic Explorations in Music*. Madison, Conn.: International Universities Press, 1993.
**P**

Feininger, Karl. *An Experimental Psychology of Music*. New York: A. Gemunder, 1909.
**CI, P**

Feldman, David Henry, Mihaly Csikszentmihalyi, and Howard Gardner. *Changing the World: A Framework for the Study of Creativity*. Westport, Conn.: Praeger, 1994.
**CI, P**

*First Music Assessment: An Overview*. Washington: United States Government Printing Office, 1974.
**CI, P, RSC**

Fisher, Frederic I. *The Science of Music: An Essay in Prehistory.* Denton, Tex.: C/G Productions, 1981.
**FPA, P**

Fisher, Henry. *Psychology for Music Teachers: The Laws of Thought Applied to Sounds and Their Symbols, with Other Relevant Matter.* 3rd ed. London: Curwen, 1905.
**CI, P**

Fiske, Harold E. *Music and Mind: Philosophical Essays on the Cognition and Meaning of Music.* Lewiston, N.Y.: Edwin Mellen Press, 1990.
**FPA, P**

_____. *Music Cognition and Aesthetic Attitudes.* Lewiston, N.Y.: Edwin Mellen Press, 1993.
**FPA, P**

_____. "Structure of Cognition and Music Decision-Making." In *Handbook of Research on Music Teaching and Learning*, ed. Richard J. Colwell, 360-76. New York: Schirmer Books, 1992.
**P, R**

Flagg, Marion Elizabeth. *Musical Learning: A Guide to Child Growth.* Boston: C. C. Birchard, 1949.
**BR, CI, P**

Fletcher, Peter. *Roll over Rock: A Study of Music in Contemporary Culture.* London: Stainer and Bell, 1981.
**CI, P**

Fox, Donna Brink. "Teaching Tots and Toddlers." In *Music and Child Development: The Biology of Music Making - Proceedings of the 1987 Denver Conference*, ed. Frank R. Wilson and Franz L. Roehmann, 384-88. St. Louis, Mo.: MMB Music, 1990.
**CI, P, R**

Frances, Robert. *The Perception of Music.* Transl. W. Jay Dowling. Hillsdale, N.Y.: L. Erlbaum, 1988.
**FPA, P**

Franklin, Erik. *Music Education: Psychology and Method.* London: Harrap, 1972.
**CI, P**

Freund, Hans-Joachim, and Harald Hefter. "Timing Mechanisms in Skilled Hand Movements." In *Music and Child Development: The Biology of Music Making - Proceedings of the 1987 Denver Conference*, ed. Frank R. Wilson and Franz L. Roehmann, 179-90. St. Louis, Mo.: MMB Music, 1990.
**P**

Frith, Simon. *Sound Effects: Youth, Leisure, and the Politics of Rock 'n' Roll.* New York: Pantheon Books, 1981.

**P**

————. "Towards an Aesthetic of Popular Music." In *Music and Society: The Politics of Composition, Performance, and Reception,* ed. Richard D. Leppert and Susan McClary, 133-49. New York: Cambridge University Press, 1987.

**FPA, P**

————, ed. *World Music, Politics, and Social Change: Papers from the International Association for the Study of Popular Music.* New York: St. Martin's, 1989.

**P, RSC**

Furman, Charles E., ed. *Effectiveness of Music Therapy Procedures: Documentation of Research and Clinical Practice.* 2nd ed. Silver Spring, Md.: National Association for Music Therapy, 1996.

**P, R**

Gardner, Howard. *Art, Mind, and Brain: A Cognitive Approach to Creativity.* New York: Basic Books, 1982.

**A, CI, P**

————. *Artful Scribbles: The Significance of Children's Drawings.* New York: Basic Books, 1980.

**A, P**

————. *The Arts and Human Development: A Psychological Study of the Artistic Process.* 1973. Reprint, New York: Basic Books, 1994.

**A, CI, P**

————. *Creating Minds: An Anatomy of Creativity Seen through the Lives of Freud, Einstein, Picasso, Stravinsky, Eliot, Graham, and Gandhi.* New York: Basic Books, 1993.

**A, CI, P**

————. *Frames of Mind: The Theory of Multiple Intelligences.* 10th anniv. ed. New York: Basic Books, 1993.

**CI, P**

————. *The Mind's New Science: A History of the Cognitive Revolution.* New York: Basic Books, 1985.

**CI, P**

————. "Multiple Intelligences: Implications for Art and Creativity." In *Artistic Intelligences: Implications for Education*, ed. William J. Moody, 11-27. New York: Teachers College, 1990.

**A, CI, P**

————. *Multiple Intelligences: The Theory in Practice*. New York: Basic Books, 1993.

**CI, P**

————. *The Quest for Mind: Piaget, Levi-Strauss, and the Structuralist Movement*. 2nd ed. Chicago: University of Chicago Press, 1981.

**P**

————. *To Open Minds: Chinese Clues to the Dilemma of Contemporary Education*. New York: Basic Books, 1989.

**CI, P**

————. *The Unschooled Mind: How Children Think and How Schools Should Teach*. New York: Basic Books, 1991.

**CI, P**

Gardner, Howard, and David N. Perkins, eds. *Art, Mind, and Education: Research from Project Zero*. Urbana: University of Illinois Press, 1989.

**A, CI, P, R**

Garfias, Robert. "Thoughts on the Processes of Language and Music Acquisition." In *Music and Child Development: The Biology of Music Making - Proceedings of the 1987 Denver Conference*, ed. Frank R. Wilson and Franz L. Roehmann, 100-05. St. Louis, Mo.: MMB Music, 1990.

**P**

Gaston, E. Thayer. "Functional Music." In *Basic Concepts in Music Education: 57th Yearbook of the National Society for the Study of Education*, ed. Nelson B. Henry, 292-309. Chicago: University of Chicago Press, 1958.

**P**

————. *Test of Musicality*. Lawrence, Kans.: O'Dell's Instrumental Service, 1957.

**P**

————, ed. *Music in Therapy*. Lawrence, Kans.: Allen, 1968.

**P**

Gaston, E. Thayer, and Erwin H. Schneider, eds. *An Analysis, Evaluation, and Selection of Clinical Uses of Music in Therapy*. Lawrence: University of Kansas, 1965.

**P**

Geerdes, Harold P. *TIPS: Improving Acoustics for Music Teaching.* Reston, Va.: Music Educators National Conference, 1991.
P

Gelber, Gary. "Psychological Development of the Conservatory Student." In *The Biology of Music Making: Proceedings of the 1984 Denver Conference*, ed. Franz L. Roehmann and Frank R. Wilson, 3-15. St. Louis, Mo.: MMB Music, 1988.
CI, P

George, Warren E. "Measurement and Evaluation of Musical Behavior." In *Handbook of Music Psychology*, ed. Donald A. Hodges, 291-392. Lawrence, Kans.: National Association for Music Therapy, 1980.
P, R

George, Warren, E., and Donald A. Hodges. "The Nature of Musical Attributes." In *Handbook of Music Psychology*, ed. Donald A. Hodges, 401-14. Lawrence, Kans.: National Association for Music Therapy, 1980.
P, R

Gerber, Linda L. "Music in Early Childhood: Postscript and Preview." In *Symposium in Music Education: A Festschrift for Charles Leonhard*, ed. Richard J. Colwell, 45-57. Urbana-Champaign: University of Illinois, 1982.
CI, P

Gfeller, Kate. "Research Regarding Students with Disabilities." In *Handbook of Research on Music Teaching and Learning*, ed. Richard J. Colwell, 615-32. New York: Schirmer Books, 1992.
P, R

Gildersleeve, Glenn. "Standards and the Evaluation and Measurement of Achievement in Music." In *Music Education: 35th Yearbook of the National Society for the Study of Education (Part II)*, ed. Guy Montrose Whipple, 195-206. Bloomington, Ill.: Public School Publishing, 1936.
CI, FPA, P

Ginsburg, David D. "Popular Music and Society." In *International Music Journals*, ed. Linda M. Fidler and Richard S. James, 346-48. New York: Greenwood, 1990.
J, P, R

Godwin, Joscelyn, ed. *The Harmony of the Spheres: A Sourcebook of the Pythagorean Tradition in Music.* Rochester, Vt.: Inner Traditions International, 1993.
FPA, P

————, ed. *Music, Mysticism, and Magic: A Sourcebook.* New York: Arkana, 1987.
BR, FPA, P

Goehr, Lydia. "Music Has No Meaning to Speak Of': On the Politics of Musical Interpretation." In *The Interpretation of Music: Philosophical Essays*, ed. Michael Krausz, 177-90. New York: Oxford University Press, 1992.

**FPA, P**

Goodlad, John I. "Beyond the Rhetoric of Promise." In *Arts and the Schools*, ed. Jerome J. Hausman and Joyce Wright, 205-36. New York: McGraw-Hill, 1980.

**A, CI, P**

Gordon, Edwin E. *Advanced Measures of Music Audiation.* Chicago: G.I.A. Publications, 1989.

**P**

————. *Designing Objective Research in Music Education: Fundamental Considerations.* Chicago: G.I.A. Publications, 1986.

**P, R**

————. *Guiding Your Child's Musical Development.* Chicago: G.I.A. Publications, 1991.

**CI, P**

————. *Instrument Timbre Preference Test.* Chicago: G.I.A Publications, 1985.

**P**

————. *Intermediate Measures of Music Audiation.* Chicago: G.I.A. Publications, 1982.

**P**

————. *Iowa Tests of Music Literacy.* Rev. ed. Chicago: G.I.A. Publications, 1991.

**P**

————. *Learning Sequences in Music: Skill, Content, and Patterns.* Chicago: G.I.A. Publications, 1993.

**P**

————. "Music Learning and Learning Theory." In *Documentary Report of the Ann Arbor Symposium: National Symposium on the Applications of Psychology to the Teaching and Learning of Music (Sessions I and II)*, 62-68. Reston, Va.: Music Educators National Conference, 1981.

**P**

————. *A Music Learning Theory for Newborn and Young Children.* Chicago: G.I.A. Publications, 1990.

**CI, P**

————. *Musical Aptitude Profile.* Rev. ed. Chicago: G.I.A. Publications, 1995.

**P**

_____. *Primary Measures of Music Audiation.* Chicago: G.I.A. Publications, 1979.
**P**

_____. "The Nature and Description of Developmental and Stabilized Music Aptitudes: Implications for Music Learning." In *Music and Child Development: The Biology of Music Making - Proceedings of the 1987 Denver Conference*, ed. Frank R. Wilson and Franz L. Roehmann, 325-35. St. Louis, Mo.: MMB Music, 1990.
**P**

_____. *The Nature, Description, Measurement, and Evaluation of Music Aptitudes.* Chicago: G.I.A. Publications, 1987.
**P**

_____. *The Psychology of Music Teaching.* Englewood Cliffs, N.J.: Prentice-Hall, 1971.
**P**

_____. *Tonal and Rhythm Patterns: An Objective Analysis.* Albany: State University of New York Press, 1976.
**P**

Graham, C. Ray. "Music and Learning of Language in Early Childhood." In *Music and Child Development*, ed. J. Craig Peery, Irene W. Peery, and Thomas W. Draper, 177-83. New York: Springer-Verlag, 1987.
**CI, P**

Graham, Richard M. "Music Education of Exceptional Children." In *Basic Concepts in Music Education II*, ed. Richard J. Colwell, 222-36. Niwot: University Press of Colorado, 1991.
**CI, P**

_____. "Music Methodology for Exceptional Children: Current View of Professional Activity in Music Education and Music Therapy." In *Music Education in the United States: Contemporary Issues*, ed. J. Terry Gates, 224-39. Tuscaloosa: University of Alabama Press, 1988.
**CI, P**

_____, comp. *Music for the Exceptional Child.* Reston, Va.: Music Educators National Conference, 1975.
**CI, P**

Graham, Richard M., and Alice S. Beer. *Teaching Music to the Exceptional Child: A Handbook for Mainstreaming.* Englewood Cliffs, N.J.: Prentice-Hall, 1980.
**BR, CI, P**

Green, Barry, and Timothy W. Gallwey. *The Inner Game of Music.* Garden City, N.Y.: Anchor, 1986.

**CI, P**

Green, Lucy. *Music on Deaf Ears: Musical Meaning, Ideology, Education.* New York: Manchester University Press, 1988.

**CI, FPA, P**

Greenberg, Norman C. "Conclusion: The Influence of Cultural Forces on Music and Art." In *Racial and Ethnic Directions in American Music*, CMS Report No. 3, 61-75. Boulder, Colo.: College Music Society, 1982.

**CI, P**

Greer, R. Douglas. "An Operant Approach to Motivation and Affect: Ten Years of Research in Music Learning." In *Documentary Report of the Ann Arbor Symposium: National Symposium on the Applications of Psychology to the Teaching and Learning of Music (Sessions I and II)*, 102-21. Reston, Va.: Music Educators National Conference, 1981.

**P, R**

————. *Design for Music Learning.* New York: Teachers College, 1980.

**CI, FPA, P**

Grindea, Carola. *Tensions in the Performance of Music.* Enl. ed. White Plains, N.Y.: Pro/Am Music Resources, 1995.

**P, RSC**

Grossman, Sebastian P. "The Biology of Motivation." In *Education and the Brain: 77th Yearbook of the National Society for the Study of Education (Part II)*, ed. Jeanne S. Chall and Allan F. Mirsky, 103-42. Chicago: University of Chicago Press, 1978.

**P**

Gryskiewicz, Stanley S. "Directing Creativity: Marching with Different Drummers." In *Documentary Report of the Ann Arbor Symposium on the Applications of Psychology to the Teaching and Learning of Music: Motivation and Creativity (Session III)*, 13-15. Reston, Va.: Music Educators National Conference, 1983.

**CI, P**

Gurney, Edmund. *The Power of Sound.* 1880. Reprint, New York: Basic Books, 1966.

**FPA, P**

Haack, Paul. "The Acquisition of Music Listening Skills." In *Handbook of Research on Music Teaching and Learning*, ed. Richard J. Colwell, 451-65. New York: Schirmer Books, 1992.

**CI, P, R**

————. "The Behavior of Music Listeners." In *Handbook of Music Psychology*, ed. Donald A. Hodges, 141-82. Lawrence, Kans.: National Association for Music Therapy, 1980.
P

Hall, Donald E. *Musical Acoustics.* 2nd ed. Pacific Grove, Calif.: Brooks/Cole, 1991.
P

Hall, Manly Palmer. *The Therapeutic Value of Music Including the Philosophy of Music.* Los Angeles: Philosophical Research Society, 1982.
FPA, P

Halpern, Steven. *Tuning the Human Instrument: An Owner's Manual.* Palo Alto, Calif.: Spectrum Research Institute, 1978.
P

Hamann, Donald L., ed. *Creativity in the Music Classroom: The Best of MEJ.* Reston, Va.: Music Educators National Conference, 1992.
CI, P

Hamburg, Jeannine W. *Where Is That Music Coming from? A Path to Creativity.* Cherry Hill, N.J.: Myrte, 1989.
P

Handel, Stephen. *Listening: An Introduction to the Perception of Auditory Events.* Cambridge: MIT, 1989.
P

Hanslick, Eduard. *On the Musically Beautiful: A Contribution towards the Revision of the Aesthetics of Music.* Transl. and ed. Geoffrey Payzant from 8th ed., 1891. Reprint, Indianapolis, Ind.: Hackett, 1986.
A, FPA, P

Hargreaves, David J. "Developmental Psychology and the Arts." In *Children and the Arts,* ed. David J. Hargreaves, 3-21. Philadelphia: Open University Press, 1989.
A, P

————. *The Developmental Psychology of Music.* Cambridge: Cambridge University Press, 1986.
P

————, ed. *Children and the Arts.* Philadelphia: Open University Press, 1989.
A, P

Hargreaves, David J., and Marilyn P. Zimmerman. "Developmental Theories of Music Learning." In *Handbook of Research on Music Teaching and Learning*, ed. Richard J. Colwell, 377-91. New York: Schirmer Books, 1992.
**CI, P, R**

Hargreaves, David J., and Maurice J. Galton. "Aesthetic Learning: Psychological Theory and Educational Practice." In *The Arts, Education, and Aesthetic Knowing: 91st Yearbook of the National Society for the Study of Education (Part II)*, ed. Bennett Reimer and Ralph A. Smith, 124-50. Chicago: University of Chicago Press, 1992.
**A, CI, P**

Harre, Rom. "Is There a Semantics for Music? In *The Interpretation of Music: Philosophical Essays*, ed. Michael Krausz, 203-13. New York: Oxford University Press, 1992.
**FPA, P**

Harrell, Jean Gabbert. *Soundtracks: A Study of Auditory Perception, Memory, and Valuation.* Buffalo, N.Y.: Prometheus Books, 1986.
**FPA, P**

Harris, Pamela. *Music and Self: Living Your Inner Sound.* Albuquerque, N.M.: Intermountain, 1989.
**P**

Hartshorn, William C. "The Role of Listening." In *Basic Concepts in Music Education: 57th Yearbook of the National Society for the Study of Education*, ed. Nelson B. Henry, 261-91. Chicago: University of Chicago Press, 1958.
**CI, P**

Harvey, Nigel. "Vocal Control in Singing: A Cognitive Approach." In *Musical Structure and Cognition*, ed. Peter Howell, Ian Cross, and Robert West, 287-332. London: Academic Press, 1985.
**P**

Havas, Kato. *Stage Fright: Its Causes and Cures with Special Reference to Violin Playing.* London: Bosworth Publishers, 1973.
**CI, P**

Healy, Jane M. "Musical Brains for the World of Tomorrow." In *Toward Tomorrow: New Visions for General Music*, ed. Sandra L. Stauffer, 15-19. Reston, Va.: Music Educators National Conference, 1995.
**CI, P**

Hedden, Steven K. "The Physical Basis of Music." In *Handbook of Music Psychology*, ed. Donald A. Hodges, 37-42. Lawrence, Kans.: National Association for Music Therapy, 1980.
**P**

————. "Psychoacoustical Parameters of Music." In *Handbook of Music Psychology*, ed. Donald A. Hodges, 63-92. Lawrence, Kans.: National Association for Music Therapy, 1980.

**P**

————. "Psychomotor Skills." In *Documentray Report of the Ann Arbor Symposium: National Symposium on the Applications of Psychology to the Teaching and Learning of Music (Sessions I and II)*, 22-28. Reston, Va.: Music Educators National Conference, 1981.

**CI, P, R**

Heilman, Kenneth M. "Language and the Brain: Relationship of Localization of Language Function to the Acquisition and Loss of Various Aspects of Language." In *Education and the Brain: 77th Yearbook of the National Society for the Study of Education (Part II)*, ed. Jeanne S. Chall and Allan F. Mirsky, 143-68. Chicago: University of Chicago Press, 1978.

**P**

Heller, Jack J., and Warren C. Campbell. "Auditory Perception in Music Teaching and Learning." In *Documentary Report of the Ann Arbor Symposium: National Symposium on the Applications of Psychology to the Teaching and Learning of Music (Sessions I and II)*, 8-15. Reston, Va.: Music Educators National Conference, 1981.

**CI, P, R**

————. "Models of Language and Intellect in Music Research." In *Music Education for Tomorrow's Society*, ed. Arthur Motycka, 40-49. Jamestown, R.I.: GAMT Music, 1976.

**FPA, P, R**

Helmholtz, Hermann von. *On the Sensations of Tone as a Physiological Basis for the Theory of Music*. 2nd English ed., transl. Alexander J. Ellis, 1862. Reprint, New York: Dover, 1954.

**P, R**

Herman, Joan L., Pamela R. Aschbacher, and Lynn Winters. *A Practical Guide to Alternative Assessment*. Alexandria, Va.: Association for Supervision and Curriculum Development, 1992.

**BR, CI, P**

Herndon, Marcia, and Susanne Ziegler, eds. *Music, Gender, and Culture*. New York: C. F. Peters, 1990.

**CI, P**

Heyfron, Victor. "The Objective Status of Aesthetic Knowing." In *The Arts: A Way of Knowing*, ed. Malcolm Ross, 43-72. New York: Pergamon, 1983.

**A, FPA, P**

Higgins, Kathleen Marie. *The Music of Our Lives.* Philadelphia: Temple University Press, 1991.
**FPA, P**

Hilgard, Ernest Ropiequet, ed. *Theories of Learning and Instruction: 63rd Yearbook of the National Society for the Study of Education.* Chicago: University of Chicago Press, 1964.
**BR, CI, P**

Hodges, Donald A. "The Acquisition of Music Reading Skills." In *Handbook of Research on Music Teaching and Learning,* ed. Richard J. Colwell, 466-71. New York: Schirmer Books, 1992.
**CI, P, R**

————. "Human Hearing." In *Handbook of Music Psychology,* ed. Donald A. Hodges, 43-62. Lawrence, Kans.: National Association for Music Therapy, 1980.
**P**

————. "Neurophysiology and Musical Behavior." In *Handbook of Music Psychology,* ed. Donald A. Hodges, 195-224. Lawrence, Kans.: National Association for Music Therapy, 1980.
**P**

————. "Physiological Responses to Music." In *Handbook of Music Psychology,* ed. Donald A. Hodges, 392-400. Lawrence, Kans.: National Association for Music Therapy, 1980.
**P**

————, ed. *Handbook of Music Psychology.* Lawrence, Kans.: National Association for Music Therapy, 1980.
**BR, P, R**

Hoffer, Charles R. "Artistic Intelligences and Music Education." In *Artistic Intelligences: Implications for Education,* ed. William J. Moody, 135-40. New York: Teachers College, 1991.
**A, CI, P**

————. "Sociology and Music Education." In *Handbook of Research on Music Teaching and Learning,* ed. Richard J. Colwell, 713-23. New York: Schirmer Books, 1992.
**P, R**

Hollander, Lorin. "The Price of Stress in Education." In *The Biology of Music Making: Proceedings of the 1984 Denver Conference,* ed. Franz L. Roehmann and Frank R. Wilson, 47-51. St. Louis, Mo.: MMB Music, 1988.
**P**

Honigsheim, Paul. *Sociologists and Music: An Introduction to the Study of Music and Society.* 2nd ed., ed. K. Peter Etzkorn. New Brunswick, N.J.: Transaction Publishers, 1989.
**P**

Howard, Vernon A. "Music as Educating Imagination." In *The Crane Symposium: Toward an Understanding of the Teaching and Learning of Music Performance,* ed. Charles Fowler, 25-35. Potsdam: Potsdam College of the State University of New York, 1988.
**FPA, P**

Howell, Peter. "Auditory Feedback of the Voice in Singing." In *Musical Structure and Cognition,* ed. Peter Howell, Ian Cross, and Robert West, 259-86. London: Academic Press, 1985.
**P**

Howell, Peter, Ian Cross, and Robert West. *Musical Structure and Cognition.* London: Academic Press, 1985.
**P**

Howes, Frank Stewart. *The Borderland of Music and Psychology.* New York: Oxford University Press, 1927.
**P**

_____. *Man, Mind and Music.* 1948. Reprint, Freeport, N.Y.: Books for Libraries, 1970.
**FPA, P**

Hulse, Stewart H. "Comparative Psychology and Music Perception." In *Music and Child Development: The Biology of Music Making - Proceedings of the 1987 Denver Conference,* ed. Frank R. Wilson and Franz L. Roehmann, 139-56. St. Louis, Mo.: MMB Music, 1990.
**P**

Inglefield, Ruth K. "International Review of the Aesthetics and Sociology of Music." In *International Music Journals,* ed. Linda M. Fidler and Richard S. James, 172-74. New York: Greenwood, 1990.
**A, FPA, J, P, R**

_____. "Psychomusicology." In *International Music Journals,* ed. Linda M. Fidler and Richard S. James, 468-69. New York: Greenwood, 1990.
**J, P, R**

*International Journal of Behavioral Development.* London, England: Erlbaum Associates, 1978-.
**J, P, R**

*International Journal of Music Education.* Huddersfield, England: International Society for Music Education, 1983-.

**CI, FPA, J, P, R**

Jackendoff, Ray S., and Fred Lerdahl. *A Deep Parallel between Music and Language.* Bloomington: Indiana Univerity Linguistics Club, 1980.

**FPA, P**

James, Jamie. *The Music of the Spheres: Music, Science, and the Natural Order of the Universe.* New York: Grove, 1993.

**FPA, P**

Jeans, Sir James Hopwood. *Science and Music.* 1937. Reprint, New York: Dover, 1968.

**P**

Jones, Elizabeth. "Applications of Research to Pedagogy." In *The Biology of Music Making: Proceedings of the 1984 Denver Conference,* ed. Franz L. Roehmann and Frank R. Wilson, 287-90. St. Louis, Mo.: MMB Music, 1988.

**CI, P**

————. "What Children Teach Us about Learning Music." In *Music and Child Development: The Biology of Music Making - Proceedings of the 1987 Denver Conference,* ed. Frank R. Wilson and Franz L. Roehmann, 366-76. St. Louis, Mo.: MMB Music, 1990.

**CI, P**

Jones, Mari Riess, and Susan Holleran, eds. *Cognitive Bases of Musical Communication.* Washington: American Psychological Association, 1992.

**P, RSC**

Jones, Sharon. "Teaching Music for Life." In *Music and Child Development: The Biology of Music Making - Proceedings of the 1987 Denver Conference,* ed. Frank R. Wilson and Franz L. Roehmann, 389-99. St. Louis, Mo.: MMB Music, 1990.

**CI, P**

*Journal of Educational Psychology.* Washington: American Psychological Association, 1910-.

**CI, J, P, R**

*Journal of Experimental Psychology: General.* Washington: American Psychological Association, 1975-.

**J, P, R**

*Journal of Experimental Psychology: Human Perception and Performance.* Washington: American Psychological Association, 1975-.

**J, P, R**

*Journal of Experimental Psychology: Learning, Memory and Cognition.* Washington: American Psychological Association, 1975-.

**J, P, R**

*Journal of the Acoustical Society of America.* New York: American Institute of Physics for the Acoustical Society of America, 1929-.

**J, P, R**

Judd, Tedd. "A Neuropsychologist Looks at Musical Behavior." In *The Biology of Music Making: Proceedings of the 1984 Denver Conference*, ed. Franz L. Roehmann and Frank R. Wilson, 57-76. St. Louis, Mo.: MMB Music, 1988.

**P**

Kaemmer, John E. *Music in Human Life: Anthropological Perspectives on Music.* Austin: University of Texas Press, 1993.

**P**

Kantorski, Vincent J. "The Council for Research in Music Education Bulletin." In *International Music Journals*, ed. Linda M. Fidler and Richard S. James, 100-02. New York: Greenwood, 1990.

**CI, FPA, J, P, R**

———. "Journal of Research in Music Education." In *International Music Journals*, ed. Linda M. Fidler and Richard S. James, 203-05. New York: Greenwood, 1990.

**CI, J, P, R**

———. "Update: The Applications of Research in Music Education." In *International Music Journals*, ed. Linda M. Fidler and Richard S. James, 469-70. New York: Greenwood, 1990.

**CI, J, P, R**

Kaplan, Max. "Society, Sociology, and Music Education." In *Music Education in the United States: Contemporary Issues*, ed. J. Terry Gates, 3-32. Tuscaloosa: University of Alabama Press, 1988.

**CI, P**

Kasha, Michael. "Science, Art, and a Box with the Sound You Dream About." In *The Biology of Music Making: Proceedings of the 1984 Denver Conference*, ed. Franz L. Roehmann and Frank R. Wilson, 205-07. St. Louis, Mo.: MMB Music, 1988.

**P**

Katsh, Shelley, and Carol Merle-Fishman. *The Music within You.* New York: Simon and Schuster, 1985.

**P**

Kennell, Richard P. "Contributions to Music Education." In *International Music Journals*, ed. Linda M. Fidler and Richard S. James, 98-100. New York: Greenwood, 1990.
**CI, J, P, R**

————. "Musical Thinking in the Instrumental Rehearsal." In *Dimensions of Musical Thinking*, ed. Eunice Boardman, 83-89. Reston, Va.: Music Educators National Conference, 1989.
**CI, P**

Kessen, William. "Encounters: The American Child's Meeting with Music." In *Documentary Report of the Ann Arbor Symposium: National Symposium on the Applications of Psychology to the Teaching and Learning of Music (Sessions I and II)*, 353-61. Reston, Va.: Music Educators National Conference, 1981.
**FPA, P, R**

Kingsbury, Henry. *Music, Talent, and Performance: A Conservatory Cultural System.* Philadelphia: Temple University Press, 1988.
**CI, P**

Kinsbourne, Marcel, and Merrill Hiscock. "Cerebral Lateralization and Cognitive Development." In *Education and the Brain: 77th Yearbook of the National Society for the Study of Education (Part II)*, ed. Jeanne S. Chall and Allan F. Mirsky, 169-222. Chicago: University of Chicago Press, 1978.
**P**

Kivy, Peter. *Sound and Semblance: Reflections on Musical Representation.* 1984. Reprint, Ithaca, N.Y.: Cornell University Press, 1991.
**FPA, P**

Knieter, Gerard L. "Cognition and Musical Development." In *Documentary Report of the Ann Arbor Symposium: National Symposium on the Applications of Psychology to the Teaching and Learning of Music (Sessions I and II)*, 68-76. Reston, Va.: Music Educators National Conference, 1981.
**P**

————. "Humanistic Dimensions of Aesthetic Education." In *Music Education for Tomorrow's Society*, ed. Arthur Motycka, 1-11. Jamestown, R.I.: GAMT Music, 1976.
**FPA, P**

————. "The Nature of Aesthetic Education." In *Toward an Aesthetic Education: A Report*, 3-19. Washington: Music Educators National Conference, 1971.
**A, CI, FPA, P**

Knuth, William E. *Knuth Achievement Tests in Music: Recognition of Rhythm and Melody.* 1936. Philadelphia: Educational Test Bureau, 1968.

**P**

Kohut, Daniel L. *Musical Performance: Learning Theory and Pedagogy.* Champaign, Ill.: Stipes Publishing, 1992.

**CI, P**

Koza, Julia Eklund. "Sex Equity and Policy in Music Education: A Change of Vision, A Change of Values." In *Policy Issues in Music Education: A Report of the Proceedings of the Robert Petzold Symposium*, ed. Gerald Olson, Anthony L. Barresi, and David Nelson, 135-45. Madison: School of Music, University of Wisconsin, 1991.

**FPA, P**

Kramer, Jack J., and Jane Close Conoley, eds. *The Eleventh Mental Measurements Yearbook.* Lincoln: University of Nebraska Press, 1992.

**BR, P**

Krathwohl, David R. "Reflections on the Taxonomy: Its Past, Present, and Future." In *Bloom's Taxonomy—A Forty-Year Retrospective: 93rd Yearbook of the National Society for the Study of Education (Part II)*, ed. Lorin W. Anderson and Lauren A. Sosniak, 181-202. Chicago: University of Chicago Press, 1994.

**CI, FPA, P**

Kratus, John K. "College Music Symposium." In *International Music Journals*, ed. Linda M. Fidler and Richard S. James, 90-93. New York: Greenwood, 1990.

**CI, J, P, R**

————. "Music Perception." In *International Music Journals*, ed. Linda M. Fidler and Richard S. James, 464-65. New York: Greenwood, 1990.

**J, P, R**

————. "Psychology of Music." In *International Music Journals*, ed. Linda M. Fidler and Richard S. James, 348-51. New York: Greenwood, 1990.

**J, P, R**

Kraus, Egon. *The Present State of Music Education in the World.* Washington: International Society for Music Education, 1960.

**P, R, RSC**

Krausz, Michael, ed. *The Interpretation of Music: Philosophical Essays.* New York: Oxford University Press, 1992.

**FPA, P**

Krout, Robert. *Music Therapy in Special Education: Developing and Maintaining Social Skills Necessary for Mainstreaming.* St. Louis, Mo.: MMB Music, 1986.
P

Krumhansl, Carol L. *Cognitive Foundations of Musical Pitch.* New York: Oxford University Press, 1990.
P

Kwalwasser, Jacob. "The Composition of Musical Ability." In *Music Education: 35th Yearbook of the National Society for the Study of Education (Part II)*, ed. Guy Montrose Whipple, 35-42. Bloomington, Ill.: Public School Publishing, 1936.
P

_____. *Exploring the Musical Mind.* New York: Coleman Ross, 1955.
P

_____. *Kwalwasser Music Talent Test.* Melville, N.Y.: Belwin Mills, 1953.
P

_____. *Tests and Measurements in Music.* Boston: Birchard, 1927.
P

LaBerge, David. "Perceptual and Motor Schemas in the Performance of Musical Pitch." In *Documentary Report of the Ann Arbor Symposium: National Symposium on the Applications of Psychology to the Teaching and Learning of Music (Sessions I and II)*, 179-96. Reston, Va.: Music Educators National Conference, 1981.
CI, P, R

Lanfer, Helen. *The Music within Us: An Exploration in Creative Music Education.* New York: Hebrew Arts Music Publications, 1979.
CI, P

Lanza, Joseph. *Elevator Music: A Surreal History of Muzak, Easy-Listening, and Other Moodsong.* New York: St. Martin's, 1994.
P

Laske, Otto E. *Music, Memory, and Thought: Explanations in Cognitive Musicology.* Ann Arbor, Mich.: University Microfilms International for the University of Pittsburgh Music Dept., 1977.
P

Lawrence, Ian. *Composers and the Nature of Music Education.* London: Scolar, 1978.
CI, FPA, P

Lawrence, Sidney L. *Everyone's Musical, Psychologically Speaking.* New York: Clayton F. Summy, 1946.
P

LeBlanc, Albert. "The Culture as Educator: Elements in the Development of Individual Music Preference." In *Music Education in the United States: Contemporary Issues*, ed. J. Terry Gates, 33-43. Tuscaloosa: University of Alabama Press, 1988.
P, R

————. "The Development of Music Preference in Children." In *Music and Child Development*, ed. J. Craig Peery, Irene W. Peery, and Thomas W. Draper, 137-57. New York: Springer-Verlag, 1987.
P

Lee, C. S. "The Rhythmic Interpretation of Simple Musical Sequences: Toward a Perceptual Model." In *Musical Structure and Cognition*, ed. Peter Howell, Ian Cross, and Robert West, 53-69. London: Academic Press, 1985.
P

Lehman, Paul R. "Issues of Assessment." In *Perspectives on Implementation: Arts Education Standards for America's Students*, ed. Bruce O. Boston, 47-54. Reston, Va.: Music Educators National Conference, 1994.
A, CI, P

————. *Tests and Measurements in Music.* Englewood Cliffs, N.J.: Prentice-Hall, 1968.
P

Lehrer, Paul. "The Causes and Cures of Performance Anxiety: A Review of the Psychological Literature." In *The Biology of Music Making: Proceedings of the 1984 Denver Conference*, ed. Franz L. Roehmann and Frank R. Wilson, 32-46. St. Louis, Mo.: MMB Music, 1988.
P, R

Leonhard, Charles. "Evaluation in Music Education." In *Basic Concepts in Music Education: 57th Yearbook of the National Society for the Study of Education*, ed. Nelson B. Henry, 310-38. Chicago: University of Chicago Press, 1958.
CI, P

Leppert, Richard D. *The Sight of Sound: Music, Representation, and the History of the Body.* Berkeley: University of California Press, 1993.
FPA, P

Leppert, Richard D., and Susan McClary, eds. *Music and Society: The Politics of Composition, Performance, and Reception.* New York: Cambridge University Press, 1987.
FPA, P

Lerdahl, Fred, and Ray S. Jackendoff. *A Generative Theory of Tonal Music.* Cambridge: MIT, 1983.

**P**

Licht, Sidney Herman. *Music in Medicine.* Boston: New England Conservatory of Music, 1946.

**P**

Lieberman, Julie Lyonn. *You Are Your Instrument: The Definitive Musician's Guide to Practice and Performance.* 3rd ed. New York: Huiksi Music, 1995.

**BR, CI, P**

Lipps, Theodor. *Psychological Studies.* 1926. Reprint, New York: Arno, 1973.

**P**

Long, Newell H. *Indiana-Oregon Music Discrimination Test.* Rev. ed. Bloomington, Ind.: Midwest Music Tests, 1970.

**P**

Lundin, Robert W. *An Objective Psychology of Music.* 3rd ed. Malabar, Fla.: R. E. Kreiger, 1985.

**P**

MacLean, Paul D. "A Mind of Three Minds: Educating the Triune Brain." In *Education and the Brain: 77th Yearbook of the National Society for the Study of Education (Part II),* ed. Jeanne S. Chall and Allan F. Mirsky, 308-42. Chicago: University of Chicago Press, 1978.

**P**

Madeja, Stanley S., ed. *The Arts, Cognition and Basic Skills.* St. Louis, Mo.: CEMREL, 1978.

**A, CI, P, RSC**

Madsen, Charles H., Jr., and Clifford K. Madsen. *Teaching/Discipline: A Positive Approach for Educational Development.* 3rd ed. Raleigh, N.C.: Contemporary Publishing, 1983.

**CI, P, R**

Madsen, Clifford K. *Music Therapy: A Behavioral Guide for the Mentally Retarded.* Lawrence, Kans.: National Association for Music Therapy, 1981.

**BR, CI, P**

Madsen, Clifford K., and Charles H. Madsen, Jr. *Experimental Research in Music.* Raleigh, N.C.: Contemporary Publishing, 1978.

**P, R**

Madsen, Clifford K., and Carol A. Prickett, eds. *Applications of Research in Music Behavior.* Tuscaloosa: Ala.: University of Alabama Press, 1987.
**CI, P, R, RSC**

Madsen, Clifford K., and Randall S. Moore, eds. *Experimental Research in Music: Workbook in Design and Statistical Tests.* Rev. ed. Raleigh, N.C.: Contemporary Publishing, 1978.
**P, R**

Madsen, Clifford K., R. Douglas Greer, and Charles H. Madsen, Jr., eds. *Research in Music Behavior: Modifying Music Behavior in the Classroom.* New York: Teachers College, 1975.
**CI, P, R**

Maehr, Martin L. "The Development of Continuing Interests in Music." In *Documentary Report of the Ann Arbor Symposium on the Applications of Psychology to the Teaching and Learning of Music: Motivation and Creativity (Session III)*, 5-11. Reston, Va.: Music Educators National Conference, 1983.
**CI, P**

Mark, Michael L. "Aesthetics and Utility Reconciled: The Importance to Society of Education in Music." In *Music Education in the United States: Contemporary Issues*, ed. J. Terry Gates, 111-29. Tuscaloosa: University of Alabama Press, 1988.
**CI, FPA, P**

Martin, Peter. *Sounds and Society: Themes in the Sociology of Music.* New York: St. Martin's, 1995.
**P**

Marzano, Robert J., et al. *Dimensions of Thinking: A Framework for Curriculum and Instruction.* Alexandria, Va.: Association for Supervision and Curriculum Development, 1988.
**CI, P, R**

Maus, Fred Everett. "Recent Ideas and Activities of James K. Randall and Benjamin Boretz: A New Social Role for Music." In *Perspectives on Musical Aesthetics*, ed. John Rahn, 107-15. New York: Norton, 1994.
**A, FPA, P**

May, William V., ed. *Research Symposium on the Psychology and Acoustics of Music, 1979.* Lawrence: University of Kansas Department of Art and Music Education and Music Therapy, 1980.
**P, R, RSC**

Mazziotta, John. "Visualization of Brain Metabolism in Skilled Movements." In *The Biology of Music Making: Proceedings of the 1984 Denver Conference*, ed. Franz L. Roehmann and Frank R. Wilson, 100-03. St. Louis, Mo.: MMB Music, 1988.
**P**

McAllester, David P., ed. *Becoming Human through Music: The Wesleyan Symposium on the Perspectives of Social Anthropology in the Teaching and Learning of Music.* Reston, Va.: Music Educators National Conference, 1985.
**CI, P, RSC**

McDonald, Dorothy T., and Gene M. Simons. *Musical Growth and Development: Birth through Six.* New York: Schirmer Books, 1988.
**CI, P**

McMullen, Patrick T. "Music as a Perceived Stimulus Object and Affective Responses: An Alternative Theoretical Framework." In *Handbook of Music Psychology*, ed. Donald A. Hodges, 183-94. Lawrence, Kans.: National Association for Music Therapy, 1980.
**FPA, P**

Merriam, Alan P. *The Anthropology of Music.* Evanston, Ill.: Northwestern University Press, 1964.
**P**

Merrion, Margaret D. *Instructional and Classroom Management for Music Educators.* Washington: University Press of America, 1982.
**CI, P**

Merritt, Stephanie. *Mind, Music, and Imagery: Unlocking the Treasures of Your Mind.* 2nd ed. Santa Rosa, Calif.: Aslan, 1996.
**P**

Meske, Eunice Boardman. "Educating the Music Teacher: Participation in a Metamorphosis." In *Symposium in Music Education: A Festschrift for Charles Leonhard*, ed. Richard J. Colwell, 249-65. Urbana-Champaign: University of Illinois, 1982.
**CI, FPA, P, R**

Meyer, Leonard B. *Emotion and Meaning in Music.* Chicago: University of Chicago Press, 1956.
**FPA, P**

————. *Explaining Music: Essays and Explorations.* Chicago: University of Chicago Press, 1978.
**FPA, P**

————. *Music, the Arts, and Ideas.* 1967. Reprint, Chicago: University of Chicago Press, 1994.
**A, FPA, P**

————. *Style and Music: Theory, History, and Ideology.* Philadelphia: University of Pennsylvania Press, 1989.
**FPA, P**

Meyer, Max F. *Contributions to a Psychological Theory of Music*. Columbia: University of Missouri, 1901.
P


————. *How We Hear: How Tones Make Music*. Boston: C. T. Branford, 1950.
P


Michel, Donald E. *Music Therapy: An Introduction, Including Music in Special Education*. 2nd ed. Springfield, Ill.: C. C. Thomas, 1985.
CI, P


Miller, Dayton Clarence. *The Science of Musical Sounds*. 2nd ed. 1922. Reprint, St. Clair Shores, Mich.: Scholarly Press, 1980.
P


Miller, Leon K. *Musical Savants: Exceptional Skill in the Mentally Retarded*. Hillsdale, N.J.: Erlbaum Association, 1989.
P


Miller, Linda Bryant. "Children's Musical Behaviors in the Natural Environment." In *Music and Child Development*, ed. J. Craig Peery, Irene W. Peery, and Thomas W. Draper, 206-24. New York: Springer-Verlag, 1987.
CI, P


Miller, Robert F. "Affective Reponse." In *Handbook of Research on Music Teaching and Learning*, ed. Richard J. Colwell, 414-24. New York: Schirmer Books, 1992.
P, R


Mirsky, Allen F. "Attention: A Neuropsychological Perspective." In *Education and the Brain: 77th Yearbook of the National Society for the Study of Education (Part II)*, ed. Jeanne S. Chall and Allan F. Mirsky, 33-60. Chicago: University of Chicago Press, 1978.
P


*Missouri Journal of Research in Music Education*. Jefferson City: Missouri State Department of Education, 1962-.
CI, J, P, R


Mitchell, Ruth, ed. *Measuring Up to the Challenge: What Standards and Assessment Can Do for Arts Education*. New York: ACA Books, 1994.
A, CI, P, RSC

Moles, Abraham A. *Information Theory and Esthetic Perception.* Transl. Joel F. Cohen. Urbana-Champaign: University of Illinois, 1966.
**FPA, P**

Monelle, Raymond. *Linguistics and Semiotics in Music.* Philadelphia: Harwood Academic Press, 1992.
**FPA, P**

Moody, William J., ed. *Artistic Intelligences: Implications for Education.* New York: Teachers College, 1990.
**A, CI, FPA, P, RSC**

Moog, Helmut. *The Musical Experience of the Pre-School Child.* Transl. Claudia Clarke. London: Schott Music, 1976.
**CI, P**

Moore, Brian. "Musical Thinking Processes." In *Dimensions of Musical Thinking*, ed. Eunice Boardman, 33-44. Reston, Va.: Music Educators National Conference, 1989.
**CI, P**

Moore, George. "The Study of Skilled Performance in Musicians." In *The Biology of Music Making: Proceedings of the 1984 Denver Conference*, ed. Franz L. Roehmann and Frank R. Wilson, 77-91. St. Louis, Mo.: MMB Music, 1988.
**P**

Mueller, John H. "Music and Education: A Sociological Approach." In *Basic Concepts in Music Education: 57th Yearbook of the National Society for the Study of Education*, ed. Nelson B. Henry, 88-122. Chicago: University of Chicago Press, 1958.
**P**

Mullins, Shirley. *Teaching Music: The Human Experience.* Yellow Springs, Ohio: S. Mullins, 1985.
**CI, P**

Murphy, Linda L., Jane Close Conoley, and James C. Impara, eds. *Tests in Print IV: An Index to Tests, Test Reviews, and the Literature on Specific Tests.* Lincoln: University of Nebraska Press, 1994.
**BR, P**

Mursell, James L. *Education for Musical Growth.* Boston, Mass.: Ginn, 1948.
**CI, P**

_____. "Growth Processes in Music Education." In *Basic Concepts in Music Education II*, ed. Richard J. Colwell, 111-29. Niwot: University Press of Colorado, 1991.
**CI, P**

_____. "Growth Processes in Music Education." In *Basic Concepts in Music Education: 57th Yearbook of the National Society for the Study of Education*, ed. Nelson B. Henry, 140-62. Chicago: University of Chicago Press, 1958.
**CI, P**

_____. *Human Values in Music Education*. New York: Silver Burdett, 1934.
**CI, FPA, P**

_____. *The Psychology of Music*. 1937. Reprint, New York: Norton, 1976.
**P**

Mursell, James L., and Mabelle Glenn. *The Psychology of School Music Teaching*. New York: Silver Burdett, 1938.
**CI, P**

*Music Education in the Modern World: Materials of the Ninth Conference of the International Society for Music Education*. Moscow: Progress Publishers, 1974.
**CI, P, R, RSC**

*Music in Special Education*. Washington: Music Educators National Conference, 1972.
**CI, P**

*Music Psychology Index*. Vol. 2. Ed. Charles T. Eagle, Jr. Denton, Tex.: Institute for Therapeutics Research, 1978.
**BR, J, P, R**

*Music Psychology Index*. Vol. 3. Ed. Charles T. Eagle, Jr., and John J. Miniter. Phoenix, Ariz.: Oryx, 1984.
**BR, J, P, R**

*Music Therapy Index*. Vol. 1. Ed. Charles T. Eagle, Jr. Lawrence, Kans.: National Association for Music Therapy, 1976.
**BR, J, P, R**

Narmour, Eugene. *The Analysis and Cognition of Basic Melodic Structures: The Implication-Realization Model*. Chicago: University of Chicago Press, 1990.
**P**

_____. *The Analysis and Cognition of Melodic Complexity: The Implication-Realization Model*. Chicago: University of Chicago Press, 1992.
**P**

National Assessment of Educational Progress. *Music 1971-79: Results from the Second National Music Assessment.* Denver, Colo.: Education Commission of the States, 1981.
**P, RSC**

Nettl, Bruno. *The Western Impact on World Music: Change, Adaptation, and Survival.* New York: Schirmer Books, 1985.
**FPA, P**

Newman, Warren Bennett. "The Effect of Standardized Testing in the Arts." In *Artistic Intelligences: Implications for Education*, ed. William J. Moody, 52-56. New York: Teachers College, 1990.
**A, P**

Nicholls, John G. "Task Involvement in Music." In *Documentary Report of the Ann Arbor Symposium on the Applications of Psychology to the Teaching and Learning of Music: Motivation and Creativity (Session III)*, 1-4. Reston, Va.: Music Educators National Conference, 1983.
**P**

Nordoff, Paul, and Clive Robbins. *Music Therapy in Special Education.* 2nd ed. St. Louis, Mo.: MMB, 1983.
**P**

Norris, Christopher, ed. *Music and the Politics of Culture.* New York: St. Martin's, 1989.
**FPA, P**

O'Connor, Joseph. *Not Pulling Strings: An Exploration of Music and Instrumental Teaching Using Neuro-Linguistic Programming.* Portland, Ore.: Metamorphous, 1989.
**CI, P**

Ostwald, Peter F. "Music in the Organization of Childhood Experience and Emotion." In *Music and Child Development: The Biology of Music Making - Proceedings of the 1987 Denver Conference*, ed. Frank R. Wilson and Franz L. Roehmann, 11-27. St. Louis, Mo.: MMB Music, 1990.
**P**

Overby, Lynnette Young, Ann Richardson, Lillian S. Hasko, and Luke Kahlich, eds. *Early Childhood Creative Arts: Proceedings of the International Early Childhood Creative Arts Conference.* Reston, Va.: Music Educators National Conference and National Dance Association, 1991.
**A, CI, P, RSC**

Paddison, Max. *Adorno's Aesthetics of Music.* New York: Cambridge Univerity Press, 1993.
**FPA, P**

Parsons, Michael J. "Cognition as Interpretation in Art Education." In *The Arts, Education, and Aesthetic Knowing: 91st Yearbook of the National Society for the Study of Education (Part II)*, ed. Bennett Reimer and Ralph A. Smith, 70-91. Chicago: University of Chicago Press, 1992.

**A, CI, P**

Pautz, Mary P. "Musical Thinking in the General Music Classroom." In *Dimensions of Musical Thinking*, ed. Eunice Boardman, 65-72. Reston, Va.: Music Educators National Conference, 1989.

**CI, P**

————. "Musical Thinking in the Teacher Education Classroom." In *Dimensions of Musical Thinking*, ed. Eunice Boardman, 101-09. Reston, Va.: Music Educators National Conference, 1989.

**CI, P**

Peery, Irene Weiss, Dale Nyboer, and J. Craig Peery. "The Virtue and Vice of Musical Performance Competitions for Children." In *Music and Child Development*, ed. J. Craig Peery, Irene W. Peery, and Thomas W. Draper, 225-36. New York: Springer-Verlag, 1987.

**CI, P**

Peery, J. Craig, and Irene Weiss Peery. "The Role of Music in Child Development." In *Music and Child Development*, ed. J. Craig Peery, Irene W. Peery, and Thomas W. Draper, 3-31. New York: Springer-Verlag, 1987.

**CI, P**

Peery, J. Craig, Irene W. Peery, and Thomas W. Draper, eds. *Music and Child Development*. New York: Springer-Verlag, 1987.

**P**

Perris, Arnold. *Music as Propaganda: Art to Persuade, Art to Control*. Westport, Conn.: Greenwood, 1985.

**FPA, P**

Peters, G. David, and Robert F. Miller. *Music Teaching and Learning*. New York: Longman, 1982.

**CI, P**

Peters, Jacqueline Schmidt. *Music Therapy: An Introduction*. Springfield, Ill.: C. C. Thomas, 1987.

**P**

Petzold, Robert G. "Child Development." In *Documentary Report of the Ann Arbor Symposium: National Symposium on the Applications of Psychology to the Teaching and Learning of Music (Sessions I and II)*, 42-48. Reston, Va.: Music Educators National Conference, 1981.
**P, R**

Piaget, Jean. *The Child and Reality: Problems of Genetic Psychology.* Transl. Arnold Rosin. New York: Penguin Books, 1976.
**P**

_____. *The Child's Conception of the World.* Transl. Joan and Andrew Tomlinson. 1929. Reprint, Totowa, N.J.: Rowman and Littlefield, 1989.
**P**

_____. *Judgment and Reasoning in the Child.* 1928. Reprint, Totowa, N.J.: Littlefield, Adams, 1976.
**P**

_____. *The Language and Thought of the Child.* 1926. 3rd ed., rev. New York: Humanities Press, 1989.
**P**

_____. *Logic and Psychology.* Transl. W. Mays and F. Whitehead. 1953. Reprint, Manchester, England: Manchester University Press, 1965.
**P**

_____. *The Origins of Intelligence in Children.* Transl. Margaret Cook. 1952. Reprint, New York: International Universities Press, 1974.
**P**

_____. *The Psychology of Intelligence.* Transl. Malcolm Piercy and D. E. Berlyne. 1947. Reprint, Totowa, N.J.: Littlefield, Adams, 1981.
**P**

_____. *To Understand Is to Invent: The Future of Education.* Transl. George-Anne Roberts. 1948. Reprint, New York: Penguin, 1976.
**CI, P**

Piaget, Jean, and Barbel Inhelder. *The Psychology of the Child.* Transl. Helen Weaver. New York: Basic Books, 1969.
**P**

Pierce, John Robinson. *The Science of Musical Sound.* Rev. ed. New York. W. H. Freeman, 1992.
**P**

Pike, Alfred John. *A Phenomenological Analysis of Musical Experience and Other Related Essays.* New York: St. John's, 1970.
**FPA, P**

Podolsky, Edward, ed. *Music Therapy.* New York: Philosophical Library, 1954.
**P**

Pogonowski, Lenore. "Metacognition: A Dimension of Musical Thinking." In *Dimensions of Musical Thinking*, ed. Eunice Boardman, 9-19. Reston, Va.: Music Educators National Conference, 1989.
**CI, P**

Pratt, Carroll C. *The Meaning of Music: A Study in Psychological Aesthetics.* 1931. Reprint, Ann Arbor, Mich.: University Microfilms International, 1979.
**FPA, P**

Pratt, Rosalie R., ed. *International Symposium on Music in Medicine, Education, and Therapy for the Handicapped.* Lanham, Md.: University Press of America, 1985.
**CI, P, RSC**

_____, ed. *Music Therapy and Music Education for the Handicapped: Developments and Limitations in Practice and Research.* St. Louis, Mo.: MMB Music, 1993.
**CI, P, RSC**

Pratt, Rosalie R., and Barbara Hesser, eds. *Music Therapy and Music in Special Education: The International State of the Art.* St. Louis, Mo.: MMB Music for the International Society for Music Education, 1989.
**P, RSC**

Priestley, Mary. *Music Therapy in Action.* 2nd ed. St. Louis, Mo.: MMB Music, 1985.
**P**

Pring, Richard. "Creative Development at 14 + ." In *The Aesthetic in Education*, ed. Malcolm Ross, 115-31. New York: Pergamon, 1985.
**A, P**

*Quarterly Journal of Music Teaching and Learning.* Greeley: University of Northern Colorado School of Music, 1990-.
**CI, FPA, J, P, R**

Radocy, Rudolf E. "The Perception of Melody, Harmony, Rhythm, and Form." In *Handbook of Music Psychology*, ed. Donald A. Hodges, 93-104. Lawrence, Kans.: National Association for Music Therapy, 1980.
**P**

Radocy, Rudolf E., and J. David Boyle. *Psychological Foundations of Musical Behaviors.* 2nd ed. Springfield, Ill.: Charles C. Thomas, 1988.
**P, R**

Raffman, Diana. "Goodman, Density, and the Limits of Sense Peception." In *The Interpretation of Music: Philosophical Essays*, ed. Michael Krausz, 215-27. New York: Oxford University Press, 1992.
**FPA, P**

_____. *Language, Music, and Mind.* Cambridge, Mass.: MIT, 1993.
**FPA, P**

Raynor, Joel O. "Motivational Determinants of Music-Related Behavior: Psychological Careers of Student, Teacher, Performer, and Listener." In *Documentary Report of the Ann Arbor Symposium: National Symposium on the Applications of Psychology to the Teaching and Learning of Music (Sessions I and II)*, 332-51. Reston, Va.: Music Educators National Conference, 1981.
**P, R**

_____. "Step-Path Theory and the Motivation for Achievement." In *Documentary Report of the Ann Arbor Symposium on the Applications of Psychology to the Teaching and Learning of Music: Motivation and Creativity (Session III)*, 17-22. Reston, Va.: Music Educators National Conference, 1983.
**P**

Redfield, John. *Music: A Science and an Art.* New ed. New York: Tudor Publishing, 1935.
**FPA, P**

Regelski, Thomas A. *Arts Education and Brain Research.* Reston, Va.: Music Educators National Conference, 1978.
**A, CI, P**

Reid, Louis Arnaud. "Aesthetic Knowledge in the Arts." In *The Arts: A Way of Knowing*, ed. Malcolm Ross, 19-41. New York: Pergamon, 1983.
**A, FPA, P**

_____. "Assessment and Aesthetic Education." In *The Aesthetic Imperative: Relevance and Responsibility in Arts Education*, ed. Malcolm Ross, 8-24. New York: Pergamon, 1981.
**A, CI, FPA, P**

_____. *Meaning in the Arts.* New York: Humanities Press, 1969.
**A, CI, FPA, P**

Reimer, Bennett. "Aesthetic Behaviors in Music." In *Toward an Aesthetic Education: A Report*, 65-87. Washington: Music Educators National Conference, 1971.

**A, CI, FPA, P**

_____. "Designing Effective Arts Programs." In *Arts and the Schools*, ed. Jerome J. Hausman and Joyce Wright, 117-56. New York: McGraw-Hill, 1980.

**A, CI, FPA, P**

_____. "Music Education Philosophy and Psychology after Mursell." In *Basic Concepts in Music Education II*, ed. Richard J. Colwell, 130-56. Niwot: University Press of Colorado, 1991.

**FPA, P**

_____. "What Knowledge Is of Most Worth in the Arts?" In *The Arts, Education, and Aesthetic Knowing: 91st Yearbook of the National Society for the Study of Education (Part II)*, ed. Bennett Reimer and Ralph A. Smith, 20-50. Chicago: University of Chicago Press, 1992.

**A, CI, FPA, P**

Reimer, Bennett, and Ralph A. Smith, eds. *The Arts, Education, and Aesthetic Knowing: 91st Yearbook of the National Society for the Study of Education (Part II)*. Chicago: National Society for the Study of Education, 1992.

**A, BR, CI, FPA, P**

Resnick, Lauren B., and Leopold E. Klopfer, eds. *Toward the Thinking Curriculum: Current Cognitive Research*. Alexandria, Va.: Association for Supervision and Curriculum Development, 1989.

**CI, P, R**

Revesz, Geza. *Introduction to the Psychology of Music*. Transl. G. I. C. De Courcy. Norman: University of Oklahoma Press, 1954.

**P**

_____. *The Psychology of a Musical Prodigy*. 1925. Reprint, Westport, Conn.: Greenwood, 1970.

**P**

Richardson, Carol P., and Nancy L. Whitaker. "Critical Thinking and Music Education." In *Handbook of Research on Music Teaching and Learning*, ed. Richard J. Colwell, 546-57. New York: Schirmer Books, 1992.

**CI, P, R**

Rideout, Roger R. "The Role of Mental Presets in Skill Acquisition." In *Handbook of Research on Music Teaching and Learning*, ed. Richard J. Colwell, 472-79. New York: Schirmer Books, 1992.
**CI, P, R**

Ristad, Eloise. *A Soprano on Her Head: Right-Side-Up Reflections on Life and Other Performances.* Moab, Utah: Real People, 1982.
**CI, P**

Rivas, Frank W. *The First National Assessment of Musical Performance - National Assessment of Educational Progress: A Project of the Education Commission of the States.* Washington: United States Government Printing Office, 1974.
**CI, P, RSC**

Rochlitz, Rainer. "Language for One, Language for All: Adorno and Modernism." In *Perspectives on Musical Aesthetics*, ed. John Rahn, 21-39. New York: Norton, 1994.
**FPA, P**

Roederer, Juan G. *Introduction to the Physics and Psychophysics of Music.* 2nd ed. New York: Springer-Verlag, 1979.
**P**

Roehmann, Franz L., and Frank R. Wilson, eds. *The Biology of Music Making: Proceedings of the 1984 Denver Conference.* St. Louis, Mo.: MMB Music, 1988.
**P, RSC**

Rogers, Sally J. "Theories of Child Development and Musical Ability." In *Music and Child Development: The Biology of Music Making - Proceedings of the 1987 Denver Conference*, ed. Frank R. Wilson and Franz L. Roehmann, 1-10. St. Louis, Mo.: MMB Music, 1990.
**P**

Rohwer, William D., Jr., and Kathryn Sloane. "Psychological Perspectives." In *Bloom's Taxonomy—A Forty-Year Retrospective: 93rd Yearbook of the National Society for the Study of Education (Part II)*, ed. Lorin W. Anderson and Lauren A. Sosniak, 41-63. Chicago: University of Chicago Press, 1994.
**CI, P**

Ross, Malcolm, ed. *Assessment in Arts Education: A Necessary Discipline or a Loss of Happiness?* New York: Pergamon, 1986.
**A, CI, P**

Rossing, Thomas D. *The Science of Sound.* 2nd ed. Reading, Mass.: Addison-Wesley, 1990.
**P**

Rossman, R. Louis, comp. *TIPS: Discipline in the Music Classroom.* Reston, Va.: Music Educators National Conference, 1989.
CI, P

Rubinstein, Michael. *Music to My Ear: Reflections on Music and Digressions on Metaphysics.* London: Quartet, 1985.
FPA, P

Rudel, Rita G. "Neuroplasticity: Implications for Development and Education." In *Education and the Brain: 77th Yearbook of the National Society for the Study of Education (Part II),* ed. Jeanne S. Chall and Allan F. Mirsky, 269-307. Chicago: University of Chicago Press, 1978.
P

Ruud, Even. *Music Therapy and Its Relationship to Current Treatment Theories.* Rev. ed. St. Louis, Mo.: Magnamusic-Baton, 1980.
P

Schaberg, Gail, comp. *TIPS: Teaching Music to Special Learners.* Reston, Va.: Music Educators National Conference, 1988.
CI, P

Schafer, R. Murray. *Ear Cleaning: Notes for an Experimental Music Course.* Toronto: Clark and Cruickshank, 1969.
CI, P

_____. *The Soundscape: Our Sonic Environment and the Tuning of the World.* 1977. Reprint, Rochester, Vt.: Destiny Books, 1994.
CI, FPA, P

_____. *The Thinking Ear: Complete Writings on Music Education.* Toronto: Arcana Editions, 1986.
CI, P

Schiller Institute. *A Manual on the Rudiments of Tuning and Registration.* Washington: Schiller Institute, 1992.
BR, P

Schleuter, Stanley and Lois. "Teaching and Learning Music Performance: What, When, and How." In *The Crane Symposium: Toward an Understanding of the Teaching and Learning of Music Performance,* ed. Charles Fowler, 63-87. Potsdam: Potsdam College of the State University of New York, 1988.
CI, P

Schmitt, Cecilia. *Rapport and Success: Human Relations in Music Education.* Philadelphia: Dorrance, 1976.
**CI, P**

Schneiderman, Barbara. *Confident Music Performance: The Art of Preparing.* St. Louis, Mo.: MMB Music, 1991.
**CI, P**

Schoen, Max. *The Psychology of Music.* New York: Ronald, 1940.
**P**

_____. *The Understanding of Music.* 1945. Reprint, Ann Arbor, Mich.: University Microfilms, 1962.
**FPA, P**

_____, ed. *The Effects of Music: A Series of Essays.* 1927. Reprint, Freeport, N.Y.: Books for Libraries, 1968.
**P**

Schulberg, Cecilia H. *The Music Therapy Sourcebook: A Collection of Activities Categorized and Analyzed.* New York: Human Sciences, 1981.
**BR, CI, P**

Schullian, Dorothy M., and Max Shoen, eds. *Music and Medicine.* 1948. Reprint, Freeport, N.Y.: Books for Libraries, 1971.
**P**

Schwartz, Herbert. "Music and Emotion." In *Perspectives on Musical Aesthetics*, ed. John Rahn, 293-96. New York: Norton, 1994.
**FPA, P**

Scott, Carol Rogel. "Getting There from Here: The Examination of Musical Growth in Young Children." In *Research in Music Education: A Festschrift for Arnold Bentley*, ed. Anthony E. Kemp, 74-80. London: International Society for Music Education, 1988.
**P, R**

Scott-Kassner, Carol. "Research on Music in Early Childhood." In *Handbook of Research on Music Teaching and Learning*, ed. Richard J. Colwell, 633-50. New York: Schirmer Books, 1992.
**CI, P, R**

Seashore, Carl Emil. *In Search of Beauty in Music: A Scientific Approach to Music Esthetics.* 1947. Reprint, Westport, Conn.: Greenwood, 1981.
**FPA, P**

————. *Pioneering in Psychology.* Iowa City: University of Iowa Press, 1942.
P

————. *Psychology of Music.* 1938. Reprint, New York: Dover, 1967.
P

————. *The Psychology of Musical Talent.* New York: Silver Burdett, 1919.
P

————. *Psychology of the Vibrato in Voice and Instrument.* Iowa City: University Press, 1936.
P

————. *Why We Love Music.* Philadelphia: Oliver Ditson, 1941.
FPA, P

————, ed. *Objective Analysis of Musical Performance.* Iowa City: University Press, 1936.
P

————, ed. *The Vibrato.* Iowa City: University Press, 1932.
P

Seashore, Carl Emil, Don Lewis, and Joseph G. Seatveit. *Seashore Measures of Musical Talents.* Rev. ed. New York: Psychological Corp., 1960.
P

Serafine, Mary Louise. "Music." In *Cognition and Instruction,* ed. Ronna F. Dillon and Robert J. Sternberg, 299-341. New York: Academic Press, 1986.
CI, P

————. *Music as Cognition: The Development of Thought in Sound.* New York: Columbia University Press, 1988.
P

Sessions, Roger. *The Musical Experience of Composer, Performer, Listener.* Princeton, N.J.: Princeton University Press, 1950, 1974.
FPA, P

Shehan, Patricia K. "Movement in the Music Education of Children." In *Music and Child Development: The Biology of Music Making - Proceedings of the 1987 Denver Conference,* ed. Frank R. Wilson and Franz L. Roehmann, 354-65. St. Louis, Mo.: MMB Music, 1990.
CI, P, R

Shepard, Roger N. "Individual Differences in the Perception of Musical Pitch." In *Documentary Report of the Ann Arbor Symposium: National Symposium on the Applications of Psychology to the Teaching and Learning of Music (Sessions I and II)*, 152-74. Reston, Va.: Music Educators National Conference, 1981.

**P, R**

Shepherd, John. "Media, Social Process and Music." In *Whose Music? A Sociology of Musical Languages*, ed. John Shepherd, Phil Virden, Graham Vulliamy, and Trevor Wishart, 7-51. London: Latimer, 1977.

**FPA, P**

————. "Music and Male Hegemony." In *Music and Society: The Politics of Composition, Performance, and Reception*, ed. Richard D. Leppert and Susan McClary, 151-72. New York: Cambridge University Press, 1987.

**FPA, P**

————. *Music as Social Text*. Cambridge, England: Polity, 1991.

**P**

————. "The Musical Coding of Ideologies." In *Whose Music? A Sociology of Musical Languages*, ed. John Shepherd, Phil Virden, Graham Vulliamy, and Trevor Wishart, 69-124. London: Latimer, 1977.

**FPA, P**

Shepherd, John, Phil Virden, Graham Vulliamy, and Trevor Wishart, eds. *Whose Music? A Sociology of Musical Languages*. London: Latimer, 1977.

**FPA, P**

Shetler, Donald J. "The Inquiry into Prenatal Musical Experience." In *Music and Child Development: The Biology of Music Making - Proceedings of the 1987 Denver Conference*, ed. Frank R. Wilson and Franz L. Roehmann, 44-62. St. Louis, Mo.: MMB Music, 1990.

**P**

Shuell, Thomas. "The Role of Transfer in the Learning and Teaching of Music: A Cognitive Perspective." In *The Crane Symposium: Toward an Understanding of the Teaching and Learning of Music Performance*, ed. Charles Fowler, 143-67. Potsdam: Potsdam College of the State University of New York, 1988.

**CI, P**

Shuler, Scott C. "Assessment in General Music: Trends and Innovations in Local, State, and National Assessment." In *Toward Tomorrow: New Visions for General Music*, ed. Sandra L. Stauffer, 51-66. Reston, Va.: Music Educators National Conference, 1995.

**A, CI, P**

Shuter-Dyson, Rosamund. "Musical Ability." In *The Psychology of Music*, ed. Diana Deutsch, 391-412. New York: Academic Press, 1982.
**P, R**

Shuter-Dyson, Rosamund, and Clive Gabriel. *The Psychology of Musical Ability.* 2nd ed., rev. New York: Methuen, 1981.
**P**

Sibley, Frank. "Making Music Our Own." In *The Interpretation of Music: Philosophical Essays*, ed. Michael Krausz, 165-76. New York: Oxford University Press, 1992.
**FPA, P**

Sidnell, Robert G. "Motor Learning in Music Education." In *Documentary Report of the Ann Arbor Symposium: National Symposium on the Applications of Psychology to the Teaching and Learning of Music (Sessions I and II)*, 28-35. Reston, Va.: Music Educators National Conference, 1981.
**CI, P, R**

Siegel, Jane A. "Culturally Defined Learning Experience." In *Documentary Report of the Ann Arbor Symposium: National Symposium on the Applications of Psychology to the Teaching and Learning of Music (Sessions I and II)*, 200-16. Reston, Va.: Music Educators National Conference, 1981.
**P, R**

Siegmeister, Elie. *Music and Society.* 1938. Reprint, New York: Haskell House, 1974.
**FPA, P**

Silbermann, Alphons. *The Sociology of Music.* Transl. Corbet Stewart. 1963. Reprint, Westport, Conn.: Greenwood, 1977.
**P**

Silvers, Anita. "Show and Tell: The Arts, Cognition, and Basic Modes of Referring." In *The Arts, Cognition and Basic Skills*, ed. Stanley S. Madeja, 31-50. St. Louis, Mo.: CEMREL, 1978.
**A, P**

Simons, Gene M. *Early Childhood Musical Development: A Bibliography of Research Abstracts, 1960-1975, with Implications and Recommendations for Teaching and Research.* Reston, Va.: Music Educators National Conference, 1978.
**BR, CI, P, R**

―――――. *Simons Measurements of Music Listening Skills.* Chicago: Stoelting, 1974.
**P**

Simonton, Dean Keith. "Aesthetics, Biography, and History in Musical Creativity." In *Documentary Report of the Ann Arbor Symposium on the Applications of Psychology to the Teaching and Learning of Music: Motivation and Creativity (Session III)*, 41-48. Reston, Va.: Music Educators National Conference, 1983.

**FPA, P**

Simpson, Elizabeth Jane. *The Classification of Educational Objectives: Psychomotor Domain.* Urbana: University of Illinois, 1966.

**CI, P**

Sink, Patricia E., ed. *Research Symposium on the Psychology and Acoustics of Music, 1982.* Lawrence: University of Kansas Department of Art and Music Education and Music Therapy, 1982.

**P, R, RSC**

Slawson, Wayne. *Sound Color.* Berkeley: University of California Press, 1985.

**P**

Sloboda, John A. "Music as a Language." In *Music and Child Development: The Biology of Music Making - Proceedings of the 1987 Denver Conference*, ed. Frank R. Wilson and Franz L. Roehmann, 28-43. St. Louis, Mo.: MMB Music, 1990.

**FPA, P**

————. *The Musical Mind: The Cognitive Psychology of Music.* New York: Oxford University Press, 1989.

**P**

————, ed. *Generative Processes in Music: The Psychology of Performance, Improvisation and Composition.* New York: Oxford University Press, 1988.

**CI, P**

Small, Christopher. *Music, Society, Education: A Radical Examination of the Prophetic Function of Music in Western, Eastern, and African Cultures with Its Impact on Society and Its Use in Education.* 2nd rev. ed. London: J. Calder, 1980.

**CI, P**

Smith, Charles Thomas. *Music and Reason: The Art of Listening, Appreciating and Composing.* New York: Social Sciences Publishers, 1948.

**P**

————. *Music and Reason: The Basis of Listening, Composing and Assessing.* London: Watts, 1947.

**P**

Smith, F. Joseph. "Music Educating as Phenomenologist: An Overview." In *Music Education for Tomorrow's Society*, ed. Arthur Motycka, 73-83. Jamestown, R.I.: GAMT Music, 1976.
**FPA, P**

Smith, Nancy R. "Classroom Practice: Creating Meaning in the Arts." In *Arts and the Schools*, ed. Jerome J. Hausman and Joyce Wright, 79-115. New York: McGraw-Hill, 1980.
**A, CI, P**

Snyder Knuth, Alice. *Snyder Knuth Music Achievement Test*. San Francisco: Creative Arts Research Associates, 1968.
**P**

Soibelman, Doris. *Therapeutic and Industrial Uses of Music: A Review of the Literature*. New York: Columbia University Press, 1948.
**P, R**

Sosniak, Lauren A. "The Taxonomy, Curriculum, and Their Relations." In *Bloom's Taxonomy—A Forty-Year Retrospective: 93rd Yearbook of the National Society for the Study of Education (Part II)*, ed. Lorin W. Anderson and Lauren A. Sosniak, 103-25. Chicago: University of Chicago Press, 1994.
**CI, P**

*Southeastern Journal of Music Education*. Athens: University of Georgia Center for Continuing Education, 1990-.
**CI, J, P, R**

Stanton, Hazel Martha. *Measurement of Musical Talent: The Eastman Experiment*. Ed. Carl Emil Seashore. Iowa City: University of Iowa, 1935.
**P**

Stebbing, Lionel, comp. *Music Therapy: A New Anthology*. Sussex, England: New Knowledge Books, 1975.
**BR, P**

Storr, Anthony. *Music and the Mind*. New York: Maxwell Macmillan International, 1992.
**FPA, P**

Stringham, Mary, comp. *Orff-Schulwerk, Background and Commentary: Articles from German and Austrian Periodicals*. Transl. Mary Stringham. St. Louis, Mo.: MMB Music, 1976.
**CI, P**

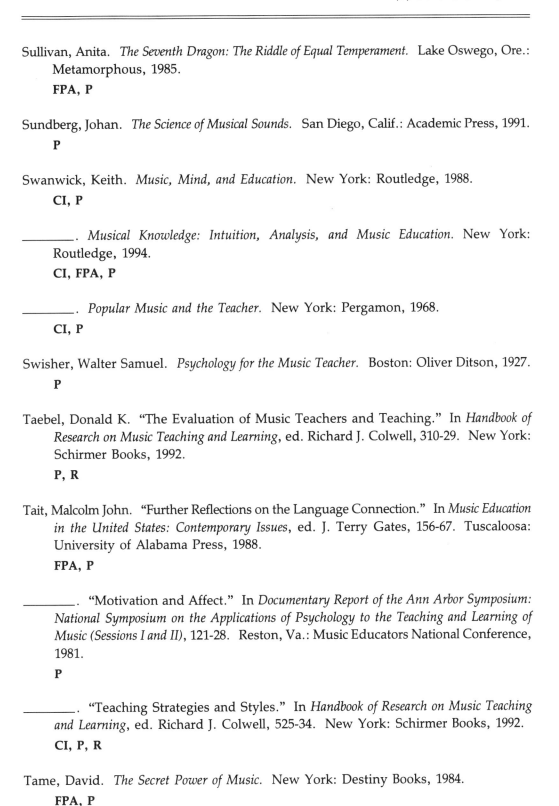

Sullivan, Anita. *The Seventh Dragon: The Riddle of Equal Temperament.* Lake Oswego, Ore.: Metamorphous, 1985.
**FPA, P**

Sundberg, Johan. *The Science of Musical Sounds.* San Diego, Calif.: Academic Press, 1991.
**P**

Swanwick, Keith. *Music, Mind, and Education.* New York: Routledge, 1988.
**CI, P**

————. *Musical Knowledge: Intuition, Analysis, and Music Education.* New York: Routledge, 1994.
**CI, FPA, P**

————. *Popular Music and the Teacher.* New York: Pergamon, 1968.
**CI, P**

Swisher, Walter Samuel. *Psychology for the Music Teacher.* Boston: Oliver Ditson, 1927.
**P**

Taebel, Donald K. "The Evaluation of Music Teachers and Teaching." In *Handbook of Research on Music Teaching and Learning*, ed. Richard J. Colwell, 310-29. New York: Schirmer Books, 1992.
**P, R**

Tait, Malcolm John. "Further Reflections on the Language Connection." In *Music Education in the United States: Contemporary Issues*, ed. J. Terry Gates, 156-67. Tuscaloosa: University of Alabama Press, 1988.
**FPA, P**

————. "Motivation and Affect." In *Documentary Report of the Ann Arbor Symposium: National Symposium on the Applications of Psychology to the Teaching and Learning of Music (Sessions I and II)*, 121-28. Reston, Va.: Music Educators National Conference, 1981.
**P**

————. "Teaching Strategies and Styles." In *Handbook of Research on Music Teaching and Learning*, ed. Richard J. Colwell, 525-34. New York: Schirmer Books, 1992.
**CI, P, R**

Tame, David. *The Secret Power of Music.* New York: Destiny Books, 1984.
**FPA, P**

Taubman, Dorothy. "A Teacher's Perspectives on Musicians' Injuries." In *The Biology of Music Making: Proceedings of the 1984 Denver Conference*, ed. Franz L. Roehmann and Frank R. Wilson, 144-53. St. Louis, Mo.: MMB Music, 1988.
**CI, P**

Taylor, Charles Alfred. *Exploring Music: The Science and Technology of Tones and Tunes.* Philadelphia: Institute of Physics Publishing, 1992.
**P**

————. *The Physics of Musical Sounds.* New York: American Elsevier, 1965.
**P**

Taylor, Dale B. "Childhood Sequential Development of Rhythm, Melody and Pitch." In *Music and Child Development: The Biology of Music Making - Proceedings of the 1987 Denver Conference*, ed. Frank R. Wilson and Franz L. Roehmann, 241-53. St. Louis, Mo.: MMB Music, 1990.
**CI, P**

Taylor, Jack A. "The Development of Musical Performance Skills in Children." In *Music and Child Development: The Biology of Music Making - Proceedings of the 1987 Denver Conference*, ed. Frank R. Wilson and Franz L. Roehmann, 214-24. St. Louis, Mo.: MMB Music, 1990.
**P**

Tenney, James. *A History of "Consonance" and "Dissonance."* New York: Excelsior, 1988.
**FPA, P**

Teyler, Timothy J. "The Brain Sciences: An Introduction." In *Education and the Brain: 77th Yearbook of the National Society for the Study of Education (Part II)*, ed. Jeanne S. Chall and Allan F. Mirsky, 1-32. Chicago: University of Chicago Press, 1978.
**P**

Thomas, Nancy G. "Motivation." In *Handbook of Research on Music Teaching and Learning*, ed. Richard J. Colwell, 425-36. New York: Schirmer Books, 1992.
**P, R**

Thorpe, Louis P. "Learning Theory and Music Teaching." In *Basic Concepts in Music Education: 57th Yearbook of the National Society for the Study of Education*, ed. Nelson B. Henry, 163-94. Chicago: University of Chicago Press, 1958.
**CI, P**

Tighe, Thomas J., and W. Jay Dowling, eds. *Psychology and Music: The Understanding of Melody and Rhythm.* Hillsdale, N.J.: Erlbaum, 1992.
**P**

Tolbert, Mary R., ed. *Evaluating the Arts in Schools: New Concepts.* Columbus: Ohio State University, 1974.
**A, P**

Tonkin, Humphrey. "Sound, Meaning, and Sanity." In *The Crane Symposium: Toward an Understanding of the Teaching and Learning of Music Performance*, ed. Charles Fowler, 21-24. Potsdam: Potsdam College of the State University of New York, 1988.
**FPA, P**

Treffinger, Donald J. "Fostering Creativity and Problem Solving." In *Documentary Report of the Ann Arbor Symposium on the Applications of Psychology to the Teaching and Learning of Music: Motivation and Creativity (Session III)*, 55-59. Reston, Va.: Music Educators National Conference, 1983.
**CI, P**

Trotter, T. H. Yorke. *Music and Mind.* London: Methuen, 1924.
**CI, P**

Tunks, Thomas W. "Applications of Psychological Positions on Learning and Development to Musical Behavior." In *Handbook of Music Psychology*, ed. Donald A. Hodges, 275-90. Lawrence, Kans.: National Association for Music Therapy, 1980.
**CI, P**

————. "The Transfer of Music Learning." In *Handbook of Research on Music Teaching and Learning*, ed. Richard J. Colwell, 437-47. New York: Schirmer Books, 1992.
**CI, P, R**

Turk, Gayla C., ed. *Proceedings of the Research Symposium on the Psychology and Acoustics of Music, 1985.* Lawrence: University of Kansas Department of Art and Music Education and Music Therapy, 1985.
**P, R, RSC**

Tyndall, John. *The Science of Sound.* 1867. Reprint, New York: Philosophical Library, 1964.
**P**

Upitis, Rena. *Can I Play You My Song? The Compositions and Invented Notations of Children.* Portsmouth, N.H.: Heinemann, 1992.
**CI, P**

Vallance, Elizabeth. "Artistic Intelligences and General Education." In *Artistic Intelligences: Implications for Education*, ed. William J. Moody, 79-84. New York: Teachers College, 1990.
**A, CI, P**

Van de Wall, Willem. *Music in Hospitals.* New York: Russell Sage Foundation, 1946.
P

Virden, Phil, and Trevor Wishart. "Some Observations on the Social Stratification of Twentieth-Century Music." In *Whose Music? A Sociology of Musical Languages,* ed. John Shepherd, Phil Virden, Graham Vulliamy, and Trevor Wishart, 155-77. London: Latimer, 1977.
FPA, P

Vulliamy, Graham. "Music and the Mass Culture Debate." In *Whose Music? A Sociology of Musical Languages,* ed. John Shepherd, Phil Virden, Graham Vulliamy, and Trevor Wishart, 179-200. London: Latimer, 1977.
FPA, P

————. "Music as a Case Study in the 'New Sociology of Education'." In *Whose Music? A Sociology of Musical Languages,* ed. John Shepherd, Phil Virden, Graham Vulliamy, and Trevor Wishart, 201-32. London: Latimer, 1977.
FPA, P

Vulliamy, Graham, and Ed Lee, eds. *Pop, Rock and Ethnic Music in School.* New York: Cambridge University Press, 1982.
CI, P

Wade, Michael G. "Motor Skills and the Making of Music." In *Music and Child Development: The Biology of Music Making - Proceedings of the 1987 Denver Conference,* ed. Frank R. Wilson and Franz L. Roehmann, 157-78. St. Louis, Mo.: MMB Music, 1990.
P

Wagner, Michael J. *Introductory Musical Acoustics.* 3rd ed. Raleigh, N.C.: Contemporary Publishing, 1994.
P

Walker, Edward L. "Hedgehog Theory and Music Education." In *Documentary Report of the Ann Arbor Symposium: National Symposium on the Applications of Psychology to the Teaching and Learning of Music (Sessions I and II),* 317-28. Reston, Va.: Music Educators National Conference, 1981.
P, R

Walker, Robert. "Auditory-Visual Perception and Musical Behavior." In *Handbook of Research on Music Teaching and Learning,* ed. Richard J. Colwell, 344-59. New York: Schirmer Books, 1992.
P, R

_____. *Musical Beliefs: Psychoacoustic, Mythical, and Educational Perspectives.* New York: Teachers College, 1990.
**FPA, P**

Wallach, Michael A. "Creativity and Talent." In *Documentary Report of the Ann Arbor Symposium on the Applications of Psychology to the Teaching and Learning of Music: Motivation and Creativity (Session III)*, 23-29. Reston, Va.: Music Educators National Conference, 1983.
**P**

Wallin, Nils Lennart. *Biomusicology: Neurophysiological, Neuropsychological, and Evolutionary Perspectives on the Origins and Purposes of Music.* Stuyvesant, N.Y.: Pendragon, 1991.
**P**

Walters, Darrel L. "Sequencing for Efficient Learning." In *Handbook of Research on Music Teaching and Learning*, ed. Richard J. Colwell, 535-45. New York: Schirmer Books, 1992.
**CI, P, R**

Walters, Darrel L., and Cynthia Crump Taggart, eds. *Readings in Music Learning Theory.* Chicago: G.I.A. Publications, 1989.
**CI, P**

Walton, Kendall. "Understanding Humour and Understanding Music." In *The Interpretation of Music: Philosophical Essays*, ed. Michael Krausz, 259-69. New York: Oxford University Press, 1992.
**FPA, P**

Ward, David. "The Arts and Special Needs." In *The Claims of Feeling: Readings in Aesthetic Education*, ed. Malcolm Ross, 99-118. Philadelphia: Falmer, 1989.
**A, CI, P**

Watkins, Anthony J., and Mary C. Dyson. "On the Perceptual Organization of Tone Sequences and Melodies." In *Musical Structure and Cognition*, ed. Peter Howell, Ian Cross, and Robert West, 71-119. London: Academic Press, 1985.
**P**

Watkins, John G. *Objective Measurement of Instrumental Performance.* 1942. Reprint, New York: AMS, 1972.
**P**

Watkins, John G., and Stephen E. Farnum. *The Watkins-Farnum Performance Scale: A Standardized Achievement Test for All Band Instruments.* Rev. ed. Winona, Minn.: Hal Leonard, 1962.
**P**

Watson, Andrew, and Nevill Drury. *Healing Music.* Garden City Park, N.Y.: Avery, 1988.
   **P**

Webster, Peter R. "Conceptual Bases for Creative Thinking in Music." In *Music and Child Development*, ed. J. Craig Peery, Irene W. Peery, and Thomas W. Draper, 158-74. New York: Springer-Verlag, 1987.
   **P, R**

_____. "Creative Thinking in Music: Approaches to Research." In *Music Education in the United States: Contemporary Issues*, ed. J. Terry Gates, 66-81. Tuscaloosa: University of Alabama Press, 1988.
   **P, R**

_____. "Research on Creative Thinking in Music: The Assessment Literature." In *Handbook of Research on Music Teaching and Learning*, ed. Richard J. Colwell, 266-80. New York: Schirmer Books, 1992.
   **P, R**

Welsbacher, Betty. "Musical Thinking in the Special Education Classroom." In *Dimensions of Musical Thinking*, ed. Eunice Boardman, 91-99. Reston, Va.: Music Educators National Conference, 1989.
   **CI, P**

West, Robert, Peter Howell, and Ian Cross. "Modelling Perceived Musical Structure." In *Musical Structure and Cognition*, ed. Peter Howell, Ian Cross, and Robert West, 21-52. London: Academic Press, 1985.
   **P**

Whipple, Guy Montrose, ed. *Music Education: 35th Yearbook of the National Society for the Study of Education (Part II).* Bloomington, Ill.: Public School Publishing, 1936.
   **BR, CI, FPA, P**

White, Harvey E. and Donald H. *Physics and Music: The Science of Musical Sound.* Philadelphia: Saunders College, 1980.
   **P**

Whitehead, Alfred North. *The Aims of Education, and Other Essays.* 1929. Reprint, New York: Free Press, 1967.
   **CI, FPA, P**

Whybrew, William Ernest. *Measurement and Evaluation in Music.* 2nd ed. Dubuque, Iowa: William C. Brown, 1971.
   **P**

Williams, David Brian. "Music Information Processing and Memory." In *Documentary Report of the Ann Arbor Symposium: National Symposium on the Applications of Psychology to the Teaching and Learning of Music (Sessions I and II)*, 87-93. Reston, Va.: Music Educators National Conference, 1981.
**P, R**

Wilson, Frank R. "Brain Mechanisms in Highly Skilled Movements." In *The Biology of Music Making: Proceedings of the 1984 Denver Conference*, ed. Franz L. Roehmann and Frank R. Wilson, 92-99. St. Louis, Mo.: MMB Music, 1988.
**P**

_____. *Mind, Muscle, and Music: Physiological Clues to Better Teaching*. Elkhart, Ind.: Selmer, 1981.
**CI, P**

_____. *Tone Deaf and All Thumbs? An Introduction to Music Making for Late Bloomers and Non-Prodigies*. New York: Viking-Penguin, 1986.
**CI, P**

Wilson, Frank R., and Franz L. Roehmann. "The Study of Biomechanical and Physiological Processes in Relation to Musical Performance." In *Handbook of Research on Music Teaching and Learning*, ed. Richard J. Colwell, 509-24. New York: Schirmer Books, 1992.
**CI, P, R**

_____, eds. *Music and Child Development: The Biology of Music Making - Proceedings of the 1987 Denver Conference*. St. Louis, Mo.: MMB Music, 1990.
**CI, P, RSC**

Winckel, Fritz. *Music, Sound, and Sensation: A Modern Exposition*. Transl. Thomas Binkley. New York: Dover, 1967.
**P**

Wing, Herbert Daniel. *Tests of Musical Ability and Appreciation: An Investigation into the Measurement, Distribution, and Development of Musical Capacity*. 2nd ed. London: Cambridge University Press, 1968.
**P**

_____. *Wing Standardised Tests of Musical Intelligence*. 1939. Rev. ed. The Mere, England: National Foundation for Educational Research, 1961.
**P**

Winick, Steven. *Rhythm: An Annotated Bibliography*. Metuchen, N.J.: Scarecrow, 1974.
**BR, P, R**

Wishart, Trevor. "Musical Writing, Musical Speaking." In *Whose Music? A Sociology of Musical Languages*, ed. John Shepherd, Phil Virden, Graham Vulliamy, and Trevor Wishart, 125-53. London: Latimer, 1977.

**FPA, P**

Wittrock, M. C. "Education and the Cognitive Processes of the Brain." In *Education and the Brain: 77th Yearbook of the National Society for the Study of Education (Part II)*, ed. Jeanne S. Chall and Allan F. Mirsky, 61-102. Chicago: University of Chicago Press, 1978.

**P**

Wolf, Dennie, and Howard Gardner. "Beyond Playing or Polishing: A Developmental View of Artistry." In *Arts and the Schools*, ed. Jerome J. Hausman and Joyce Wright, 47-77. New York: McGraw-Hill, 1980.

**A, P**

Woodruff, Asahel D. "Toward a Linkage System between Psychology and Music Education." In *Documentary Report of the Ann Arbor Symposium: National Symposium on the Applications of Psychology to the Teaching and Learning of Music (Sessions I and II)*, 286-98. Reston, Va.: Music Educators National Conference, 1981.

**P**

Xenakis, Iannis. "Creativity." In *Perpectives on Musical Aesthetics*, ed. John Rahn, 158-64. New York: Norton, 1994.

**FPA, P**

Yardley, Alice. *Senses and Sensitivity*. New York: Citation, 1973.

**CI, P**

Zimmerman, Marilyn P. "Child Development and Music Education." In *Documentary Report of the Ann Arbor Symposium: National Symposium on the Applications of Psychology to the Teaching and Learning of Music (Sessions I and II)*, 49-56. Reston, Va.: Music Educators National Conference, 1981.

**P, R**

_____. "Developmental Processes in Music Learning." In *Symposium in Music Education: A Festschrift for Charles Leonhard*, ed. Richard J. Colwell, 25-44. Urbana-Champaign: University of Illinois, 1982.

**CI, P**

_____. *Musical Characteristics of Children: From Research to the Music Classroom No. 1*. Washington: Music Educators National Conference, 1971.

**CI, P, R**

_____. "Psychological Theory and Music Learning." In *Basic Concepts in Music Education II*, ed. Richard J. Colwell, 157-76. Niwot: University Press of Colorado, 1991.
**CI, P**

Zimmerman, Marilyn P., and Lee Sechrest. *How Children Conceptually Organize Musical Sounds*. Evanston, Ill.: Northwestern University, 1968.
**P**

# (R)

## RESEARCH

Abeles, Harold F. "A Guide to Interpreting Research in Music Education." In *Handbook of Research on Music Teaching and Learning*, ed. Richard J. Colwell, 227-43. New York: Schirmer Books, 1992.
**BR, R**

Adelman, Clem, and Anthony E. Kemp. "Case Study and Action Research." In *Some Approaches to Research in Music Education*, ed. Anthony E. Kemp, 111-37. Reading, England: International Society for Music Education, 1992.
**R**

*American Educational Research Journal*. Washington: American Educational Research Association, 1964-.
**CI, J, R**

Anderson, Lorin W. "Research on Teaching and Teacher Education." In *Bloom's Taxonomy— A Forty-Year Retrospective: 93rd Yearbook of the National Society for the Study of Education (Part II)*, ed. Lorin W. Anderson and Lauren A. Sosniak, 126-45. Chicago: University of Chicago Press, 1994.
**CI, R**

*Arts Education Research Agenda for the Future*. Washington: U.S. Department of Education, 1994.
**A, CI, R, RSC**

*Arts in Education: Research Report*. Washington: National School Boards Association, 1978.
**A, CI, R, RSC**

Asmus, Edward P., Jr., ed. *Proceedings of the Research Symposium on the Psychology and Acoustics of Music, 1978.* Lawrence: University of Kansas Department of Art and Music Education and Music Therapy, 1978.
P, R

————, ed. *Psychology and Acoustics of Music: A Collection of Papers.* Lawrence: University of Kansas Department of Art and Music Education and Music Therapy, 1977.
P, R, RSC

Asmus, Edward P., Jr., and Rudolf E. Radocy. "Quantitative Analysis." In *Handbook of Research on Music Teaching and Learning*, ed. Richard J. Colwell, 141-83. New York: Schirmer Books, 1992.
R

Atterbury, Betty W. "Research on the Teaching of Elementary General Music." In *Handbook of Research on Music Teaching and Learning*, ed. Richard J. Colwell, 594-601. New York: Schirmer Books, 1992.
CI, R

Barnes, Stephen H., ed. *A Cross-Section of Research in Music Education.* Washington: University Press of America, 1982.
CI, R

Barresi, Anthony L., and Gerald Olson. "The Nature of Policy and Music Education." In *Handbook of Research on Music Teaching and Learning*, ed. Richard J. Colwell, 760-72. New York: Schirmer Books, 1992.
FPA, R

Baxter, Steve, and Sandra L. Stauffer. "Music Teaching: A Review of Common Practice." In *The Crane Symposium: Toward an Understanding of the Teaching and Learning of Music Performance*, ed. Charles Fowler, 49-62. Potsdam: Potsdam College of the State University of New York, 1988.
CI, R

Benner, Charles H. *Teaching Performing Groups: From Research to the Music Classroom No. 2.* Washington: Music Educators National Conference, 1972.
CI, R

Bentley, Arnold, Kurt E. Eicke, and Robert G. Petzold, eds. *The Third International Seminar on Research in Music Education.* London: Bärenreiter, 1973.
CI, R, RSC

Best, John W., and James V. Kahn. *Research in Education.* 7th ed. Boston: Allyn and Bacon, 1993.
R

Bloom, Kathryn. "Research and Development Needs for Comprehensive Programs in the Arts in Education at the Precollegiate Level." In *Arts and Aesthetics: An Agenda for the Future*, ed. Stanley S. Madeja, 317-30. St. Louis, Mo.: CEMREL, 1977.

**A, CI, R**

Boardman, Eunice. "Music Teacher Education." In *Handbook of Research on Teacher Education*, ed. W. Robert Houston, Martin Haberman, and John P. Sikula, 730-45. New York: Macmillan, 1990.

**CI, R**

Boyle, J. David. "Evaluation of Music Ability." In *Handbook of Research on Music Teaching and Learning*, ed. Richard J. Colwell, 247-65. New York: Schirmer Books, 1992.

**P, R**

Bresler, Liora, and Robert E. Stake. "Qualitative Research Methodology in Music Education." In *Handbook of Research on Music Teaching and Learning*, ed. Richard J. Colwell, 75-90. New York: Schirmer Books, 1992.

**R**

*British Journal of Aesthetics.* London: Oxford University Press, 1960-.

**A, FPA, J, R**

*British Journal of Music Education.* Cambridge: Cambridge University Press, 1984-.

**CI, J, P, R**

Brown, Roger. "Music and Language." In *Documentary Report of the Ann Arbor Symposium: National Symposium on the Applications of Psychology to the Teaching and Learning of Music (Sessions I and II)*, 233-65. Reston, Va.: Music Educators National Conference, 1981.

**P, R**

Buckwell, Patricia J. "Journal of Music Therapy." In *International Music Journals*, ed. Linda M. Fidler and Richard S. James, 198-200. New York: Greenwood, 1990.

**J, P, R**

*Bulletin of Historical Research in Music Education.* Lawrence: University of Kansas Department of Art and Music Education and Music Therapy, 1980-.

**FPA, J, R**

Busch, John Christian, and James W. Sherbon. "Experimental Research Methodology." In *Handbook of Research on Music Teaching and Learning*, ed. Richard J. Colwell, 124-40. New York: Schirmer Books, 1992.

**R**

Bussis, Anne M., Edward A. Chittenden, and Marianne Amarel. "Collaborative Research." In *The Teaching Process, Arts and Aesthetics*, ed. Gerard L. Knieter and Jane Stallings, 70-91. St. Louis, Mo.: CEMREL, 1979.
**A, R**

Buttram, Joe B. "An Overview of Learning Theory and Related Developments." In *Handbook of Music Psychology*, ed. Donald A. Hodges, 235-74. Lawrence, Kans.: National Association for Music Therapy, 1980.
**P, R**

Cady, Henry L. "Sources of Theory for Research in School Music." In *Handbook of Research on Music Teaching and Learning*, ed. Richard J. Colwell, 60-72. New York: Schirmer Books, 1992.
**R**

Campbell, Donald T., and Julian C. Stanley. *Experimental and Quasi-Experimental Designs for Research.* Chicago: Rand McNally, 1963.
**R**

*Canadian Music Educator.* St. Catherines, Ontario: Canadian Music Educators' Association, 1959-.
**CI, J, P, R**

Capurso, Alexander, ed. *Music and Your Emotions: A Practical Guide to Music Selections Associated with Desired Emotional Responses.* 1952. Reprint, New York: Liveright, 1970.
**BR, P, R**

Carlsen, James C. "Auditory Perception: Concerns for Musical Learning." In *Documentary Report of the Ann Arbor Symposium: National Symposium on the Applications of Psychology to the Teaching and Learning of Music (Sessions I and II)*, 2-8. Reston, Va.: Music Educators National Conference, 1981.
**P, R**

Casey, Donald E. "Descriptive Research: Techniques and Procedures." In *Handbook of Research on Music Teaching and Learning*, ed. Richard J. Colwell, 115-23. New York: Schirmer Books, 1992.
**R**

*Challenges in Music Education: Proceedings of the XI International Conference of the International Society for Music Education.* Ed. Frank Callaway. Perth: University of Western Australia, 1976.
**CI, R, RSC**

Clifford, Geraldine Joncich. "An Historical Review of Teaching and Research: Perspectives for Arts and Aesthetic Education." In *The Teaching Process, Arts and Aesthetics*, ed. Gerard L. Knieter and Jane Stallings, 11-39. St. Louis, Mo.: CEMREL, 1979.
**A, FPA, R**

*Cognition and Emotion.* Hove, East Sussex, England: Erlbaum Associates, 1987-.
**J, P, R**

*Cognition: International Journal of Cognitive Psychology.* New York: Elsevier Science, 1972-.
**J, P, R**

Colwell, Richard J. *A Critique of Research Studies in Music Education.* Urbana: University of Illinois, 1972.
**BR, R**

_____, ed. *Handbook of Research on Music Teaching and Learning.* New York: Schirmer Books, 1992.
**BR, CI, P, R**

_____, ed. *Symposium in Music Education: A Festschrift for Charles Leonhard.* Urbana-Champaign: University of Illinois, 1982.
**CI, FPA, R, RSC**

*Comparative Music Education: Proceedings of the Fourth International Conference of the International Society for Music Education.* Mainz: International Society for Music Education, 1962.
**CI, R, RSC**

*Comprehensive Dissertation Index, 1861-1972.* 37 vols. Ann Arbor, Mich.: Xerox University Microfilms, 1973.
**BR, R**

Corrigan, Vincent J. "The Opera Quarterly." In *International Music Journals*, ed. Linda M. Fidler and Richard S. James, 465-66. New York: Greenwood, 1990.
**J, R**

Costanza, Peter, and Timothy Russell. "Methodologies in Music Education." In *Handbook of Research on Music Teaching and Learning*, ed. Richard J. Colwell, 498-508. New York: Schirmer Books, 1992.
**CI, R**

Cuddy, Lola L., and Rena Upitis. "Aural Perception." In *Handbook of Research on Music Teaching and Learning*, ed. Richard J. Colwell, 333-43. New York: Schirmer Books, 1992.
**P, R**

Cutietta, Robert A. "The Measurement of Attitudes and Preferences in Music Education." In *Handbook of Research on Music Teaching and Learning*, ed. Richard J. Colwell, 295-309. New York: Schirmer Books, 1992.
**P, R**

Davidson, Lyle, and Larry Scripp. "Surveying the Coordinates of Cognitive Skills in Music." In *Handbook of Research on Music Teaching and Learning*, ed. Richard J. Colwell, 392-413. New York: Schirmer Books, 1992.

**CI, P, R**

Day, Ruth S. "Music Ability and Patterns of Cognition." In *Documentary Report of the Ann Arbor Symposium: National Symposium on the Applications of Psychology to the Teaching and Learning of Music (Sessions I and II)*, 270-84. Reston, Va.: Music Educators National Conference, 1981.

**P, R**

Deutsch, Diana. "Musical Illusions and Handedness." In *Documentary Report of the Ann Arbor Symposium: National Symposium on the Applications of Psychology to the Teaching and Learning of Music (Sessions I and II)*, 218-31. Reston, Va.: Music Educators National Conference, 1981.

**P, R**

————. "The Perception of Musical Configurations." In *The Biology of Music Making: Proceedings of the 1984 Denver Conference*, ed. Franz L. Roehmann and Frank R. Wilson, 112-30. St. Louis, Mo.: MMB Music, 1988.

**P, R**

*Dissertation Abstracts International.* Ann Arbor, Mich.: University Microfilms International, 1938-.

**BR, R**

Dobbs, Jack P. B., ed. *Music Education - Facing the Future: Proceedings of the 19th World Conference of the International Society for Music Education.* Reading, England: International Society for Music Education, 1990.

**CI, R, RSC**

*Documentary Report of the Ann Arbor Symposium: National Symposium on the Applications of Psychology to the Teaching and Learning of Music (Sessions I and II).* Reston, Va.: Music Educators National Conference, 1981.

**CI, P, R, RSC**

*Documentary Report of the Ann Arbor Symposium on the Applications of Psychology to the Teaching and Learning of Music: Motivation and Creativity (Session III).* Reston, Va.: Music Educators National Conference, 1983.

**CI, P, R, RSC**

Dowling, W. Jay. "Mental Structures through Which Music Is Perceived." In *Documentary Report of the Ann Arbor Symposium: National Symposium on the Applications of Psychology to the Teaching and Learning of Music (Sessions I and II)*, 144-49. Reston, Va.: Music Educators National Conference, 1981.
**P, R**

Druesedow, John E., Jr. *Library Research Guide to Music: Illustrated Search Strategy and Sources.* Ann Arbor, Mich.: Pierian, 1982.
**BR, R**

Duckles, Vincent H., and Ida Reed. *Music Reference and Research Materials: An Annotated Bibliography.* 5th ed. New York: Schirmer Books, 1997.
**BR, R**

Duerksen, George L. *Teaching Instrumental Music: From Research to the Music Classroom, No. 3.* Washington: Music Educators National Conference, 1972.
**CI, R**

Eagle, Charles T., Jr. "An Introductory Perspective of Music Psychology." In *Handbook of Music Psychology*, ed. Donald A. Hodges, 1-28. Lawrence, Kans.: National Association for Music Therapy, 1980.
**P, R**

Edwards, Roger H. "Model Building." In *Handbook of Research on Music Teaching and Learning*, ed. Richard J. Colwell, 38-47. New York: Schirmer Books, 1992.
**CI, P, R**

Eisner, Elliot W. "Thoughts on an Agenda for Research and Development in Arts Education." In *Arts and Aesthetics: An Agenda for the Future*, ed. Stanley S. Madeja, 411-22. St. Louis, Mo.: CEMREL, 1977.
**A, CI, R**

*Encyclopedia of Adolescence.* Ed. Richard Lerner, Anne C. Petersen, and Jeanne Brooks-Gunn. New York: Garland, 1991.
**BR, CI, R**

*Encyclopedia of Educational Research.* Ed. Marvin C. Alkin, Michele Linden, Jana Noel, and Karen Ray. 6th ed. New York: Macmillan, 1992.
**BR, CI, R**

Engel, Martin. "An Informal Framework for Cognitive Research in Arts Education." In *The Arts, Cognition and Basic Skills*, ed. Stanley S. Madeja, 23-30. St. Louis, Mo.: CEMREL, 1978.
**A, P, R**

Engel, Martin, and Jerome J. Hausman, eds. *Curriculum and Instruction in Arts and Aesthetic Education.* St. Louis, Mo.: CEMREL, 1981.

**A, FPA, R, RSC**

Fidler, Linda M. "Black Music Research Journal." In *International Music Journals*, ed. Linda M. Fidler and Richard S. James, 55-57. New York: Greenwood, 1990.

**J, R**

Fiske, Harold E. "Experimental Research." In *Some Approaches to Research in Music Education*, ed. Anthony E. Kemp, 57-85. Reading, England: International Society for Music Education, 1992.

**R**

————. "Structure of Cognition and Music Decision-Making." In *Handbook of Research on Music Teaching and Learning*, ed. Richard J. Colwell, 360-76. New York: Schirmer Books, 1992.

**P, R**

Forsythe, Jere L. "The Blind Musicians and the Elephant." In *Applications of Research in Music Behavior*, ed. Clifford K. Madsen and Carol A. Prickett, 329-38. Tuscaloosa: University of Alabama Press, 1987.

**R**

Foshay, Arthur W. "Inquiry into Aesthetics Education for Curriculum-Making." In *Arts and Aesthetics: An Agenda for the Future*, ed. Stanley S. Madeja, 243-50. St. Louis, Mo.: CEMREL, 1977.

**A, CI, FPA, R**

Fowler, Charles B., ed. *The Crane Symposium: Toward an Understanding of the Teaching and Learning of Music Performance.* New York: Potsdam College of the State University of New York, 1988.

**CI, R, RSC**

Fox, Donna Brink. "Teaching Tots and Toddlers." In *Music and Child Development: The Biology of Music Making - Proceedings of the 1987 Denver Conference*, ed. Frank R. Wilson and Franz L. Roehmann, 384-88. St. Louis, Mo.: MMB Music, 1990.

**CI, P, R**

Froehlich, Hildegard C. "Issues and Characteristics Common to Research on Teaching in Instructional Settings." In *Handbook of Research on Music Teaching and Learning*, ed. Richard J. Colwell, 561-67. New York: Schirmer Books, 1992.

**CI, R**

Furman, Charles E., ed. *Effectiveness of Music Therapy Procedures: Documentation of Research and Clinical Practice.* 2nd ed. Silver Spring, Md.: National Association for Music Therapy, 1996.

**P, R**

Gardner, Howard. "Sifting the Special from the Shared: Notes toward an Agenda for Research in Arts Education." In *Arts and Aesthetics: An Agenda for the Future*, ed. Stanley S. Madeja, 267-78. St. Louis, Mo.: CEMREL, 1977.

**A, CI, R**

Gardner, Howard, and David N. Perkins, eds. *Art, Mind, and Education: Research from Project Zero.* Urbana: University of Illinois Press, 1989.

**A, CI, P, R**

George, Warren E. "Measurement and Evaluation of Musical Behavior." In *Handbook of Music Psychology*, ed. Donald A. Hodges, 291-392. Lawrence, Kans.: National Association for Music Therapy, 1980.

**P, R**

George, Warren E., and Donald A. Hodges. "The Nature of Musical Attributes." In *Handbook of Music Psychology*, ed. Donald A. Hodges, 401-14. Lawrence, Kans.: National Association for Music Therapy, 1980.

**P, R**

Gfeller, Kate. "Research Regarding Students with Disabilities." In *Handbook of Research on Music Teaching and Learning*, ed. Richard J. Colwell, 615-32. New York: Schirmer Books, 1992.

**P, R**

Ginsburg, David D. "Popular Music and Society." In *International Music Journals*, ed. Linda M. Fidler and Richard S. James, 346-48. New York: Greenwood, 1990.

**J, P, R**

Gonzo, Carroll. "Toward a Rational Critical Process." In *Handbook of Research on Music Teaching and Learning*, ed. Richard J. Colwell, 218-26. New York: Schirmer Books, 1992.

**FPA, R**

Gordon, Edwin E. *Designing Objective Research in Music Education: Fundamental Considerations.* Chicago: G.I.A. Publications, 1986.

**P, R**

Greer, R. Douglas. "An Operant Approach to Motivation and Affect: Ten Years of Research in Music Learning." In *Documentary Report of the Ann Arbor Symposium: National Symposium on the Applications of Psychology to the Teaching and Learning of Music (Sessions I and II)*, 102-21. Reston, Va.: Music Educators National Conference, 1981.

**P, R**

Haack, Paul. "The Acquisition of Music Listening Skills." In *Handbook of Research on Music Teaching and Learning*, ed. Richard J. Colwell, 451-65. New York: Schirmer Books, 1992.
**CI, P, R**

Hargreaves, David J., and Marilyn P. Zimmerman. "Developmental Theories of Music Learning." In *Handbook of Research on Music Teaching and Learning*, ed. Richard J. Colwell, 377-91. New York: Schirmer Books, 1992.
**CI, P, R**

Hedden, Steven K. "Psychomotor Skills." In *Documentary Report of the Ann Arbor Symposium: National Symposium on the Applications of Psychology to the Teaching and Learning of Music (Sessions I and II)*, 22-28. Reston, Va.: Music Educators National Conference, 1981.
**CI, P, R**

Hedden, Steven K., and David G. Woods. "Student Outcomes of Teaching Systems for General Music, Grades K-8." In *Handbook of Research on Music Teaching and Learning*, ed. Richard J. Colwell, 669-75. New York: Schirmer Books, 1992.
**CI, R**

Heintze, James R. *American Music Studies: A Classified Bibliography of Master's Theses.* Bibliographies in American Music, 8. Detroit: Information Coordinators, 1984.
**BR, R**

Heller, George N. *Historical Research in Music Education: A Bibliography.* 2nd ed. Lawrence: University of Kansas Department of Art and Music Education and Music Therapy, 1992.
**BR, FPA, R**

Heller, George N., and Bruce D. Wilson. "Historical Research." In *Handbook of Research on Music Teaching and Learning*, ed. Richard J. Colwell, 102-14. New York: Schirmer Books, 1992.
**R**

Heller, Jack J., and Warren C. Campbell. "Auditory Perception in Music Teaching and Learning." In *Documentary Report of the Ann Arbor Symposium: National Symposium on the Applications of Psychology to the Teaching and Learning of Music (Sessions I and II)*, 8-15. Reston, Va.: Music Educators National Conference, 1981.
**CI, P, R**

————. "Models of Language and Intellect in Music Research." In *Music Education for Tomorrow's Society*, ed. Arthur Motycka, 40-49. Jamestown, R.I.: GAMT Music, 1976.
**FPA, P, R**

Helmholtz, Hermann von. *On the Sensations of Tone as a Physiological Basis for the Theory of Music.* 2nd English ed., transl. Alexander J. Ellis. 1862. Reprint, New York: Dover, 1954.

**P, R**

Hodges, Donald A. "The Acquisition of Music Reading Skills." In *Handbook of Research on Music Teaching and Learning*, ed. Richard J. Colwell, 466-71. New York: Schirmer Books, 1992.

**CI, P, R**

———, ed. *Handbook of Music Psychology.* Lawrence, Kans.: National Association for Music Therapy, 1980.

**BR, P, R**

Hoffer, Charles R. "Sociology and Music Education." In *Handbook of Research on Music Teaching and Learning*, ed. Richard J. Colwell, 713-23. New York: Schirmer Books, 1992.

**P, R**

Horner, V. *Music Education: The Background of Research and Opinion.* Hawthorn: Australian Council for Educational Research, 1965.

**CI, R**

Horowitz, Harold. "The Research Division of the National Endowment for the Arts: Background and Highlights of the First Year." In *Arts and Aesthetics: An Agenda for the Future*, ed. Stanley S. Madeja, 178-201. St. Louis, Mo.: CEMREL, 1977.

**A, R**

Houston, W. Robert, Martin Haberman, and John P. Sikula, eds. *Handbook of Research on Teacher Education.* 2nd ed. New York: Macmillan, 1996.

**BR, CI, R**

Humphreys, Jere T., William V. May, and David Nelson. "Research on Music Ensembles." In *Handbook of Research on Music Teaching and Learning*, ed. Richard J. Colwell, 651-68. New York: Schirmer Books, 1992.

**CI, R**

Inglefield, Ruth K. "International Review of the Aesthetics and Sociology of Music." In *International Music Journals*, ed. Linda M. Fidler and Richard S. James, 172-74. New York: Greenwood, 1990.

**A, FPA, J, P, R**

———. "Journal of Aesthetics and Art Criticism." In *International Music Journals*, ed. Linda M. Fidler and Richard S. James, 187-88. New York: Greenwood, 1990.

**A, FPA, J, R**

_____. "The Musical Quarterly." In *International Music Journals*, ed. Linda M. Fidler and Richard S. James, 274-77. New York: Greenwood, 1990.
**J, R**

_____. "Psychomusicology." In *International Music Journals*, ed. Linda M. Fidler and Richard S. James, 468-69. New York: Greenwood, 1990.
**J, P, R**

*International Directory of Approved Music Education Dissertations in Progress*. Urbana, Ill.: Council for Research in Music Education, 1989-.
**BR, J, R**

*International Journal of Behavioral Development*. London, England: Erlbaum Associates, 1978-.
**J, P, R**

*International Journal of Music Education*. Huddersfield, England: International Society for Music Education, 1983-.
**CI, FPA, J, P, R**

Jackson, Philip W., ed. *Handbook of Research on Curriculum: A Project of the American Educational Research Association*. New York: Macmillan, 1992.
**BR, CI, R**

James, Richard S. "American Music." In *International Music Journals*, ed. Linda M. Fidler and Richard S. James, 458-60. New York: Greenwood, 1990.
**J, R**

Johnston, J. Howard, and Glenn C. Markle. *What Research Says to the Middle Level Practitioner*. Columbus, Ohio: National Middle School Association, 1986.
**CI, R**

Jones, L. JaFran. "Yearbook for Traditional Music." In *International Music Journals*, ed. Linda M. Fidler and Richard S. James, 449-51. New York: Greenwood, 1990.
**J, R**

Jordan, Joyce. "Multicultural Music Education in a Pluralistic Society." In *Handbook of Research on Music Teaching and Learning*, ed. Richard J. Colwell, 735-48. New York: Schirmer Books, 1992.
**CI, R**

Jorgensen, Estelle R. "On Philosophical Method." In *Handbook of Research on Music Teaching and Learning*, ed. Richard J. Colwell, 91-101. New York: Schirmer Books, 1992.
**FPA, R**

*Journal of Aesthetic Education.* Urbana: University of Illinois Press, 1966-.

**A, CI, FPA, J, R**

*Journal of Educational Psychology.* Washington: American Psychological Association, 1910-.

**CI, J, P, R**

*Journal of Educational Research.* Washington: Heldref, 1920-.

**CI, J, R**

*Journal of Experimental Psychology: General.* Washington: American Psychological Association, 1975-.

**J, P, R**

*Journal of Experimental Psychology: Human Perception and Performance.* Washington: American Psychological Association, 1975-.

**J, P, R**

*Journal of Experimental Psychology: Learning, Memory and Cognition.* Washington: American Psychological Association, 1975-.

**J, P, R**

*Journal of Music Teacher Education.* Reston, Va.: Music Educators National Conference, 1991-.

**CI, J, R**

*Journal of the Acoustical Society of America.* New York: American Institute of Physics for the Acoustical Society of America, 1929-.

**J, P, R**

Kantorski, Vincent J. "The Council for Research in Music Education Bulletin." In *International Music Journals,* ed. Linda M. Fidler and Richard S. James, 100-02. New York: Greenwood, 1990.

**CI, FPA, J, P, R**

_____. "Journal of Band Research." In *International Music Journals,* ed. Linda M. Fidler and Richard S. James, 189-90. New York: Greenwood, 1990.

**CI, J, R**

_____. "Journal of Research in Music Education." In *International Music Journals,* ed. Linda M. Fidler and Richard S. James, 203-05. New York: Greenwood, 1990.

**CI, J, P, R**

————. "Update: The Applications of Research in Music Education." In *International Music Journals*, ed. Linda M. Fidler and Richard S. James, 469-70. New York: Greenwood, 1990.
**CI, J, P, R**

Kemp, Anthony E. "Approaching Research." In *Some Approaches to Research in Music Education*, ed. Anthony E. Kemp, 7-18. Reading, England: International Society for Music Education, 1992.
**R**

————. "Writing Research Reports." In *Some Approaches to Research in Music Education*, ed. Anthony E. Kemp, 138-58. Reading, England: International Society for Music Education, 1992.
**R**

————, ed. *Research in Music Education: A Festschrift for Arnold Bentley*. London: International Society for Music Education, 1988.
**R, RSC**

————, ed. *Some Approaches to Research in Music Education*. Reading, England: International Society for Music Education, 1992.
**R**

Kemp, Anthony E., and Laurence Lepherd. "Research Methods in International and Comparative Music Education." In *Handbook of Research on Music Teaching and Learning*, ed. Richard J. Colwell, 773-88. New York: Schirmer Books, 1992.
**CI, R**

Kennell, Richard P. "Contributions to Music Education." In *International Music Journals*, ed. Linda M. Fidler and Richard S. James, 98-100. New York: Greenwood, 1990.
**CI, J, P, R**

————. "Dialogue in Instrumental Music Education." In *International Music Journals*, ed. Linda M. Fidler and Richard S. James, 114-16. New York: Greenwood, 1990.
**CI, J, R**

Kessen, William. "Encounters: The American Child's Meeting with Music." In *Documentary Report of the Ann Arbor Symposium: National Symposium on the Applications of Psychology to the Teaching and Learning of Music (Sessions I and II)*, 353-61. Reston, Va.: Music Educators National Conference, 1981.
**FPA, P, R**

Knowles, Rosalind. "American Choral Review." In *International Music Journals*, ed. Linda M. Fidler and Richard S. James, 14-16. New York: Greenwood, 1990.
**CI, J, R**

Koehler, Virginia. "Research on Teaching: Implications for Research on the Teaching of the Arts." In *The Teaching Process, Arts and Aesthetics*, ed. Gerard L. Knieter and Jane Stallings, 40-63. St. Louis, Mo.: CEMREL, 1979.
**A, R**

Kratus, John K. "College Music Symposium." In *International Music Journals*, ed. Linda M. Fidler and Richard S. James, 90-93. New York: Greenwood, 1990.
**CI, J, P, R**

————. "Music Perception." In *International Music Journals*, ed. Linda M. Fidler and Richard S. James, 464-65. New York: Greenwood, 1990.
**J, P, R**

————. "Psychology of Music." In *International Music Journals*, ed. Linda M. Fidler and Richard S. James, 348-51. New York: Greenwood, 1990.
**J, P, R**

Kraus, Egon. *The Present State of Music Education in the World*. Washington: International Society for Music Education, 1960.
**P, R, RSC**

Kreitzer, Amelia E., and George F. Madaus. "Empirical Investigations of the Hierarchical Structure of the Taxonomy." In *Bloom's Taxonomy—A Forty-Year Retrospective: 93rd Yearbook of the National Society for the Study of Education (Part II)*, ed. Lorin W. Anderson and Lauren A. Sosniak, 64-81. Chicago: University of Chicago Press, 1994.
**CI, R**

L'Hommedieu, Randi. "Regression-Based Research Designs." In *Handbook of Research on Music Teaching and Learning*, ed. Richard J. Colwell, 184-95. New York: Schirmer Books, 1992.
**R**

LaBerge, David. "Perceptual and Motor Schemas in the Performance of Musical Pitch." In *Documentary Report of the Ann Arbor Symposium: National Symposium on the Applications of Psychology to the Teaching and Learning of Music (Sessions I and II)*, 179-96. Reston, Va.: Music Educators National Conference, 1981.
**CI, P, R**

Larson, William S., ed. *Bibliography of Research Studies in Music Education, 1932-1948*. Chicago: Music Educators National Conference, 1949.
**BR, R**

————, ed. *Bibliography of Research Studies in Music Education, 1949-1956*. Chicago: Music Educators National Conference, 1958.
**BR, R**

LeBlanc, Albert. "The Culture as Educator: Elements in the Development of Individual Music Preference." In *Music Education in the United States: Contemporary Issues*, ed. J. Terry Gates, 33-43. Tuscaloosa: University of Alabama Press, 1988.
**P, R**

Lehman, Paul R. "Curriculum and Program Evaluation." In *Handbook of Research on Music Teaching and Learning*, ed. Richard J. Colwell, 281-94. New York: Schirmer Books, 1992.
**CI, R**

Lehrer, Paul. "The Causes and Cures of Performance Anxiety: A Review of the Psychological Literature." In *The Biology of Music Making: Proceedings of the 1984 Denver Conference*, ed. Franz L. Roehmann and Frank R. Wilson, 32-46. St. Louis, Mo.: MMB Music, 1988.
**P, R**

Leonhard, Charles, and Richard J. Colwell. "Research in Music Education." In *Arts and Aesthetics: An Agenda for the Future*, ed. Stanley S. Madeja, 81-108. St. Louis, Mo.: CEMREL, 1977.
**R**

Lepherd, Laurence. "Comparative Research." In *Some Approaches to Research in Music Education*, ed. Anthony E. Kemp, 33-56. Reading, England: International Society for Music Education, 1992.
**R**

Madeja, Stanley S. "Structure a Research Agenda for the Arts and Aesthetics." In *Arts and Aesthetics: An Agenda for the Future*, ed. Stanley S. Madeja, 374-91. St. Louis, Mo.: CEMREL, 1977.
**A, FPA, R**

Madsen, Charles H., Jr., and Clifford K. Madsen. *Teaching/Discipline: A Positive Approach for Educational Development*. 3rd ed. Raleigh, N.C.: Contemporary Publishing, 1983.
**CI, P, R**

Madsen, Clifford K., and Charles H. Madsen, Jr. *Experimental Research in Music*. Raleigh, N.C.: Contemporary Publishing, 1978.
**P, R**

Madsen, Clifford K., and Carol A. Prickett, eds. *Applications of Research in Music Behavior*. Tuscaloosa: University of Alabama Press, 1987.
**CI, P, R, RSC**

Madsen, Clifford K., and Randall S. Moore, eds. *Experimental Research in Music: Workbook in Design and Statistical Tests.* Rev. ed. Raleigh, N.C.: Contemporary Publishing, 1978.
**P, R**

Madsen, Clifford K., R. Douglas Greer, and Charles H. Madsen, Jr., eds. *Research in Music Behavior: Modifying Music Behavior in the Classroom.* New York: Teachers College, 1975.
**CI, P, R**

Mark, Desmond, ed. *Stock-Taking of Musical Life - Music Sociography and Its Relevance to Music Education: Report on a Seminar Organized by the ISME Commission on Music in Cultural, Educational and Mass Media Policies.* Vienna, Austria: Doblinger, 1981.
**CI, R, RSC**

Mark, Michael L. "A History of Music Education Research." In *Handbook of Research on Music Teaching and Learning,* ed. Richard J. Colwell, 48-59. New York: Schirmer Books, 1992.
**FPA, R**

Marzano, Robert J., et al. *Dimensions of Thinking: A Framework for Curriculum and Instruction.* Alexandria, Va.: Association for Supervision and Curriculum Development, 1988.
**CI, P, R**

Mast, Paul B. "Journal of Music Theory." In *International Music Journals,* ed. Linda M. Fidler and Richard S. James, 195-98. New York: Greenwood, 1990.
**CI, J, R**

————. "Perspectives of New Music." In *International Music Journals,* ed. Linda M. Fidler and Richard S. James, 339-42. New York: Greenwood, 1990.
**J, R**

May, William V., ed. *Research Symposium on the Psychology and Acoustics of Music, 1979.* Lawrence: University of Kansas Department of Art and Music Education and Music Therapy, 1980.
**P, R, RSC**

Merrion, Margaret D., ed. *What Works: Instructional Strategies for Music Education.* Reston, Va.: Music Educators National Conference, 1989.
**CI, R**

Meske, Eunice Boardman. "Educating the Music Teacher: Participation in a Metamorphosis." In *Symposium in Music Education: A Festschrift for Charles Leonhard,* ed. Richard J. Colwell, 249-65. Urbana-Champaign: University of Illinois, 1982.
**CI, FPA, P, R**

Miller, Robert F. "Affective Response." In *Handbook of Research on Music Teaching and Learning*, ed. Richard J. Colwell, 414-24. New York: Schirmer Books, 1992.

**P, R**

*Missouri Journal of Research in Music Education.* Jefferson City: Missouri State Department of Education, 1962-.

**CI, J, P, R**

Mixter, Keith E. *General Bibliography for Music Research.* 3rd ed. Warren, Mich.: Harmonie Park Press, 1996.

**BR, R**

*Music Education in the Modern World: Materials of the Ninth Conference of the International Society for Music Education.* Moscow: Progress Publishers, 1974.

**CI, P, R, RSC**

*Music Psychology Index.* Vol. 2. Ed. Charles T. Eagle, Jr. Denton, Tex.: Institute for Therapeutics Research, 1978.

**BR, J, P, R**

*Music Psychology Index.* Vol. 3. Ed. Charles T. Eagle, Jr., and John J. Miniter. Phoenix, Ariz.: Oryx, 1984.

**BR, J, P, R**

*Music Therapy Index.* Vol. 1. Ed. Charles T. Eagle, Jr. Lawrence, Kans.: National Association for Music Therapy, 1976.

**BR, J, P, R**

Olson, Gerald, Anthony L. Barresi, and David Nelson, eds. *Policy Issues in Music Education: A Report of the Proceedings of the Robert Petzold Research Symposium.* Madison: School of Music, University of Wisconsin, 1991.

**FPA, R, RSC**

Pankratz, David. "Adults and Arts Education: A Literature Review." In *Arts Education beyond the Classroom*, ed. Judith H. Balfe and Joni Cherbo Heine, 11-22. New York: American Council for the Arts, 1988.

**A, R**

Pankratz, David, and Kevin V. Mulcahy, eds. *The Challenge to Reform Arts Education: What Role Can Research Play?* New York: ACA Books, 1989.

**A, CI, FPA, R**

Petzold, Robert G. "Child Development." In *Documentary Report of the Ann Arbor Symposium: National Symposium on the Applications of Psychology to the Teaching and Learning of Music (Sessions I and II)*, 42-48. Reston, Va.: Music Educators National Conference, 1981.

**P, R**

Phelps, Roger P., Lawrence Ferrara, and Thomas W. Goolsby. *A Guide to Research in Music Education*. 4th ed. Metuchen, N.J.: Scarecrow, 1993.

**BR, R**

Phillips, Kenneth H. "Research on the Teaching of Singing." In *Handbook of Research on Music Teaching and Learning*, ed. Richard J. Colwell, 568-76. New York: Schirmer Books, 1992.

**CI, R**

*Philosophy of Music Education Review*. Bloomington: Indiana University School of Music, 1993-.

**FPA, J, R**

*Quarterly Journal of Music Teaching and Learning*. Greeley: University of Northern Colorado School of Music, 1990-.

**CI, FPA, J, P, R**

Radocy, Rudolf E., and J. David Boyle. *Psychological Foundations of Musical Behaviors*. 2nd ed. Springfield, Ill.: Charles C. Thomas, 1988.

**P, R**

Rainbow, Bernarr. "Historical Research." In *Some Approaches to Research in Music Education*, ed. Anthony E. Kemp, 19-32. Reading, England: International Society for Music Education, 1992.

**R**

Rainbow, Edward L., and Hildegard C. Froehlich. *Research in Music Education: An Introduction to Systematic Inquiry*. New York: Schirmer Books, 1987.

**R**

Raynor, Joel O. "Motivational Determinants of Music-Related Behavior: Psychological Careers of Student, Teacher, Performer, and Listener." In *Documentary Report of the Ann Arbor Symposium: National Symposium on the Applications of Psychology to the Teaching and Learning of Music (Sessions I and II)*, 332-51. Reston, Va.: Music Educators National Conference, 1981.

**P, R**

Reimer, Bennett. "Toward a Philosophical Foundation for Music Education Research." In *Handbook of Research on Music Teaching and Learning*, ed. Richard J. Colwell, 21-37. New York: Schirmer Books, 1992.
**FPA, R**

Resnick, Lauren B., and Leopold E. Klopfer, eds. *Toward the Thinking Curriculum: Current Cognitive Research*. Alexandria, Va.: Association for Supervision and Curriculum Development, 1989.
**CI, P, R**

*Restructuring and Reform: Selected Bibliography*. Reston, Va.: Music Educators National Conference, 1993.
**BR, CI, R, RSC**

*Review of Educational Research*. Washington: American Educational Research Association, 1931-.
**CI, J, R**

Richardson, Carol P., and Nancy L. Whitaker. "Critical Thinking and Music Education." In *Handbook of Research on Music Teaching and Learning*, ed. Richard J. Colwell, 546-57. New York: Schirmer Books, 1992.
**CI, P, R**

Rideout, Roger R. "The Role of Mental Presets in Skill Acquisition." In *Handbook of Research on Music Teaching and Learning*, ed. Richard J. Colwell, 472-79. New York: Schirmer Books, 1992.
**CI, P, R**

Riis, Thomas L. "Black Perspective in Music." In *International Music Journals*, ed. Linda M. Fidler and Richard S. James, 57-59. New York: Greenwood, 1990.
**J, R**

Runfola, Maria, and Joanne Rutkowski. "General Music Curriculum." In *Handbook of Research on Music Teaching and Learning*, ed. Richard J. Colwell, 697-709. New York: Schirmer Books, 1992.
**CI, R**

Schneider, Erwin H., and Henry L. Cady. *Evaluation and Synthesis of Research Studies Related to Music Education*. Columbus: Ohio State University, 1965.
**CI, R**

Schurk, William L. "Recorded Sound." In *International Music Journals*, ed. Linda M. Fidler and Richard S. James, 360-62. New York: Greenwood, 1990.
**BR, J, R**

Scott, Carol Rogel. "Getting There from Here: The Examination of Musical Growth in Young Children." In *Research in Music Education: A Festschrift for Arnold Bentley*, ed. Anthony E. Kemp, 74-80. London: International Society for Music Education, 1988.
**P, R**

Scott-Kassner, Carol. "Research on Music in Early Childhood." In *Handbook of Research on Music Teaching and Learning*, ed. Richard J. Colwell, 633-50. New York: Schirmer Books, 1992.
**CI, P, R**

Shehan, Patricia K. "Movement in the Music Education of Children." In *Music and Child Development: The Biology of Music Making - Proceedings of the 1987 Denver Conference*, ed. Frank R. Wilson and Franz L. Roehmann, 354-65. St. Louis, Mo.: MMB Music, 1990.
**CI, P, R**

Shepard, Roger N. "Individual Differences in the Perception of Musical Pitch." In *Documentary Report of the Ann Arbor Symposium: National Symposium on the Applications of Psychology to the Teaching and Learning of Music (Sessions I and II)*, 152-74. Reston, Va.: Music Educators National Conference, 1981.
**P, R**

Shulman, Lee S. "Research on Teaching in the Arts: Review, Analysis, Critique." In *The Teaching Process, Arts and Aesthetics*, ed. Gerard L. Knieter and Jane Stallings, 244-64. St. Louis, Mo.: CEMREL, 1979.
**A, CI, R**

Shuter-Dyson, Rosamund. "Musical Ability." In *The Psychology of Music*, ed. Diana Deutsch, 391-412. New York: Academic Press, 1982.
**P, R**

Sidnell, Robert G. "Motor Learning in Music Education." In *Documentary Report of the Ann Arbor Symposium: National Symposium on the Applications of Psychology to the Teaching and Learning of Music (Sessions I and II)*, 28-35. Reston, Va.: Music Educators National Conference, 1981.
**CI, P, R**

Siegel, Jane A. "Culturally Defined Learning Experience." In *Documentary Report of the Ann Arbor Symposium: National Symposium on the Applications of Psychology to the Teaching and Learning of Music (Sessions I and II)*, 200-16. Reston, Va.: Music Educators National Conference, 1981.
**P, R**

Simons, Gene M. *Early Childhood Musical Development: A Bibliography of Research Abstracts, 1960-1975, with Implications and Recommendations for Teaching and Research.* Reston, Va.: Music Educators National Conference, 1978.
**BR, CI, P, R**

Sink, Patricia E. "Research on Teaching Junior High and Middle School General Music." In *Handbook of Research on Music Teaching and Learning*, ed. Richard J. Colwell, 602-12. New York: Schirmer Books, 1992.
**CI, R**

_____, ed. *Research Symposium on the Psychology and Acoustics of Music, 1982.* Lawrence: University of Kansas Department of Art and Music Education and Music Therapy, 1982.
**P, R, RSC**

Small, Arnold M., ed. *Bibliography of Research Studies in Music Education, 1932-1944.* Iowa City: State University of Iowa Press, 1944.
**BR, R**

Smith, Ralph A. "Trends and Issues in Policy-Making for Arts Education." In *Handbook of Research on Music Teaching and Learning*, ed. Richard J. Colwell, 749-59. New York: Schirmer Books, 1992.
**A, CI, FPA, R**

Soibelman, Doris. *Therapeutic and Industrial Uses of Music: A Review of the Literature.* New York: Columbia University Press, 1948.
**P, R**

*Southeastern Journal of Music Education.* Athens: University of Georgia Center for Continuing Education, 1990-.
**CI, J, P, R**

Steinel, Daniel V., comp. *Data on Music Education.* Reston, Va.: Music Educators National Conference, 1990.
**BR, R**

_____, comp. *Music and Music Education: Data and Information.* Reston, Va.: Music Educators National Conference, 1984.
**BR, R**

Stubley, Eleanor V. "Philosophical Foundations." In *Handbook of Research on Music Teaching and Learning*, ed. Richard J. Colwell, 3-20. New York: Schirmer Books, 1992.
**FPA, R**

Taebel, Donald K. "The Evaluation of Music Teachers and Teaching." In *Handbook of Research on Music Teaching and Learning*, ed. Richard J. Colwell, 310-29. New York: Schirmer Books, 1992.

**P, R**

Tait, Malcolm John. "Teaching Strategies and Styles." In *Handbook of Research on Music Teaching and Learning*, ed. Richard J. Colwell, 525-34. New York: Schirmer Books, 1992.

**CI, P, R**

Tallarico, P. Thomas, ed. *Contributions to Symposium/80: The Bowling Green State University Symposium on Music Teaching and Research*. Bowling Green, Ohio: Bowling Green State University, 1980.

**R, RSC**

_____, ed. *Contributions to Symposium/83: The Bowling Green State University Symposium on Music Teaching and Research*. Bowling Green, Ohio: Bowling Green State University, 1983.

**R, RSC**

Thomas, Nancy G. "Motivation." In *Handbook of Research on Music Teaching and Learning*, ed. Richard J. Colwell, 425-36. New York: Schirmer Books, 1992.

**P, R**

Tunks, Thomas W. "The Transfer of Music Learning." In *Handbook of Research on Music Teaching and Learning*, ed. Richard J. Colwell, 437-47. New York: Schirmer Books, 1992.

**CI, P, R**

Turk, Gayla C., ed. *Proceedings of the Research Symposium on the Psychology and Acoustics of Music, 1985*. Lawrence: University of Kansas Department of Art and Music Education and Music Therapy, 1985.

**P, R, RSC**

Uszler, Marienne. "Research on the Teaching of Keyboard Music." In *Handbook of Research on Music Teaching and Learning*, ed. Richard J. Colwell, 584-93. New York: Schirmer Books, 1992.

**CI, R**

Verrastro, Ralph, and Mary Leglar. "Music Teacher Education." In *Handbook of Research on Music Teaching and Learning*, ed. Richard J. Colwell, 676-96. New York: Schirmer Books, 1992.

**CI, R**

Wagner, Christoph. "Success and Failure in Musical Performance: Biomechanics of the Hand." In *The Biology of Music Making: Proceedings of the 1984 Denver Conference*, ed. Franz L. Roehmann and Frank R. Wilson, 154-79. St. Louis, Mo.: MMB Music, 1988.
**CI, R**

Walker, Edward L. "Hedgehog Theory and Music Education." In *Documentary Report of the Ann Arbor Symposium: National Symposium on the Applications of Psychology to the Teaching and Learning of Music (Sessions I and II)*, 317-28. Reston, Va.: Music Educators National Conference, 1981.
**P, R**

Walker, Robert. "Auditory-Visual Perception and Musical Behavior." In *Handbook of Research on Music Teaching and Learning*, ed. Richard J. Colwell, 344-59. New York: Schirmer Books, 1992.
**P, R**

Walters, Darrel L. "Sequencing for Efficient Learning." In *Handbook of Research on Music Teaching and Learning*, ed. Richard J. Colwell, 535-45. New York: Schirmer Books, 1992.
**CI, P, R**

Warner, Thomas E. *Periodical Literature on Music in America, 1620-1920: A Classified Bibliography with Annotations*. Bibliographies in American Music, 11. Warren, Mich.: Harmonie Park Press, 1988.
**BR, R**

Watanabe, Ruth. *Introduction to Music Research*. Englewood Cliffs, N.J.: Prentice-Hall, 1967.
**R**

————. "Notes: The Quarterly Journal of the Music Library Association." In *International Music Journals*, ed. Linda M. Fidler and Richard S. James, 319-22. New York: Greenwood, 1990.
**BR, J, R**

Webster, Peter R. "Conceptual Bases for Creative Thinking in Music." In *Music and Child Development*, ed. J. Craig Peery, Irene W. Peery, and Thomas W. Draper, 158-74. New York: Springer-Verlag, 1987.
**P, R**

————. "Creative Thinking in Music: Approaches to Research." In *Music Education in the United States: Contemporary Issues*, ed. J. Terry Gates, 66-81. Tuscaloosa: University of Alabama Press, 1988.
**P, R**

_____. "Research on Creative Thinking in Music: The Assessment Literature." In *Handbook of Research on Music Teaching and Learning*, ed. Richard J. Colwell, 266-80. New York: Schirmer Books, 1992.
**P, R**

Weerts, Richard. "Research on the Teaching of Instrumental Music." In *Handbook of Research on Music Teaching and Learning*, ed. Richard J. Colwell, 577-83. New York: Schirmer Books, 1992.
**CI, R**

Weitz, Morris. "Research on the Arts and in Aesthetics: Some Pitfalls, Some Possibilities." In *Arts and Aesthetics: An Agenda for the Future*, ed. Stanley S. Madeja, 223-28. St. Louis, Mo.: CEMREL, 1977.
**A, FPA, R**

Werder, Richard H., ed. *Music Education in the Secondary School.* Washington: Catholic University of America Press, 1955.
**CI, R, RSC**

Williams, David Brian. "Music Information Processing and Memory." In *Documentary Report of the Ann Arbor Symposium: National Symposium on the Applications of Psychology to the Teaching and Learning of Music (Sessions I and II)*, 87-93. Reston, Va.: Music Educators National Conference, 1981.
**P, R**

Wilson, Frank R., and Franz L. Roehmann. "The Study of Biomechanical and Physiological Processes in Relation to Musical Performance." In *Handbook of Research on Music Teaching and Learning*, ed. Richard J. Colwell, 509-24. New York: Schirmer Books, 1992.
**CI, P, R**

Wing, Lizabeth Bradford. "Curriculum and Its Study." In *Handbook of Research on Music Teaching and Learning*, ed. Richard J. Colwell, 196-217. New York: Schirmer Books, 1992.
**CI, R**

Winick, Steven. *Rhythm: An Annotated Bibliography.* Metuchen, N.J.: Scarecrow, 1974.
**BR, P, R**

Yarbrough, Cornelia. "Good Teaching May Be in Sonata Form." In *Applications of Research in Music Behavior*, ed. Clifford K. Madsen and Carol A. Prickett, 3-11. Tuscaloosa: University of Alabama Press, 1987.
**CI, R**

_____. "Observational Research." In *Some Approaches to Research in Music Education*, ed. Anthony E. Kemp, 86-110. Reading, England: International Society for Music Education, 1992.

**R**

Zimmerman, Marilyn P. "Child Development and Music Education." In *Documentary Report of the Ann Arbor Symposium: National Symposium on the Applications of Psychology to the Teaching and Learning of Music (Sessions I and II)*, 49-56. Reston, Va.: Music Educators National Conference, 1981.

**P, R**

_____. *Musical Characteristics of Children: From Research to the Music Classroom No. 1.* Washington: Music Educators National Conference, 1971.

**CI, P, R**

# (RSC)

## R<small>EPORTS</small>, S<small>YMPOSIA</small>, <small>AND</small> C<small>ONFERENCES</small>

*Academic Preparation for College: What Students Need to Know and Be Able to Do.* New York: College Entrance Examination Board, 1983.

**CI, RSC**

*Action for Excellence: A Comprehensive Plan to Improve Our Nation's Schools.* Denver, Colo.: Education Commission of the States, 1983.

**CI, RSC**

*Agenda for Excellence at the Middle Level: A Statement by NASSP's Council on Middle Level Education.* Reston, Va.: National Association of Secondary School Principals, 1985.

**CI, RSC**

American Council for the Arts. *Why We Need the Arts: Eight Quotable Speeches by Leaders in Education, Business, and the Arts.* Reston, Va.: Music Educators National Conference, 1989.

**A, CI, RSC**

*Americans and the Arts V: Highlights from a National Survey of Public Opinion.* New York: American Council for the Arts, 1988.

**A, RSC**

*Arts Education Research Agenda for the Future.* Washington: U.S. Department of Education, 1994.

**A, CI, R, RSC**

*Arts in Education: Research Report.* Washington: National School Boards Association, 1978.

**A, CI, R, RSC**

*Arts in Schools—Perspectives from Four Nations: A Report from the National Endowment for the Arts.* Washington: National Endowment for the Arts, 1993.

**A, CI, RSC**

Arts, Education, and Americans Panel. *Coming to Our Senses: The Significance of the Arts for American Education.* New York: McGraw-Hill, 1977.

**A, CI, FPA, RSC**

Asmus, Edward P., Jr., ed. *Psychology and Acoustics of Music: A Collection of Papers.* Lawrence: University of Kansas Department of Art and Music Education and Music Therapy, 1977.

**P, R, RSC**

*Assessment of Community Education Programs in Music.* Reston, Va.: National Association of Schools of Music, 1988.

**BR, CI, P, RSC**

Baker, Nancy Kovaleff, and Barbara Russano Hanning, eds. *Musical Humanism and Its Legacy: Essays in Honor of Claude V. Palisca.* Stuyvesant, N.Y.: Pendragon, 1992.

**FPA, RSC**

Balfe, Judith H., and Joni Cherbo Heine, eds. *Arts Education beyond the Classroom.* New York: American Council for the Arts, 1988.

**A, CI, RSC**

*Basic Musical Functions and Musical Ability: Papers Given at a Seminar Arranged by the Royal Swedish Academy of Music.* 2nd ed. Stockholm: Royal Swedish Academy of Music, 1982.

**P, RSC**

Benson, Warren. *Creative Projects in Musicianship: A Report of Pilot Projects Sponsored by the Contemporary Music Project at Ithaca College and Interlochen Arts Academy.* Washington: Contemporary Music Project, Music Educators National Conference, 1967.

**CI, RSC**

Bentley, Arnold, Kurt E. Eicke, and Robert G. Petzold, eds. *The Third International Seminar on Research in Music Education.* London: Bärenreiter, 1973.

**CI, R, RSC**

Biasini, Americole, and Lenore Pogonowski. *Manhattanville Music Curriculum Program (MMCP) Interaction.* 2nd ed. Bellingham, Wash.: Americole, 1979.
**CI, RSC**

Blacking, John, and Joann W. Kealiinohomoku, eds. *The Performing Arts: Music and Dance.* New York: Mouton, 1979.
**A, CI, RSC**

Block, Adrienne Fried, ed. *Women's Studies/Women's Status, 1987.* Boulder, Colo.: College Music Society, 1988.
**BR, RSC**

Boston, Bruce O. *The American High School, Time for Reform: A Report for the Council for Basic Education.* Washington: Council for Basic Education, 1982.
**CI, RSC**

Boswell, Jacquelyn, ed. *The Young Child and Music: Contemporary Principles in Child Development and Music Education.* Reston, Va.: Music Educators National Conference, 1985.
**CI, P, RSC**

Boyer, Ernest L. *High School: A Report on Secondary Education in America - The Carnegie Foundation for the Advancement of Teaching.* New York: Harper and Row, 1983.
**CI, RSC**

_____. *Ready to Learn: A Mandate for the Nation.* Princeton, N.J.: Carnegie Foundation for the Advancement of Teaching, 1991.
**CI, RSC**

*Challenges in Music Education: Proceedings of the XI International Conference of the International Society for Music Education.* Ed. Frank Callaway. Perth: University of Western Australia, 1976.
**CI, R, RSC**

*Chamber Music: Performance and Study at Music Training Institutions.* Reston, Va.: National Association of Schools of Music, 1982.
**CI, RSC**

Choate, Robert A., ed. *Documenary Report of the Tanglewood Symposium.* Washington: Music Educators National Conference, 1968.
**CI, FPA, RSC**

Clarke, Eric, and Simon Emmerson, eds.  *Music, Mind and Structure.*  New York: Harwood Academic Publishers, 1989.

**P, RSC**

Clynes, Manfred, ed.  *Music, Mind, and Brain: The Neuropsychology of Music.*  New York: Plenum, 1982.

**P, RSC**

Colwell, Richard J., ed.  *Symposium in Music Education: A Festschrift for Charles Leonhard.*  Urbana-Champaign: University of Illinois, 1982.

**CI, FPA, R, RSC**

*Comparative Music Education: Proceedings of the Fourth International Conference of the International Society for Music Education.*  Mainz: International Society for Music Education, 1962.

**CI, R, RSC**

Dobbs, Jack P. B., ed.  *Music Education - Facing the Future: Proceedings of the 19th World Conference of the International Society for Music Education.*  Reading, England: International Society for Music Education, 1990.

**CI, R, RSC**

*Documentary Report of the Ann Arbor Symposium: National Symposium on the Applications of Psychology to the Teaching and Learning of Music (Sessions I and II).*  Reston, Va.: Music Educators National Conference, 1981.

**CI, P, R, RSC**

*Documentary Report of the Ann Arbor Symposium on the Applications of Psychology to the Teaching and Learning of Music: Motivation and Creativity (Session III).*  Reston, Va.: Music Educators National Conference, 1983.

**CI, P, R, RSC**

*Educating Americans for the 21st Century.*  Washington: National Science Board, 1983.

**CI, RSC**

Engel, Martin, and Jerome J. Hausman, eds.  *Curriculum and Instruction in Arts and Aesthetic Education.*  St. Louis, Mo.: CEMREL, 1981.

**A, FPA, R, RSC**

*Experiments in Musical Creativity: A Report of Pilot Projects Sponsored by the Contemporary Music Project in Baltimore, San Diego, and Farmingdale.*  Washington: Music Educators National Conference, 1966.

**CI, P, RSC**

*Fact and Value in Contemporary Musical Scholarship.* Boulder, Colo.: College Music Society, 1986.

**CI, RSC**

*First Music Assessment: An Overview.* Washington: United States Government Printing Office, 1974.

**CI, P, RSC**

Fonder, Mark, ed. *The Ithaca Conference on American Music Education: Centennial Profiles.* Ithaca, N.Y.: Ithaca College, 1992.

**FPA, RSC**

Foundation for College Education in Music. *Comprehensive Musicianship.* Washington: Contemporary Music Project, Music Educators National Conference, 1965.

**CI, RSC**

Fowler, Charles B., ed. *The Crane Symposium: Toward an Understanding of the Teaching and Learning of Music Performance.* New York: Potsdam College of the State University of New York, 1988.

**CI, R, RSC**

_____, ed. *Summit Conference on the Arts and Education: A Report.* Washington: Alliance for Arts Education, 1980.

**A, CI, RSC**

Frith, Simon, ed. *World Music, Politics, and Social Change: Papers from the International Association for the Study of Popular Music.* New York: St. Martin's, 1989.

**P, RSC**

*Generation of Fellows: Grants to Individuals from the National Endowment for the Arts.* Washington: National Endowment for the Arts, 1993.

**A, CI, RSC**

Gerber, Timothy, and William O. Hughes, eds. *Music in the High School: Current Approaches to Secondary General Music Instruction.* Reston, Va.: Music Educators National Conference, 1988.

**CI, RSC**

Grant, Willis, ed. *Music in Education.* London: Butterworths, 1963.

**CI, FPA, RSC**

Grindea, Carola, ed. *Tensions in the Performance of Music.* Enl. ed. White Plains, N.Y.: Pro/Am Music Resources, 1995.

**P, RSC**

*Growing Up Complete: The Imperative for Music Education.* Reston, Va.: Music Educators National Conference, 1991.
**CI, FPA, RSC**

*International Conference on the Role and Place of Music in the Education of Youth and Adults: Report of the Third International Conference.* Copenhagen, Denmark: International Society for Music Education, 1958.
**CI, RSC**

Jones, Mari Riess, and Susan Holleran, eds. *Cognitive Bases of Musical Communication.* Washington: American Psychological Association, 1992.
**P, RSC**

*Juilliard Report on Teaching the Literature and Materials of Music.* 1953. Reprint, Westport, Conn.: Greenwood, 1970.
**CI, RSC**

Kaplan, Max. *Music Education in a Changing World: A Report.* Washington: Music Educators National Conference, 1958.
**CI, RSC**

Kemp, Anthony E., ed. *Research in Music Education: A Festschrift for Arnold Bentley.* London: International Society for Music Education, 1988.
**R, RSC**

Knieter, Gerard L., and Jane Stallings, eds. *The Teaching Process, Arts and Aesthetics.* St. Louis, Mo.: CEMREL, 1979.
**A, CI, FPA, RSC**

Kraus, Egon. *The Present State of Music Education in the World.* Washington: International Society for Music Education, 1960.
**P, R, RSC**

Lawrence, Vera Brodsky. *CMP Library: Contemporary Music Project for Creativity in Music Education.* 2nd ed. Washington: Music Educators National Conference, 1969.
**BR, CI, RSC**

Leonhard, Charles. *The Status of Arts Education in American Public Schools: Report of a Survey Conducted by the National Arts Education Research Center at the University of Illinois.* Urbana: Council for Research in Music Education, School of Music, University of Illinois, 1991.
**A, BR, CI, RSC**

Madeja, Stanley S., ed. *Arts and Aesthetics: An Agenda for the Future.* St. Louis, Mo.: CEMREL, 1977.

**A, CI, FPA, RSC**

_____, ed. *The Arts, Cognition and Basic Skills.* St. Louis, Mo.: CEMREL, 1978.

**A, CI, P, RSC**

Madsen, Clifford K., and Carol A. Prickett, eds. *Applications of Research in Music Behavior.* Tuscaloosa: University of Alabama Press, 1987.

**CI, P, R, RSC**

*Making the Grade: Report of the Twentieth Century Fund Task Force on Federal Elementary and Secondary Education Policy.* New York: Twentieth Century Fund, 1983.

**CI, RSC**

Mark, Desmond, ed. *Stock-Taking of Musical Life - Music Sociography and Its Relevance to Music Education: Report on a Seminar Organized by the ISME Commission on Music in Cultural, Educational and Mass Media Policies.* Vienna, Austria: Doblinger, 1981.

**CI, R, RSC**

May, William V., ed. *Research Symposium on the Psychology and Acoustics of Music, 1979.* Lawrence: University of Kansas Department of Art and Music Education and Music Therapy, 1980.

**P, R, RSC**

McAllester, David P., ed. *Becoming Human through Music: The Wesleyan Symposium on the Perspectives of Social Anthropology in the Teaching and Learning of Music.* Reston, Va.: Music Educators National Conference, 1985.

**CI, P, RSC**

McCarthy, Marie, ed. *Winds of Change: A Colloquium in Music Education with Charles Fowler and David J. Elliott.* New York: ACA Books, University of Maryland at College Park, 1994.

**CI, FPA, RSC**

McKenna, Gerard, and William R. Schmid, eds. *The Tanglewood Symposium Revisited: Music in American Society Ten Years Later.* Milwaukee: University of Wisconsin, 1978.

**CI, FPA, RSC**

Mills, E. Andrew, and D. Ross Thompson. *A National Survey of Arts Education, 1984-85: A National Report on the State of the Arts in the States.* Reston, Va.: National Art Education Association, 1986.

**A, RSC**

Mitchell, Ruth, ed. *Measuring Up to the Challenge: What Standards and Assessment Can Do for Arts Education.* New York: ACA Books, 1994.
**A, CI, P, RSC**

Moody, William J., ed. *Artistic Intelligences: Implications for Education.* New York: Teachers College, 1990.
**A, CI, FPA, P, RSC**

Murfee, Elizabeth. *The Value of the Arts: Written for the President's Committee on the Arts and the Humanities.* Washington: The Committee, 1993.
**A, RSC**

Murphy, Judith, and George Sullivan. *Music in American Society: An Interpretive Report of the Tanglewood Symposium.* Washington: Music Educators National Conference, 1968.
**CI, FPA, RSC**

*Music Education in the Modern World: Materials of the Ninth Conference of the International Society for Music Education.* Moscow: Progress Publishers, 1974.
**CI, P, R, RSC**

*Music in Education: International Conference on the Role and Place of Music in the Education of Youth and Adults.* Paris: UNESCO, 1955.
**CI, RSC**

*Music in General Studies: A Survey of National Practice in Higher Education.* Boulder, Colo.: College Music Society, 1983.
**CI, RSC**

*Music in the Undergraduate Curriculum, A Reassessment: A Report of the Study Group on the Content of the Undergraduate Curriculum.* Boulder, Colo.: College Music Society, 1989.
**CI, RSC**

*Music Teacher Education: Partnership and Process.* Reston, Va.: Music Educators National Conference, 1987.
**CI, FPA, RSC**

*Music USA 87: 1987 Review of the Music Industry and Adult Attitudes toward Music Survey.* Chicago: American Music Conference, 1987.
**RSC**

Narmour, Eugene, and Ruth A. Solie, eds. *Explorations in Music, the Arts, and Ideas: Essays in Honor of Leonard B. Meyer.* Stuyvesant, N.Y.: Pendragon, 1988.
**A, BR, FPA, RSC**

*NASM Futureswork: Executive Summaries, 1989-1992.*  Reston, Va.: National Association of Schools of Music, 1992.
**FPA, RSC**

*Nation at Risk: The Imperative for Educational Reform.*  National Commission on Excellence in Education.  Washington: U.S. Government Printing Office, 1983.
**CI, RSC**

National Assessment of Educational Progress.  *Music 1971-79: Results from the Second National Music Assessment.*  Denver, Colo.: Education Commission of the States, 1981.
**P, RSC**

Neuls-Bates, Carol, ed.  *The Status of Women in College Music: Preliminary Studies - Proceedings of the Meeting on Women in the Profession.*  Binghamton, N.Y.: College Music Society, 1976.
**CI, RSC**

Olson, Gerald, Anthony L. Barresi, and David Nelson, eds.  *Policy Issues in Music Education: A Report of the Proceedings of the Robert Petzold Research Symposium.*  Madison: School of Music, University of Wisconsin, 1991.
**FPA, R, RSC**

Overby, Lynnette Young, Ann Richardson, Lillian S. Hasko, and Luke Kahlich, eds.  *Early Childhood Creative Arts: Proceedings of the International Early Childhood Creative Arts Conference.*  Reston, Va.: Music Educators National Conference and National Dance Association, 1991.
**A, CI, P, RSC**

*Papers from the Dearborn Conference on Music in General Studies.*  Boulder, Colo.: College Music Society, 1984.
**CI, RSC**

*Papers from the Forum on the Education of Music Consumers.*  Reston, Va.: National Association of Schools of Music, 1974.
**CI, RSC**

Paul, John B., ed.  *Music Education: The Proceedings of the Workshop on Music Education.*  Washington: Catholic University of America Press, 1954.
**CI, RSC**

Pratt, Rosalie R., ed.  *International Symposium on Music in Medicine, Education, and Therapy for the Handicapped.*  Lanham, Md.: University Press of America, 1985.
**CI, P, RSC**

————, ed. *Music Therapy and Music Education for the Handicapped: Developments and Limitations in Practice and Research.* St. Louis, Mo.: MMB Music, 1993.
**CI, P, RSC**

Pratt, Rosalie R., and Barbara Hesser, eds. *Music Therapy and Music in Special Education: The International State of the Art.* St. Louis, Mo.: MMB Music for the International Society for Music Education, 1989.
**P, RSC**

Price, Kingsley, ed. *On Criticizing Music: Five Philosophical Perspectives.* Baltimore: Johns Hopkins University Press, 1981.
**FPA, RSC**

*Racial and Ethnic Directions in American Music.* CMS Report No. 3. Boulder, Colo.: College Music Society, 1982.
**CI, RSC**

Raiman, Melvyn L., ed. *Midwest Symposium on Music Education.* Tulsa, Okla.: United States Jaycees, 1978.
**CI, RSC**

Rantala, Veikko, Lewis Eugene Rowell, and Eero Tarasti, eds. *Essays on the Philosophy of Music.* Helsinki: Philosophical Society of Finland, 1988.
**FPA, RSC**

Renton, Barbara Hampton. *Status of Women in College Music, 1976-77: A Statistical Study.* Boulder, Colo.: College Music Society, 1980.
**CI, RSC**

*Restructuring and Reform: Selected Bibliography.* Reston, Va.: Music Educators National Conference, 1993.
**BR, CI, R, RSC**

Rivas, Frank W. *The First National Assessment of Musical Performance - National Assessment of Educational Progress: A Project of the Education Commission of the States.* Washington: United States Government Printing Office, 1974.
**CI, P, RSC**

Roehmann, Franz L., and Frank R. Wilson, eds. *The Biology of Music Making: Proceedings of the 1984 Denver Conference.* St. Louis, Mo.: MMB Music, 1988.
**P, RSC**

Ross, Malcolm, ed. *The Aesthetic Imperative: Relevance and Responsibility in Arts Education.* New York: Pergamon, 1981.

**A, CI, FPA, RSC**

————, ed. *The Arts and Personal Growth.* New York: Pergamon, 1980.

**A, FPA, RSC**

————, ed. *The Arts: A Way of Knowing.* New York: Pergamon, 1983.

**A, FPA, RSC**

————, ed. *The Claims of Feeling: Readings in Aesthetic Education.* Philadelphia: Falmer, 1989.

**A, CI, FPA, RSC**

————, ed. *The Development of Aesthetic Experience.* New York: Pergamon, 1982.

**A, CI, FPA, RSC**

*School Choice: A Special Report of the Carnegie Foundation for the Advancement of Teaching.* Princeton, N.J.: Carnegie Foundation for the Advancement of Teaching, 1992.

**CI, RSC**

*Schools and the Fine Arts: What Should Be Taught in Art, Music, and Literature?* Washington: Council for Basic Education, 1965.

**A, CI, RSC**

Shetler, Donald J., ed. *The Future of Musical Education in America: Proceedings of the July 1983 Conference.* Rochester, N.Y.: Eastman School of Music Press, 1984.

**CI, FPA, RSC**

Sink, Patricia E., ed. *Research Symposium on the Psychology and Acoustics of Music, 1982.* Lawrence: University of Kansas Department of Art and Music Education and Music Therapy, 1982.

**P, R, RSC**

Sizer, Theodore R. *Horace's Compromise: The Dilemma of the American High School.* Boston: Houghton Mifflin, 1984.

**CI, RSC**

Stauffer, Sandra L., ed. *Toward Tomorrow: New Visions for General Music.* Reston, Va.: Music Educators National Conference, 1995.

**CI, RSC**

Stevens, Louise K. *Planning to Make the Arts Basic: A Report to the National Endowment for the Arts on the Impact and Results of the Arts in Schools Basic Education Grants Program.* Marion, Mass.: Artsmarket Consulting, 1991.

**A, CI, RSC**

Swanwick, Keith, ed. *The Arts and Education: Papers from the National Association for Education in the Arts, 1983-1990.* Oakham, England: National Association for Education in the Arts, 1990.

**A, CI, RSC**

Tallarico, P. Thomas, ed. *Contributions to Symposium/80: The Bowling Green State University Symposium on Music Teaching and Research.* Bowling Green, Ohio: Bowling Green State University, 1980.

**R, RSC**

————, ed. *Contributions to Symposium/83: The Bowling Green State University Symposium on Music Teaching and Research.* Bowling Green, Ohio: Bowling Green State University, 1983.

**R, RSC**

*Teacher Education in Music: Final Report.* Washington: Music Educators National Conference, 1972.

**CI, RSC**

*These People Have Passed the Test of Time, Can You? A Report on Arts Education.* Washington: National Endowment for the Arts, 1988.

**A, CI, RSC**

Thomas, Ronald. *Manhattanville Music Curriculum Program (MMCP) Synthesis.* Bardonia, N.Y.: Media Materials, 1971.

**CI, RSC**

*Toward an Aesthetic Education: A Report.* Washington: Music Educators National Conference, 1971.

**A, CI, FPA, RSC**

*Toward Civilization: A Report on Arts Education.* Washington: National Endowment for the Arts, 1988.

**A, CI, RSC**

Turk, Gayla C., ed. *Proceedings of the Research Symposium on the Psychology and Acoustics of Music, 1985.* Lawrence: University of Kansas Department of Art and Music Education and Music Therapy, 1985.

**P, R, RSC**

*Turning Points - Preparing American Youth for the 21st Century: The Report of the Task Force on Education of Young Adolescents.* Washington: Carnegie Council on Adolescent Development, 1989.

**CI, RSC**

Weber, Nathan, and Loren Renz. *Arts Funding: A Report on Foundation and Corporate Grantmaking Trends.* New York: Foundation Center, 1993.

**A, RSC**

Werder, Richard H., ed. *Music Education in the Secondary School.* Washington: Catholic University of America Press, 1955.

**CI, R, RSC**

————, ed. *Music Education Today: The Proceedings of the Workshop on Music.* Washington: Catholic University of America Press, 1966.

**CI, RSC**

White, Chappell, ed. *A Wingspread Conference on Music in General Studies.* Racine, Wisc.: Johnson Foundation, 1981.

**CI, RSC**

Wilson, Frank R., and Franz L. Roehmann, eds. *Music and Child Development: The Biology of Music Making - Proceedings of the 1987 Denver Conference.* St. Louis, Mo.: MMB Music, 1990.

**CI, P, RSC**

# INDEX

### Authors, Titles (not listed under an author)

# About the Author

*VINCENT J. KANTORSKI is professor of music education at Bowling Green State University in Ohio where he teaches graduate courses in music education research, foundations and principles, curriculum design, and psychology of music, as well as undergraduate methods classes.*

*He is a recipient of Bowling Green State University's Distinguished Teaching Award, Faculty Excellence Award, the University Master Teacher Award, and the University of Miami School of Music's Distinguished Alumni Award. His research appears in the* Journal of Research in Music Education, Bulletin of the Council for Research in Music Education, Psychomusicology, Dialogue in Instrumental Music Education, International Music Journal, *and* American String Teacher. *He has presented research at national conventions of the Music Educators National Conference and the American String Teachers Association, and at world symposia of the International Society for Music Education in Helsinki and Amsterdam. He is currently a member of the Council for Research in Music Education and the editorial committee of* American String Teacher. *He received a bachelor's degree in music education from Chicago Musical College at Roosevelt University, a master's degree in music performance from the University of Miami, and a Ph.D. in music education from Florida State University.*